LB
1028.46   Nickles, Herbert.
.N53
1988   The practical
             Apple

$17.50

	DATE		
FEB 1990			

THE PRACTICAL APPLE®

A Guide for Educators

The Brooks/Cole Series in Instructional Computing

RUN: Computer Education, Second Edition
Dennis O. Harper and James H. Stewart

An Apple for the Teacher: Fundamentals of
Instructional Computing, Second Edition
George H. Culp and Herbert L. Nickles

Instructional Computing Fundamentals for
IBM Microcomputers
George H. Culp and Herbert L. Nickles

Instructional Computing with the TRS 80
Herbert L. Nickles and George H. Culp

Instructional Computing Fundamentals for
the Commodore 64
Herbert L. Nickles and George H. Culp

The Micro Goes to School: Educational
Applications of Microcomputer Technology,
IBM Version
Andria Troutman and James White

The Micro Goes to School: Educational
Applications of Microcomputer Technology,
Apple II Version
*Andria Troutman, James White, and
Frank Breit*

Computers in Focus
Richard Austing and Lillian Cassel

Computer Education: Literacy and Beyond
*William E. Schall, Lowell Leake, Jr., and
Donald R. Whitaker*

Logo: Principles, Programming and Projects
George Lukas and Joan Lukas

To Logo: Activities Guide
George Lukas and Joan Lukas

Essential WordStar
Carl Brown

Essential dBase II
Carl Brown

Essential dBASE III
Carl Brown

THE PRACTICAL APPLE®

A Guide for Educators

Herbert L. Nickles
Loyola University, New Orleans

George H. Culp
University of Texas at Austin

with

Linda G. Polin
Pepperdine University

Brooks/Cole Publishing Company
Pacific Grove, California

Brooks/Cole Publishing Company
A Division of Wadsworth, Inc.

Printed in the United States of America
10 9 8 7 6 5 4 3 2 1

Library of Congress Cataloging in Publication Data
Nickles, Herbert.
  The practical Apple.

  Includes index.
  1. Computer-assisted instruction—Study and teaching—United States.   2. Computer managed instruction—Study and teaching.   3. Apple II (Computer)—
Study and teaching.   4. BASIC (Computer program
language)—Study and teaching.   5. Logo (Computer
program language)—Study and teaching.   I. Culp,
George H.   II. Title.
LB1028.46.N53   1988   371.3'9445   87-26784
ISBN 0-534-09036-2

Sponsoring Editor: *Cynthia C. Stormer*
Editorial Assistant: *Mary Ann Zuzow*
Production Editor: *Joan Marsh*
Manuscript Editor: *John Joyner*
Permissions Editor: *Carline Haga*
Interior Design: *Katherine Minerva*
Cover Design: *Vernon T. Boes*
Cover Illustration: *David Aguero*
Art Coordinator: *Sue C. Howard*
Interior Illustration: *Graphic Art*
Typesetting: *Graphic Typesetting Service*
Printing and Binding: *Diversified Printing and
Publishing Services, Inc.*

It has been said that there are three types of people in the world:
  —those who make things happen,
    —those who watch things happen,
      —and those who wake up one day and wonder what happened!

This book is dedicated to
  the Davy Crocketts,
    the Neil Armstrongs,
      the Jackie Robinsons,
        the Martin Luthers, and
          the John J. Audubons
of the future who will use computers as tools to make things happen!

PREFACE

This book is written for the professional or student teacher who needs to know practical ways in which the Apple II computer can be used in instructional computing. For the context of this book, *instructional computing* is defined as teaching with computers, teaching about computers, and managing information with computers. Teaching with computers is commonly known as CAI, computer assisted instruction, and includes problem solving, drill and practice, tutorial, simulation, and testing applications. Teaching about computers includes teaching the BASIC and Logo programming languages. Managing information with the computer uses the applications of word processing, spreadsheet, and data base as tools for the educator to improve productivity. Figure 1 graphically represents this concept, which forms the basic organization for the book.

Individual sections in the book provide a foundation in the BASIC programming language, provide instruction in the use of personal productivity tools contained in AppleWorks, and introduce a "language for learning," Logo. In addition, an extensive appendix with practical tips is included that makes the book a valuable reference for every computing teacher. For those readers unfamiliar with the Apple II computer, an introduction to the system and instructions on how it works are also included in the appendix.

The topics covered in the book have been selected from introductory and intermediate instructional computing courses. They represent a wide range of classroom computing techniques, applications, and issues. Not all instructors will want or have time to include all topics in a single course. The book is organized so that an instructor can choose which topics to include and in what order they be covered. *The Practical Apple* can be adopted as the required text for multiple courses that sequentially build on the student's knowledge base.

The emphasis in each chapter is to provide a brief, descrip-

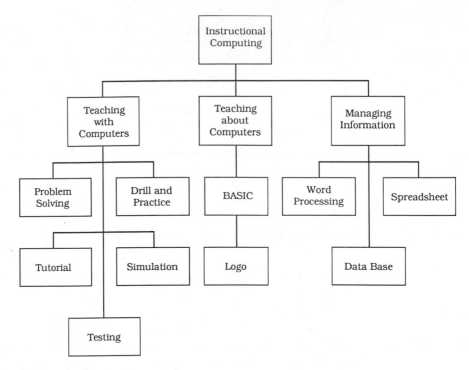

Figure 1

tive discussion of the topic followed by hands-on exercises using commonly available software. This approach not only provides the student with a theoretical foundation in instructional computing but also the tools to use the computer in the classroom as well.

In order to receive the most benefit from the book, the student will need access to certain software packages. The exercises in Part I use software that is included with each Apple II computer: Applesoft BASIC (stored in internal memory) and utility programs on the System Master diskette. Part II exercises use the popular AppleWorks program that integrates word processing, spreadsheet, and data base applications. The turtle graphics and list-processing exercises in Part III use the Apple Logo program. These packages were chosen because of their widespread use in education.

As mentioned previously, another objective of this book is to provide the student with a reference guide for future use. The appendix provides answers to the questions most commonly asked after the course is over. Step-by-step instructions are given for initializing diskettes, copying files, making back-up copies, and taking care of diskettes. Hardware maintenance and troubleshooting suggestions are provided in addition to discussions on evaluating software and setting up a computer lab. The appendix also includes summaries of Applesoft BASIC, AppleWorks, and Apple Logo commands.

A supplemental diskette is available without cost by the publisher to adopters who order twenty-five or more copies of the book. This diskette includes the example BASIC programs, AppleWorks files, and Apple Logo procedures that are referred to in the book. Answers to selected problems are also included on the diskette. It should be noted that the student cannot use the AppleWorks or Apple Logo examples without their respective software packages. We believe that the files on the supplemental diskette are very important and integral to the text; therefore, permission is hereby given to copy the diskette for class-related use.

We extend our appreciation and acknowledgment to Linda Polin of Pepperdine University for her preparation of the Logo chapters and Tip Twelve, to David Neighbours of California State University San Bernardino for his friendship, insight, and suggestions over the years, and to all of our students who have contributed to our understanding of the difficulties of learning about computers. Special thanks go to reviewers Harold Bailey, Bloomsburg University; Margaret Niess, Oregon State University; Michael Short, University of Georgia; Royal Van Horn, University of North Florida; and Wenden Waite, Boise State University, and to Joan Marsh and the publication staff at Brooks/Cole Publishing Company. An extra measure of gratitude is given to our past three editors, Mike Needham, Neil Oatley, and Cindy Stormer, who have suffered with us through what seems like years of revisions.

Herbert L. Nickles
George H. Culp

CONTENTS

ONE

A Bit
about BASIC

Introduction

More than a hundred books are available that teach BASIC (the Beginner's All-purpose Symbolic Instruction Code, developed by John G. Kemeny and Thomas E. Kurtz at Dartmouth College). Although most of these books are very thorough in describing the language, they usually emphasize problem-solving applications. Our emphasis, on the other hand, is on instruction in the use of BASIC to design and develop materials for instructional computing.

Simply put, any use of computing techniques within the classroom may be broadly defined as instructional computing (sometimes known as computer-assisted instruction, or CAI). Specifically, it includes:

1. Problem solving, in which computer programs are written to solve discipline-oriented problems.
2. Drill and practice on fundamental concepts using computer programs in a given discipline.
3. Tutorial dialog, in which computer programs provide "tutorlike" assistance in pointing out certain types of mistakes, providing review if needed, skipping areas in which proficiency is shown, and so on.
4. Simulation, in which computer programs allow manipulation and interpretation of certain elements related to given physical or social phenomena without the constraints of time, space, equipment, and environmental or logistical limits.
5. Testing, in which computer programs ask the questions, check the answers, and record the performance.

In this section we will concentrate on simple applications of instructional computing, including drill, testing, and, to a limited degree, tutorial dialog.

■ **The use of BASIC.**   An introduction to some of the fundamentals of BASIC is provided in this section. This introduction is not intended to produce highly accomplished and skilled programmers. Rather, it gives only the fundamentals needed to write simple programs for instructional computing applications. Model programs are described that illustrate this use. Most of these programs may be easily modified for, or used directly with, actual classroom activities.

■ **TOP-DOWN design.**   A general concept of a logical approach to program design is introduced in the early chapters of this section. Beginning with PROGRAM 3 in Chapter 2, each of the programs is designed in a "top-down," step-by-step, frame-by-frame approach. This is a familiar approach to instructional design for educators and facilitates program development, even for the novice computer user.

Think about This (for Fun)
Rearrange the letters of NEW DOOR to form one word. (Note: answers to Think about This (for Fun) questions may be found in Tip 14.)

Think about This (Seriously)
Is the use of computers in education just another fad?

"Nothing in life is to be feared. It is only to be understood."
Marie Curie

"In certain trying circumstances, urgent circumstances, desperate circumstances, profanity furnishes a relief denied even to prayer."
Mark Twain

"If at first you don't succeed, you are running about average."
M. H. Alderson

A Simple Instructional Computing Program: Problem Solving— What's Your Age in Days?

1.1 Objectives

For the successful completion of this chapter, you should be able to:

1. Define what (not who) composes a BASIC program (Section 1.3.1).
2. Distinguish between BASIC statements and commands (Sections 1.3.1–1.3.2).
3. Define the action of the following BASIC commands: NEW, RUN, LIST, and SAVE (Section 1.3.2).
4. Define and give at least one example of both a NUMERIC variable and a STRING variable (Section 1.3.3).
5. Describe the use of commas and semicolons in BASIC for purposes other than punctuation (Section 1.3.4).
6. Define the purpose and give at least one example of the following BASIC statements: PRINT, INPUT, LET, and END (Sections 1.4.1–1.4.4).

1.2 The Fundamental Units of Any Computer

A computer is an extremely fast and accurate processor of data. In the simplest sense, most computers may be viewed as four fundamental units connected electronically:

1. An *input* unit (such as a computer terminal keyboard), through which data is entered.
2. A *processor* unit, which stores the data input and processes it electronically.
3. An *output* unit (such as a computer terminal screen or printer), which shows the results of processing the data input.
4. A *storage/retrieval* unit (such as a disk drive), which stores information on, and retrieves information from, some magnetic medium (such as a floppy disk).

Figure 1.1 shows these units in block form.

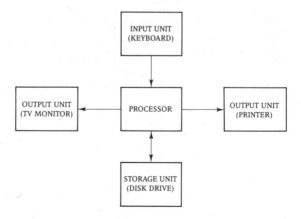

Figure 1.1 Components of a computer system

It is very important that the reader, particularly the reader new to microcomputers, become familiar with the processes needed to access (use) the system. This first involves gaining confidence in booting up the system. Refer to Tip 1 for a step-by-step procedure to accomplish this.

1.3 BASIC "Rules of the Game"

There are a few general points about BASIC that should be made early. Consider these as some of the "rules of the game" to follow for BASIC.

1.3.1 Statements

A BASIC program may be defined as at least one "instruction" performed (executed) by the computer. Instructions are written in the form of statements. These statements are words (often verbs), such as PRINT and INPUT, that make some degree of sense to both the user and the computer. (Of course, the computer has been programmed by people to "understand" these words.) The length of a BASIC statement must not exceed 255 total characters, including spaces.

BASIC statements for the Apple II series microcomputers are always numbered, generally by tens (10, 20, 30 . . .). They could be numbered 1, 2, 3, and so on, but no additional statements could be inserted into the program between, say, statements numbered 1 and 2. Statements can be inserted between lines numbered 10 and 20 (11, 12, etc.). Thus, the numbering convention is usually in increments of ten.

1.3.2 Commands

BASIC commands issue specific information to the computer system *about* the program. For example, the command NEW instructs the system to prepare for a new BASIC program to be entered at the terminal by "erasing" any program statements that are currently in the system's memory. The command LIST will produce a listing of the BASIC statements that compose the program in memory.

The command RUN executes (RUNs) the BASIC statements in their increasing numeric sequence unless one of those statements transfers the execution to another part of the program. (This transfer process is called BRANCHING and will be discussed later.) The command SAVE <filename> instructs the system to save on the disk the program in memory under the name <filename>. The program is stored on a floppy disk placed in the disk drive. (The <filename> may be just about any name, but short, descriptive names are usually best.)

1.3.3 Variables

All BASIC programs described in this text will include values that may *vary* as the program is executed (RUN). These values, called VARI- ABLES, could be students' names, test scores, responses for correct or incorrect answers, and so forth.

In BASIC, a variable may be *represented* (named) simply by any letter of the alphabet. However, the name could be as long as 255 characters *if the first* character in the name is a letter and the rest of the name contains only letters or numbers. However, only the first *two* characters are considered by the Apple. Realistically, variable names should be short and descriptive. Initially (for simplicity) we will use only one or two characters for variable names in our example programs. Later, where appropriate, longer variable names that better describe their values will be used. However, care should be taken in naming variables. Names such as AVERAGE and AVENUE appear to be differ- ent, but are really the same to the program, since both have the same first two characters (AV). Names such as LETTER and FIEND cannot be used, since they contain the letter combinations LET and END, which are two of the "reserved words" for BASIC. (Most of the reserved words are shown in Tip 10.)

For our purposes, there are two types of variables:

1. *Numeric.* The value of the variable is always numeric: 1.0, 2, 110.5, -3.1365, and so on.
2. *String* (or *alphanumeric*). The value of the variable may be alpha- betic characters or numbers or a mixture of both. Such values are always enclosed in quotation marks: "ABCDEF", "CS395T", "JOHN JONES", "NOW IS THE TIME", and so on.

A dollar sign ($) is added to the name of the string variable to distin- guish it from a numeric variable. N$, A1$, Z9$, and FL$ all represent string variable names, while N, A1, Z9, and FL all represent numeric variable names.

EXAMPLES

        A = 123

(The *numeric* variable named A has a value of 123 assigned to it.)

        A$ = "ABC"

(The *string* variable named A$ (pronounced "A-string") has a value of ABC assigned to it.)

1.3.4 Commas (,) and Semicolons (;)

Commas and semicolons have specific uses in BASIC. They can be used in the normal fashion as punctuation marks, or they can be used to instruct the system to display information in special ways. For example, every so often in a BASIC program there may be a need to have information printed in columns. Suppose that a list of student names, test score averages, and final numeric grades were to be displayed (PRINTed). Assume that the values are stored in the variables N$, T1, and F, respectively. The BASIC statement

```
PRINT N$,T1,F
```

would display this information in columns fifteen spaces apart from the start of the first value to the start of the second value, and so on. Here, the comma acts as an automatic tabulator of fifteen spaces. Thus, any line can have "fields" of display starting at column 1, column 16, and so on. This can be useful when certain types of information, such as name and grade for a series of students, are to be displayed. (See also Sections 1.4.1 and 1.4.3.)

If one wished the above information to be "close-packed" (printed without any separating spaces), the semicolon would be used in place of the comma. Or, in simple terms, the semicolon instructs the system: "Display right here whatever is PRINTed next!" In essence, then, the comma, when *not* used as a punctuation mark, instructs the system to tab fifteen spaces before printing; similarly, the semicolon instructs the system not to skip *any* spaces before printing.

Examples of these uses will be shown shortly, but for now simply be aware that the comma and semicolon can have special meanings when not used as punctuation.

1.4 BASIC Statements for This Chapter

1.4.1 Statement PRINT

PURPOSE   Displays (PRINTs) information at the computer terminal. This information may be text, numeric variable values, or string (alphanumeric) variable values (see Section 1.4.3). When text is to be displayed, it must be enclosed in quotation marks (") in the PRINT statement.

EXAMPLE
```
PRINT "Hello. What's your first name"
```

RESULT OF
EXECUTION
```
Hello. What's your first name
```

In addition, certain shorthand conventions are available for the Apple II series microcomputer. For example, the shorthand for the statement PRINT is the question mark (?). Thus, PRINT statements may be li' erally typed as

```
10 ? "Hello. What is your first name"
```

The system will automatically interpret the ? as the word PRINT.

EXAMPLE
```
10 A = 123
20 A$ = "ABC"
30 ? A, A$
```

When LISTed, this would appear:

```
10 A = 123
20 A$ = "ABC"
30 PRINT A, A$
```

When RUN, this would appear:

```
123          ABC
←15 spaces→
```

1.4.2 Statement INPUT

PURPOSE Allows numeric or alphanumeric information to be entered (INPUT) into a BASIC program during its execution. The information is entered through the terminal keyboard and is assigned to a variable specified by the program author. The variable will have the assigned value until changed by another INPUT statement or LET statement (see Section 1.4.3) for that variable.

EXAMPLES
```
INPUT N (for numeric information)
INPUT N$ (for alphanumeric information)
INPUT "Enter your name ";N$ (text with statement)
INPUT "Enter your age ";N (text with statement)
```

Note: Most BASIC systems automatically display a question mark when the INPUT statement is executed. In computer terms the question mark is called the INPUT INDICATOR or PROMPT. Program execution is stopped until the RETURN key is pressed. Note that the use of quotes discussed earlier for STRING variables (Section 1.3.3) is not required when string information is INPUT. The dollar sign ($) instructs the system that *any* input will be assigned as a string variable. Also, as noted earlier, text may be enclosed within quotation marks with the INPUT statement. In this form, the question mark will *not* be displayed, and a semicolon *must* come before the variable name.

PROGRAM
EXAMPLE

```
10 PRINT "Hello. What's your first name"
20 INPUT N$
30 PRINT N$ "is a nice name."
40 END
```

RESULT OF
EXECUTION

```
Hello. What's your first name
?SAMMY
SAMMY is a nice name.
```

(the question mark appears as a prompt, SAMMY is typed, and the RETURN key is pressed)

1.4.3 Statement LET

PURPOSE   Assigns values to variables. This action may be "direct," as in LET X = 20 (X would have a value of 20), or it may be "indirect," as in LET X = (2*Y)/3 (X would have a value equal to the result of dividing 3 into the product of 2 times the value of Y). The "*" is the symbol (character) used for multiplication; the "/" is the symbol used for division. LET may also be used to assign alphanumeric values, as in

```
LET A$ = "Here's the answer!"
```

Note: The term LET is optional; the statement X = 20 would be equivalent to LET X = 20. Note here that assignment to a string variable requires the use of quotes. The string content *must* be enclosed in quotes.

EXAMPLE

```
10 LET N$ = "JOHN JONES"
20 LET T1 = 100
30 FL = 89 (Note: LET is omitted.)
40 PRINT "STUDENT","TEST 1","FINAL"
50 PRINT "-------","------","-----"
60 PRINT N$,T1,FL
70 END
```

RESULT OF
EXECUTION

```
STUDENT         TEST 1          FINAL
-------         ------          -----
JOHN JONES      100             89
```

What would happen if the commas in statements 40–60 were replaced by semicolons? Note: answers to this and other questions found within the book are supplied under their respective chapter and section numbers in Tip 14.

1.4.4   Statement END

PURPOSE   Ends program execution. However, the END statement is not required for program execution. (See also the statement STOP in Tip 10.)

1.5   PROGRAM 1: What's Your Age in Days?

Note: In Part One of this book we will be discussing more than fifteen programs. Initially, the programs are named in the sequence of their discussion: PROGRAM 1 comes before PROGRAM 2, and so on. In Chapter 4 we will use names that reflect the specific use of the example programs that are discussed.

In creating any new program, the following sequence should be used:

1. Enter NEW.
2. Enter the program statements.
3. Enter SAVE <filename>.
4. RUN the program to test it.
5. Make any needed modifications.
6. If modified, enter SAVE <same filename>.

Step 6 *replaces* the old version of the program <filename> with the new (modified) version. If a copy of *both* versions is desired, then simply enter SAVE <different filename>. Also, the statements comprising a program in memory may be seen by entering LIST. If a specific line (statement) number or a range of line numbers is desired, enter LIST <line number> or LIST <beginning line,ending line>, respectively.

The statements discussed thus far can be combined to make a program. But what is the program to do? Some degree of design must be employed that illustrates the use of these statements. Arbitrarily, suppose that we wanted to design a program that will ask for a person's name, greet that person by the name entered, ask that person's age in years, convert that age to age in days, display the results of the conversion, and then give a farewell message. The program, designed in a step-by-step fashion, could be

Step 1. Ask for a person's (the program user's) name (PRINT).
Step 2. Assign the name entered to a string variable (INPUT).

Step 3. Greet that person with the name entered (PRINT).

Step 4. Skip a line so that the screen is not too crowded (PRINT).

Step 5. Ask for the person's age in years (PRINT).

Step 6. Assign the age entered to a numeric variable (INPUT).

Step 7. Convert the age in years to the age in days (LET).

Step 8. Skip a line to avoid crowding on the screen (PRINT).

Step 9. Display this age in days (PRINT).

Step 10. End the program (END).

Note: In the sample screen frame shown below, we have used boldface letters to emphasize important commands. Also, we have written statements in uppercase letters and used lowercase for our general text. Although the Apple IIe, Apple IIc, and Apple IIgs microcomputers allow lowercase letters in the text of PRINT statements, you should be aware that *all* commands, statement words, and INPUT must be in uppercase.

PROGRAM 1 CREATION

```
] NEW
]10 PRINT "Hello. What's your first name"
]20 INPUT N$
]30 PRINT "Howdy," N$
]40 PRINT
]50 PRINT "Tell me . . . what is your age in years";
]60 INPUT A
]70 D = A * 365
]80 PRINT
]90 PRINT "Well," N$", you have been breathing"
]100 PRINT "for at least "D" days!"
]110 PRINT, "Bye-bye," N$
]120 END
] SAVE PROGRAM 1
```

Statement-by-statement discussion of PROGRAM 1:

Step 1. Statement 10 displays a greeting and asks for the user's first name.

Step 2. Statement 20 automatically displays a "?" and waits for input from the terminal keyboard. Whatever is typed is assigned as a value to the variable N$ when the RETURN key is depressed.

Step 3. This value is displayed with the text, "Howdy," in statement 30. Carefully note that the variable N$ is *not* enclosed within the quotation marks. (Why is the blank space included within the quotation marks?)

Steps 4 and 5. Statement 40 prints a blank line, and statement 50 requests the user's age in years.

Step 6. Statement 60 automatically displays a "?" and waits until some number is typed and the RETURN key is pressed. This value is assigned to variable A.

Step 7. Statement 70 assigns a value to variable D equal to the value of A times 365 (converting years to days).

Step 8. Statement 80 prints a blank line.

Step 9. The value of variable D, with appropriate text, is then displayed in statements 90 and 100. Again, carefully note that *only* the text to be displayed, *not* the variable names (N$ and D), is enclosed within the quotation marks.

Step 10. Statement 110 skips over fifteen spaces and displays a farewell. Statement 120 ends program execution.

PROGRAM 1 SAMPLE RUN

```
]RUN
]Hello. What's your first name
]?GEORGE
]Howdy, GEORGE

]Tell me...what is your age in years? 46

]Well, GEORGE, you have been breathing
]for at least 16790 days!
]                    Bye-bye, GEORGE

]
```

For practice and review, RUN PROGRAM 1 from the text disk.

1.6 Editing BASIC Programs

Most BASIC systems have some means by which programs may be edited. For example, a PRINT statement with a misspelled word or typographic error may be corrected by editing. Three simple editing techniques are

1. Left arrow key (←). A typographic error may be corrected by using this key to backspace the cursor (the "flashing" box) over the error,

entering the correction, and then completing the line being typed. This type of editing can be used only before the RETURN key is pressed for the line currently being entered.

2. Retyping the statement. A statement may be replaced by simply retyping the line number followed by the correct statement.

3. Deleting lines. A statement may be deleted entirely by typing the line number *only* and then depressing the RETURN key. Inclusive line numbers may be deleted by typing DEL, followed by the beginning and ending line numbers to be deleted, separated by a comma. For example, the command

```
DEL 20,50
```

would delete lines 20–50, inclusive.

Although these are only three simple techniques for editing, they will get you started and can be extremely useful.

1.7 Posers and Problems

Note: Many of the "Posers and Problems" given in this book may be entered and run as programs. Where possible, this should be done, since it will be of help in arriving at the solutions. As a last resort, or to check your work, refer to Tip 14.

1. Correct any errors found in the following BASIC statements.

```
10 PRIMT "Hello
20 PRIMT What's your height in inches"
30 INPUT
40 M = 2.54 *
50 PRINT You are M centimeters tall!
60 FINISH
```

2. Mentally determine the value of X in each of the following if Y = 6.

```
X = 25
X = (2*Y)/3
X = Y
X = (2*Y)/(3*Y)
X = (Y*Y)/(Y*2)
```

3. Why is a space included within the quotation marks before or after the variable names in statements 90, 100, and 110 in PROGRAM 1? Are the variables N$ and D actually enclosed in quotation marks as they might appear in statements 90 and 100?

4. Note the different positions of the two questions marks in the sample RUN of PROGRAM 1. What caused the difference? Hint: carefully examine statements 10 and 50.

5. Modify PROGRAM 1 to output the user's age in "heartbeats" (use H as the variable), assuming a pulse rate of 72 beats per minute (and 60 minutes per hour, 24 hours per day).

6. What would result if the following statements were executed?

```
10 A$ = "NAME"
20 B$ = "SCORE"
30 C$ = "AVERAGE"
40 PRINT A$, B$, C$
50 END
```

7. What would result if the following statements were executed? (Assume you INPUT your own name and weight.)

```
10 PRINT "Your first name is";
20 INPUT N$
30 PRINT "Your weight in pounds is";
40 INPUT P
50 K = P/2.2
60 Z = P * 16
70 PRINT, "Wow, " N$ "!"
80 PRINT "That's only " K " kilograms, but, gee,"
90 PRINT, "it's " Z " ounces!"
100 END
```

(Enter and RUN it to check your results.)

8. Write a program that inputs two string variables, first name and last name, and prints out a salutation of your choice using the full name that was entered.

2

**Think
about This
(for Fun)**
What do you
sit on, sleep
on, and
brush your
teeth with?

**Think
about This
(Seriously)**
Can com-
puter pro-
grams teach?

"Even if
you're on the
right track,
you'll get run
over if you
just sit
there."
Will Rogers

"Man's mind
stretched to a
new idea
never goes
back to its
original
dimensions."
*Oliver Wendell
Holmes*

Tell It Where to Go and What to Do with It

2.1 Objectives

For the successful completion of this chapter, you should be able to

1. Define the purpose and give at least one example of each of the BASIC statements HOME, REM, GOTO, IF-THEN, and ON-GOTO (Sections 2.2.1–2.2.5).
2. Define the purpose and give at least one example of each of the BASIC functions RND(1) and INT (Section 2.3).
3. Define the purpose of the BASIC command LOAD (Section 2.4).
4. Define the purpose and give at least one example of the PRINT TAB statement (Section 2.5.1).
5. Define the purpose and give at least one example of "multiple statements per line" (Section 2.5.1).
6. Alone and unafraid, boot up a microcomputer system (Tip 1).
7. Design, enter, and RUN a BASIC program that includes the statements discussed in Chapters 1 and 2.

2.2 BASIC Statements for This Chapter

2.2.1 Statement HOME

PURPOSE   HOME erases all display and places the cursor in the upper left corner of the monitor screen. This use is particularly appropriate in instructional computing, since it allows information, examples, questions, and so on to be displayed in a screen-by-screen or frame-by-frame fashion.

EXAMPLE   HOME

2.2.2 Statement REM

PURPOSE   REM is used as a REMinder or REMark to document the listing of BASIC programs. That is, REM gives a means by which internal notes may be made in the program listing. These notes will provide information about the program and will identify special program routines or strategies, separating the program into segments so that the program listing is easy to read. The REM statement is not executed during a program RUN; thus, the only time these are displayed is after a LIST command. We will use the REM statement primarily to show the frame-by-frame and step-by-step design in the listing of each program.

EXAMPLE

```
REM -----------------------------------------
REM           Step 1 - Display a Title
REM
```

2.2.3 Statement GOTO

PURPOSE   GOTO *unconditionally* transfers (branches) program execution to a specified statement number.

EXAMPLE   GOTO 100

Note: Use of the GOTO statement in programs should be minimized. If this statement is used excessively, following the design flow of a program in a frame-by-frame fashion can become very difficult.

2.2.4 Statement IF-THEN

PURPOSE   IF-THEN *conditionally* performs the specified action following the word THEN if, and only if, the defined variable relationship is TRUE. (Note the uses and combinations of the symbols =, <, and > and their meanings.)

EXAMPLES   IF X = 1 THEN 100

(Transfer to statement 100 will occur only if X is *equal* to 1.)

                IF Y <> Z THEN 100

(Transfer to statement 100 will occur only if the value of Y is *not* equal to the value of Z.)

                IF A <= 2 THEN 100

(Transfer to statement 100 will occur only if the value of A is *less than* or *equal* to 2.)

                IF A >= 2 THEN 100

(Transfer to statement 100 will occur only if the value of A is *greater than* or *equal* to 2.)

                IF A$ = "YES" THEN 100

(Transfer to statement 100 will occur only if the value of A$ is *equal* to the same value as the character string YES.)

Also, note that IF-OR-THEN and IF-AND-THEN statements are possible:

```
IF A < 1 OR A > 10 THEN 100
```

(Transfer to statement 100 will occur only if the value of A is *less than* 1 *or greater than* 10.)

```
IF A = 2 AND B = 3 THEN 100
```

(Transfer to statement 100 will occur only if the value of A is *equal* to 2 *and* the value of B is *equal* to 3.)

Combinations of string and numeric variables also may be used:

```
IF Z$ = "YES" AND C > 8 THEN 100
```

(Transfer to statement 100 will occur only if the value of Z$ is *equal* to the string YES *and* the value of C is *greater than* 8.)

Make special note that many statements, such as PRINT, (LET), and others to be seen in later chapters, can be included in the IF-THEN statement. If the condition defined by the IF-THEN statement is TRUE, the statement included will be executed; otherwise, execution continues with the next statement in the program.

```
IF S > 69 THEN PRINT "You passed!"
```

(If the value of S is greater than 69, then "You passed!" will be PRINTed.)

```
IF Z$ = "N" THEN A = 0
```

(If the value of Z$ is equal to the string N, then the numeric variable A is set to zero.)

2.2.5 Statement ON-GOTO

PURPOSE   ON-GOTO transfers (branches) program execution to a specified statement number based on the value of a variable or numerical relationship.

EXAMPLE   ON X GOTO 100,300,600

(Transfer to statement 100 will occur if the value of X is 1; transfer to statement 300 will occur if this value is 2; transfer to statement 600 will occur if this value is 3. If X is 0 or greater than 3 in the foregoing example, execution continues with the first statement following the ON-GOTO.)

This example of the ON-GOTO is equivalent to the following *three* IF-THEN statements:

```
IF X = 1 THEN 100
IF X = 2 THEN 300
IF X = 3 THEN 600
```

By using the ON-GOTO statement, the same instructions can be given to the system by just *one* statement:

```
ON X GOTO 100,300,600
```

2.3 Some Very BASIC Functions

Functions in BASIC are essentially mathematical routines that either come with the computer system (as a library of routines or functions) or are defined by the user. Once a function has been defined, it may be used over and over again without the bother of writing out the entire routine.

Two of the most common library functions used in instructional computing applications are RND(1) and INT. When executed, the RND(1) function automatically gives some random numeric value between 0.0 and 0.99999999. The INT function reduces any number with a decimal fraction (called a REAL number) to an INTeger.

By using a combination of these functions in BASIC statements, it is possible to generate random numbers within any range desired. This capability may be used in generating different values for questions containing numbers, randomly selecting questions by number from a "bank" of questions, randomly branching to specified line numbers using ON-GOTO statements, and so on.

A general formula may be derived that will give any desired range of *positive* random numbers:

$$N = INT((H - L + 1) * RND(1) + L)$$

where N is the random number generated and H and L are the highest and lowest numbers, respectively, in the desired range. For example, a range of random numbers is desired between 100 and 25.

Highest number = 100
Lowest number = 25
100 − 25 + 1 = 76

The statement to generate this range of random numbers is

$$N = INT(76 * RND(1) + 25)$$

What statement would produce random numbers in the range 5−95, inclusive?

We will make extensive use of the statements discussed above and the INT and RND functions beginning with PROGRAM 3. But first let us modify an existing program.

2.4 Modification of Existing Programs

In Chapter 1, Problem 5 asked you to modify PROGRAM 1 to output (PRINT) the number of heartbeats equivalent to a user's age in years, assuming there were 72 beats per minute. To do this, it is necessary to

1. Retrieve PROGRAM 1 from the disk (LOAD PROGRAM 1).
2. Examine the LISTing for needed changes (LIST).
3. Make the modifications.
4. Save the modified version of PROGRAM 1 as PROGRAM 2 (SAVE PROGRAM 2).

By saving the *modified* program as PROGRAM 2, both the old version (PROGRAM 1) and the new version (PROGRAM 2) are on the disk. If only the new version is wanted, the same name (PROGRAM 1, in this case) should be used (SAVE PROGRAM 1).

In summary, we have the following commands:

Command	Example	Action
NEW	NEW	Clears memory of statements.
RUN	RUN	Executes statements in memory.
LOAD \<name>	LOAD PROGRAM 1	LOADs the program \<name> from the disk to memory.
LIST	LIST	LISTs the entire program.
LIST nn	LIST 10	LISTs line nn.
LIST nn,mm	LIST 10,100	LISTs lines nn,mm, inclusive.
SAVE \<name>	SAVE PROGRAM 1	SAVEs a NEW program in memory on the disk as \<name>.

2.4.1 PROGRAM 2: Adding Heartbeats

Recall that PROGRAM 1 was created by first typing NEW to erase any program in memory and then entering each line, statement by statement. The program was SAVEd, then RUN was entered to test it. Once a program has been SAVEd, it may be retrieved by the command

```
LOAD  <name>
```

(where \<name> is the name of the program). If any changes are made that are to be permanent in the program, the command SAVE \<name> must be entered.

Step by step then, we must

1. LOAD PROGRAM 1.
2. LIST it to see where insertions or changes must be made.
3. Insert a statement that will convert the age in days to the age in heartbeats.
4. Insert a statement(s) that will display the result of this conversion.
5. SAVE as PROGRAM 2.
6. Test the program.
7. Make any changes indicated from the results of testing the program, then repeat Steps 5 and 6 until satisfied.

PROGRAM 2 CREATION FROM PROGRAM 1

```
]LOAD PROGRAM 1
]101 REM----------------------------------
]102 REM      THESE ARE CHANGES TO PROGRAM 1
]103 REM
]104 PRINT
]105 H = D * 24 * 60 * 72
]107 PRINT "and that's a lifetime of"
]108 PRINT H "total heartbeats!"
]109 PRINT
]70 D = A * 365.25
]SAVE PROGRAM 2
```

Step-by-Step discussion of PROGRAM 1 modification:

PROGRAM 1 is first LOADed and then LISTed. Statements 101–109 are entered. (Statement 105 converts the age in days, D, to heartbeats, H, since there are 24 hours per day, 60 minutes per hour, and 72 heartbeats per minute.)

Statements 107 and 108 display the value of the variable H, along with appropriate text.

Note that statement 70 is reentered to reflect a more accurate value for the number of days per year (365.25 versus 365).

The program is SAVEd as PROGRAM 2.

The program is RUN.

**PROGRAM
2
SAMPLE
RUN**

```
]RUN
Hello. What's your first name
?GEORGE

Howdy, GEORGE

Tell me...what is your age in years? 46

Well, GEORGE, you have been breathing
for at least 16801.5 days!

And that's a lifetime of
1.74197952E+09 total heartbeats!

                    Bye-bye, GEORGE
```

Note: In the RUN of the program, the value of H is expressed as 1.74197952E+09. This is the method by which the system displays a value of 1,741,979,520. It is also the system's way of expressing scientific notation, that is, 1.741979520×10^9. This amounts to one billion, seven hundred forty one million, nine hundred seventy nine thousand, five hundred twenty heartbeats! Though easily broken, 'tis still a powerful muscle! (For practice and review, LOAD PROGRAM 2 from the text disk, then LIST it. After noting the changes made, RUN the program to see the results of the modifications.)

2.5 Incorporating the New Statements

The content design of any BASIC program is at the discretion of its author (programmer). The program can be as simple or as complex as the author desires. For example, BASIC may be used in trivial Fahrenheit-to-Celsius temperature conversions or in sophisticated modeling of population dynamics. The point is that a program does only what an author has designed it to do—nothing more or less. However, for any program, regardless of its simplicity or complexity, the author must first outline the design and "flow" of the program. On that note, the following program (PROGRAM 3) is designed to illustrate a use of the statements discussed in this unit and to introduce the frame-by-frame, step-by-step format we will use throughout this part of the book.

2.5.1 PROGRAM 3: Appropriate Responses

Suppose we wished to design a program that will ask a question and give only one chance for a correct answer. "Appropriate" responses will be made for either a correct or incorrect answer.

The program will then ask a final question related to age. The user will be informed if the answer is too low or too high. For answers that are too high, an additional comment will be randomly selected from three choices. The question will be repeated until the correct answer is given.

The preceding paragraph outlines what we want the program to do. But how is this to be translated into BASIC code? A logical, step-by-step approach is the answer. Design the overall programming "problem" as a series of small, independent steps, each accomplishing a specific task related to the complete "problem" solution. Thus, for this program we could have the steps shown on page 30.

STEP 1   Clear the screen and show a title (HOME, PRINT).

STEP 2   Ask a question and get an answer (PRINT, INPUT [with text]), and check the answer for accuracy. If correct, respond positively, then ask the next question (IF-THEN-PRINT). If incorrect, give the correct answer, then ask the next question (IF-THEN-PRINT).

STEP 3   Ask the next question and get an answer (PRINT, INPUT [with text]). Here, we will check the answer for a range of possible numbers.

STEP 4   If correct, respond positively and END the program (IF-THEN-PRINT, GOTO Step 7).

STEP 5   If the answer is too low, respond accordingly, then repeat the question (IF-THEN-PRINT, GOTO Step 3).

STEP 6   If the answer is too high, respond accordingly (IF-THEN-PRINT). Then use a method to randomly select an additional comment (LET, IF-THEN-LET, PRINT), and repeat the question (GOTO Step 3).

STEP 7   Give a closing comment and conclude the program (PRINT, END).

```
10 REM              PROGRAM 3
20 REM
30 REM -------------------------------------------------------
40 REM        STEP 1 - CLEAR THE SCREEN AND SHOW A TITLE
50 REM
60     HOME
70     PRINT "STRING AND NUMERIC ANSWER CHECKING"
80 REM -------------------------------------------------------
90 REM    STEP 2 - ASK FIRST QUESTION; CHECK INPUT
100 REM
110  PRINT
120  PRINT "WHAT STATE FOLLOWS ALASKA"
130  INPUT "IN TOTAL LAND AREA?   ";REPLY$
140  PRINT
150  IF REPLY$ = "TEXAS" THEN PRINT TAB(3) "YEEE-HAA" TAB(25)"OK!"
160  IF REPLY$ <> "TEXAS" THEN PRINT TAB(10) "NO...IT'S TEXAS"
170 REM -------------------------------------------------------
180 REM    STEP 3 - ASK SECOND QUESTION; CHECK INPUT
190 REM
200  PRINT
210  PRINT "WHAT WAS THE PERPETUAL AGE"
220  INPUT "OF THE LATE JACK BENNY?   "; REPLY
230  PRINT
240 REM -------------------------------------------------------
250 REM    STEP 4 - CORRECT? IF SO, GIVE FEEDBACK & END
260 REM
270  IF REPLY = 39 THEN PRINT "DIDN'T LOOK IT..." TAB(25) "DID HE?"
          : GOTO 440
280 REM -------------------------------------------------------
290 REM    STEP 5 - TOO LOW? IF SO, SAY SO & REPEAT
300 REM
310  IF REPLY < 39 THEN PRINT "TOO LOW..."  :   GOTO 200
320 REM -------------------------------------------------------
330 REM    STEP 6 - TOO HIGH? GIVE RANDOM FEEDBACK & REPEAT
340 REM
350  IF REPLY > 39 THEN PRINT "TOO HIGH..." ;
360  RANUM = INT (3 * RND(1) + 1)
370  IF RANUM = 1 THEN FEEDBK$ = "NOW THAT IS OLD!"
380  IF RANUM = 2 THEN FEEDBK$ = "ARE YOU TRYING TO BE CRUEL?"
390  IF RANUM = 3 THEN FEEDBK$ = "HAVE YOU NO SYMPATHY?"
400  PRINT FEEDBK$  :   GOTO 200
410 REM -------------------------------------------------------
420 REM    STEP 7 - FINAL COMMENT AND END OF PROGRAM
430 REM
440  PRINT : PRINT
450  PRINT, "BYE-BYE, FRIENDS..."
460 END
```

Carefully examine the listing of PROGRAM 3 to see how these steps are accomplished.

Note: This program also uses another "shorthand" method in BASIC: the use of multiple statements per line (statements 270, 310, 400, and 440). We have combined different BASIC statements on one line, rather than using a separate line number for each statement. The colon is used as a "delimiter," or separator, for each statement. Use of multiple statements per line makes more efficient use of the system's memory, but it can have the disadvantage of making the LISTing of the program more difficult to read in terms of its design. Therefore, the program examples will make minimal use of multiple statements on one line. However, remember as you become more experienced that this is a handy method. Also remember that the total length of a multiple-statement line must not exceed 255 characters.

Carefully note statements 150, 160, and 270 in the program listing. Each of these incorporates the PRINT TAB statement. This statement allows an automatic tabulation to a defined space before display or PRINTing occurs.

PROGRAM 3 SAMPLE RUNS— STEPS 1 AND 2

```
        STRING AND NUMERIC ANSWER CHECKING

        What state follows Alaska
        in total land area? TEXAS

          YEEE-HAA           THAT'S IT!
        -------------------------------------
        STRING AND NUMERIC ANSWER CHECKING

        What state follows Alaska
        in total land area? CALIFORNIA

                   NO...IT'S TEXAS
```

**PROGRAM
3
SAMPLE
RUN—
STEPS 3, 4
5 AND 7**

What was the perpetual age
of the late Jack Benny? 35

Too low...

What was the perpetual age
of the late Jack Benny? 39

DIDN'T LOOK IT...   DID HE?

Bye-bye, friends...

**PROGRAM
3
SAMPLE
RUN—
STEPS 3,
5 AND 6**

What was the perpetual age
of the late Jack Benny? 29

Too low...

What was the perpetual age
of the late Jack Benny? 50

Too high...have you no sympathy?

What was the perpetual age
of the late Jack Benny? 40

Too high...are you trying to be cruel?

For practice and review, RUN PROGRAM 3 from the text disk.

2.6 Posers and Problems

1. What is the difference between the variables REPLY and REPLY$ in PROGRAM 3?
2. Modify statements 370, 380, and 390 in PROGRAM 3 to give comments of your choosing.
3. What should be done to PROGRAM 3 so that it would ask for your age instead of Jack Benny's?
4. What should be done to PROGRAM 3 in order to select a random comment from five choices instead of three?
5. What changes should be made to PROGRAM 3 in order to ask for the third largest state by land area instead of the second?
6. How should PROGRAM 3 be modified to ask for the user's first name at the start of the program and then refer to the user by name instead of displaying "BYE-BYE, FRIENDS. . ." at statement 450?

7. Write a statement that will randomly give a value for variable X that is between 200 and 50, inclusive.

8. What is the RANGE of numbers that could randomly be generated by the statement

$$X = INT(25 * RND(2) + 5)$$

9. Write a program that asks for the user's height in inches and then prints "TALL" if the user is over six feet, "SHORT" if under five feet, or "AVERAGE" if between five and six feet, inclusive.

10. Write a program that inputs a number and prints "THREE" if it is a 3, "SIX" if it is a 6, "NINE" if it is a 9, or "NEITHER 3, 6, nor 9" if it is neither 3, 6, nor 9.

3

Think about This (for Fun)
What is the exact opposite of NOT IN?

Think about This (Seriously)
Should all "computer using" teachers know how to program?

"Frustration is not having anyone to blame but yourself."
Bits and Pieces

"Work spares us from three great evils: boredom, vice and need."
Voltaire

Would You Care
to Repeat That?

3.1 Objectives

For the successful completion of this chapter, you should be able to

1. Define and give at least one example of each of these BASIC statements: VTAB, HTAB, DATA-READ, FOR-NEXT, and GOSUB-RETURN (Sections. 3.2.1–3.2.4, 3.4).
2. Enter and RUN each of the BASIC programs used as statement examples in this chapter.
3. Define and give the purpose of one-dimensional arrays.
4. Design, enter, and RUN a BASIC program of your choosing that contains the statements discussed in Chapters 1–3.

3.2 BASIC Statements for This Chapter

3.2.1 Statement VTAB n

PURPOSE   VTAB vertically positions the cursor n lines on the screen, where n may be 1–24, inclusive.

EXAMPLE   VTAB 12

(The cursor would be positioned on the twelfth line in its current column.)

3.2.2 Statement HTAB n

PURPOSE   HTAB horizontally positions the cursor to column n on the screen, where n may be 1–40, inclusive.

EXAMPLES   HTAB 10

(The cursor would be positioned in the tenth column on its current line.)

```
10 HOME: VTAB 12: HTAB 18
20 PRINT "TEST 1"
```

(TEST 1 would appear in the approximate center of the screen.)

3.2.3 Statement Pair: DATA-READ

PURPOSE   DATA allows information (numeric or string) to be stored in a program for use at various stages throughout its execution. The pieces of information are generally referred to as *data elements,* with each element separated (*delimited*) by a comma. READ assigns the defined value of a data element to a specified variable and "moves" a data "marker," or "pointer," to the next data element. The data type (numeric or string) *must* match the variable type (numeric or string). For example, "ABC" cannot be assigned to a numeric variable!

One additional important note should be made in regard to the elements in the DATA statements: *never* place a comma at the end of the DATA statement. The system may take the space character following the comma as the next data element!

EXAMPLE
```
10 HOME
20 READ P1$: PRINT P1$
30 READ A: PRINT A
40 READ P2$: PRINT P2$
50 VTAB 22: HTAB 30: INPUT "RETURN =>";Z$
60 PRINT P1$; A; P2$
999 DATA "Help! I'm",47," and sinking fast!"
```

What caused the display to change from vertical to horizontal? Did the values of the variables change from one display to the next?

This example also demonstrates one method to "hold" the screen display for an indefinite period *until* the RETURN key is pressed. Note how the positioning is set in line 50. Also note that spaces are included within the quotation marks of the string elements in the DATA statement to prevent close-packing when the variable values are PRINTed in statement 60.

EXAMPLE
```
10 HOME: C = 0
20 READ N
30 C = C + N
40 PRINT "N = "N TAB(20) "C = "C
50 READ N
60 C = C + N
70 PRINT "N = "N TAB(20) "C = "C
80 DATA 10,15
```

Why did the values of variables N and C change? Note that variable C is, in effect, a cumulative total of the values assigned to variable N.

(After mentally tracing the program execution, enter and RUN the preceding example to check your mental interpretations.)

Note: On many BASIC systems, statements such as 10 . . .C = 0 (as in the previous program, for example) are not needed, because all numeric variables are automatically "initialized" (set) to zero, and string variables are set to a null value (" "). However, it is good programming practice to initialize to zero any numeric variable used.

3.2.4 Statement Pair FOR-NEXT

PURPOSE

This pair defines the number of times (loops) a series of consecutive BASIC statements is to be repeated. FOR defines the variable used as a counter for the repeats and the lower and upper limits of the count. NEXT increases the variable count by one (or the defined STEP size) and checks to see if the upper limit of the FOR is exceeded. If not, execution is transferred to the statement immediately following the FOR statement. If the upper limit is exceeded, execution is transferred to the statement immediately following the NEXT statement.

The variable names in the loop defined by a FOR-NEXT must be identical. Note that the start and limit of the loop may be defined by variable names, as in FOR X = Y TO Z.

Note also that loops may be defined in DECREASING order:

```
FOR I = 10 TO 1 STEP -1
    .
    .
NEXT I
```

In this example, the counter begins at 10 and decreases to 1 in increments (steps) of − 1.

EXAMPLES

```
10 HOME
20 FOR C = 1 TO 10
30   PRINT C,C*C
40 NEXT C
50 PRINT "That's doing a loop ten times..."

10 HOME
20 FOR C = 1 TO 30 STEP 3
30   PRINT C
40 NEXT C
50 PRINT "That's a loop in steps of threes..."
```

```
10 HOME : VTAB 12
20 INPUT "Enter your first name ";NAME$
30 FOR C = 1 TO 30
40   HOME : VTAB 12 : HTAB C
50   PRINT NAME$
60 NEXT C
70 VTAB 20 : HTAB 10 : PRINT "Wow! You move fast!"

10 HOME
20 A = 10 : B = -10
30 FOR C = A TO B STEP -2
40   PRINT C "   ";
50 NEXT C
60 PRINT "And we counted backward by twos..."
```

Note: The indentations are for clarity.

Mentally trace the execution, and then enter and RUN each program.

The FOR-NEXT loop also may be used to produce a "pausing" effect while the loop "counts" to the specified value. Approximately one second is required for the loop to "count" to 1000.

EXAMPLE

```
10 HOME : VTAB 12 : HTAB 10
20 PRINT "THE VANISHING TITLE"
30 FOR P = 1 TO 3000 : NEXT P
40 HOME
```

In the preceding example, the title will be displayed in the center of the screen for approximately three seconds.

3.3 Incorporating the New Statements and a Time-Saving Technique

With the addition of the statements in this chapter, a BASIC program may be designed that provides more utility than the earlier programs. In these programs we will also introduce "framing" into our design. Consider frames as separate screens displaying such elements as a title, information, and questions. For our purposes, each frame will begin with a HOME statement.

There may be times when a user wishes to SAVE both the old and new versions of a program. The new (modified) version of a program may be SAVEd by simply giving it a new (unique) name when the SAVE command is issued. We did this earlier in Chapter 2 when PROGRAM 1 was modified (with the heartbeats) and SAVEd as PROGRAM 2.

To illustrate this further, PROGRAM 4 will be created and SAVEd. Then it will be modified and SAVEd as PROGRAM 5. This means that both the old (PROGRAM 4) and the new (PROGRAM 5) programs will be available for future use.

3.3.1 PROGRAM 4: Subtraction Drill

Arbitrarily, this new program will be a drill on subtraction practice. Then it will be modified to be a drill on addition practice.

We will have the program display a title for a few seconds, then let the user select the number of problems (within limits) and the range of values (again, within limits). The program will present that number of problems, randomly selecting the values from within the requested range. If the problem is answered correctly, a "correct counter" will be incremented by 1, and the next problem will be presented. Otherwise, the correct answer will be displayed until the RETURN key is pressed. At the conclusion of the program the number of problems answered correctly will be displayed.

Here is the program design by frames and steps.

FRAME 1   Erase the screen and center and display a title for a few seconds (HOME, VTAB, HTAB, PRINT, FOR-NEXT).

FRAME 2,   Erase the screen and ask for the number of problems the user wishes
STEP 1   (HOME, VTAB, INPUT).

FRAME 2,   Check that the value INPUT is within our defined limits (IF-THEN-PRINT,
STEP 2   GOTO Frame 2, Step 1).

FRAME 2,   Ask for the maximum and minimum values for the problems (INPUTs).
STEP 3

FRAME 2,   Check that these values are within our defined limits (IF-THEN-PRINT,
STEP 4   GOTO Frame 2, Step 3).

Now we begin a loop asking the requested number of problems.

Carefully examine the listing of PROGRAM 4 that follows and note how each frame and step is translated into BASIC code.

```
10 REM              PROGRAM 4
20 REM
30 REM ---------------------------------------------------
40 REM   FRAME 1 - DISPLAY TITLE ABOUT 3 SECONDS
50 REM
60    HOME  :   VTAB 12  :   HTAB 10
70    PRINT "SUBTRACTION DRILL"
80    FOR P = 1 TO 3000  :   NEXT P
90 REM ---------------------------------------------------
100 REM   FRAME 2, STEP 1 - ASK FOR NUMBER OF PROBLEMS
110 REM
120    HOME  :   VTAB 12
130    INPUT "HOW MANY PROBLEMS DO YOU WANT? "; NUMBER
140 REM ---------------------------------------------------
150 REM   FRAME 2, STEP 2 - IS IT REASONABLE?
160 REM
170    IF NUMBER < 5 OR NUMBER > 20 THEN PRINT, "SELECT 5 TO 20!"
           : GOTO 130
180 REM ---------------------------------------------------
190 REM   FRAME 2, STEP 3 - GET RANGE OF PROBLEMS
200 REM
210   PRINT : INPUT "WHAT'S THE LOWEST NUMBER YOU WANT? "; LOW
220   PRINT : INPUT "WHAT'S THE HIGHEST NUMBER YOU WANT? "; HIGH
230 REM ---------------------------------------------------
240 REM   FRAME 2, STEP 4 - ARE THEY REASONABLE?
250 REM
260       IF LOW < 10 OR HIGH > 100 THEN PRINT, "SELECT 10 TO 100"
              : GOTO 210
270       IF HIGH < = LOW THEN PRINT "HIGH IS < OR = LOW NUMBER!"
              : GOTO 210
```

LOOP FRAMES, STEP 1 Erase the screen and position the cursor for each problem (FOR, HOME, VTAB, HTAB).

LOOP FRAMES, STEP 2 Randomly select two numbers within the range requested by the user. [(LET), INT, RND], and check (IF-THEN) to ensure that the first random number is larger than the second. This is done arbitrarily, since the program is a SUBTRACTION drill, and we want the answer to be positive.

LOOP FRAMES, STEP 3 Assign the difference of the second number from the first number to a variable (LET). This is the correct answer to the problem. Display the problem (PRINT).

LOOP FRAMES, STEP 4 Get the user's answer and check it for accuracy. If it is correct, increase a counter by 1 and ask the next question [INPUT, IF-THEN (LET), GOTO, NEXT].

LOOP FRAMES, STEP 5 If the answer is incorrect, display the correct answer until the RETURN key is pressed; then ask the next question (PRINT, VTAB, HTAB, INPUT, NEXT).

FINAL FRAME Erase the screen and center and display the number of problems answered correctly (HOME, VTAB, PRINT, END).

```
280 REM  --------------------------------------------------
290 REM    LOOP FRAMES, STEP 1 - START LOOP; POSITION CURSOR
300 REM
310  FOR I = 1 TO NUMBER
320   HOME : VTAB 12 : HTAB 10
330 REM  --------------------------------------------------
340 REM    LOOP FRAMES, STEP 2 - RANDOMLY SELECT 2 NUMBERS
350 REM
360       N1 = INT (((HIGH - LOW) + 1) * RND(1) + LOW)
370       N2 = INT (((HIGH - LOW) + 1) * RND(1) + LOW)
380 REM  --------------------------------------------------
390 REM    LOOP FRAMES, STEP 3 - CHECK N1 > N2; ASSIGN ANSWER
400 REM
410       IF N1 < = N2 THEN 360
420       ANSWER = N1 - N2
430       PRINT N1 " - " N2 " = ";
440 REM  --------------------------------------------------
450 REM    LOOP FRAMES, STEP 4 - CHECK REPLY; OK? COUNT IT
460 REM
470       INPUT REPLY
480       IF REPLY = ANSWER THEN CRCT = CRCT + 1 : GOTO 540
490 REM  --------------------------------------------------
500 REM    LOOP FRAMES, STEP 5 - INCORRECT? SHOW ANSWER
510 REM
520       PRINT :  PRINT "THE CORRECT ANSWER IS " ANSWER
530       VTAB 20 : HTAB 30 : INPUT "RETURN => "; Z$
540     NEXT I
550 REM  --------------------------------------------------
560 REM    FINAL FRAME - PERFORMANCE REPORT
570 REM
580       HOME  : VTAB 12
590       PRINT "YOU WERE CORRECT ON " CRCT " OF " NUMBER " PROBLEMS"
600       END
```

PROGRAM 4 SAMPLE RUN— FRAME 2, STEPS 1—4

```
          How many problems do you want? 100
                  SELECT 5 TO 20!
          How many problems do you want? 7

          What's the lowest number you want? 12

          What's the highest number you want? 12
          HIGH IS < OR = TO LOW NUMBER!

          What's the lowest number you want? 12

          What's the highest number you want? 50
```

PROGRAM 4 SAMPLE RUN— LOOP FRAME, STEPS 1—4

```
          32 - 14 = ? 18
```

PROGRAM 4 SAMPLE RUN— FINAL FRAME

```
          YOU WERE CORRECT ON 6 OF 7 PROBLEMS
```

For practice and review, RUN PROGRAM 4 from the text disk.

3.3.2 PROGRAM 5: Addition Drill (A Modification of PROGRAM 4)

For the previous program, we took a concept for the general design, broke it down into a series of steps from "top to bottom," outlined the BASIC statements needed to accomplish each step, and translated each step into program code. Now, let us see what would be necessary to take an existing program and make a minimum of modifications so that the program would present material in a similar design, but of different content.

PROGRAM 4 presented drill on subtraction. We will modify this program to present drill on addition, then SAVE it as PROGRAM 5. Careful examination of the listing of PROGRAM 4 shows that the *minimum* changes needed are statements 70, 420, and 430. After PROGRAM 4 has been LOADed from the disk, the following is entered:

```
70 PRINT "A D D I T I O N    D R I L L"
420 ANSWER = N1 + N2
430 PRINT N1 " + " N2 " = ";
SAVE PROGRAM 5
```

However, statement 10 was retyped to reflect the new program name, and statement 410 was deleted since it no longer matters if the first random number is smaller than the second.

Thus, a new program, PROGRAM 5, based on PROGRAM 4 has been created and SAVEd without the time and trouble required to completely retype the new version.

```
10 REM            PROGRAM 5
20 REM
30 REM -------------------------------------------------
40 REM    FRAME 1 - DISPLAY TITLE ABOUT 3 SECONDS
50 REM
60    HOME  :  VTAB 12  :  HTAB 10
70    PRINT "ADDITION DRILL"
80    FOR P = 1 TO 3000  :  NEXT P
90 REM -------------------------------------------------
100 REM   FRAME 2, STEP 1 - ASK FOR NUMBER OF PROBLEMS
110 REM
120    HOME  :  VTAB 12
130    INPUT "HOW MANY PROBLEMS DO YOU WANT? "; NUMBER
140 REM -------------------------------------------------
150 REM   FRAME 2, STEP 2 - IS IT REASONABLE?
160 REM
170    IF NUMBER < 5 OR NUMBER > 20 THEN PRINT, "SELECT 5 TO 20!"
           :  GOTO 130
```

```
180 REM -----------------------------------------------------
190 REM   FRAME 2, STEP 3 - GET RANGE OF PROBLEMS
200 REM
210    PRINT : INPUT "WHAT'S THE LOWEST NUMBER YOU WANT? "; LOW
220    PRINT : INPUT "WHAT'S THE HIGHEST NUMBER YOU WANT? "; HIGH
230 REM -----------------------------------------------------
240 REM   FRAME 2, STEP 4 - ARE THEY REASONABLE?
250 REM
260    IF LOW < 10 OR HIGH > 100 THEN PRINT, "SELECT 10 TO 100"
          : GOTO 210
270    IF HIGH < = LOW THEN PRINT "HIGH IS < OR = LOW NUMBER!"
          : GOTO 210
280 REM -----------------------------------------------------
290 REM   LOOP FRAMES, STEP 1 - START LOOP; POSITION CURSOR
300 REM
310    FOR I = 1 TO NUMBER
320    HOME  :  VTAB 12  :  HTAB 10
330 REM -----------------------------------------------------
340 REM   LOOP FRAMES, STEP 2 - RANDOMLY SELECT 2 NUMBERS
350 REM
360      N1 = INT (((HIGH - LOW) + 1) * RND (1) + LOW)
370      N2 = INT (((HIGH - LOW) + 1) * RND (1) + LOW)
380 REM -----------------------------------------------------
390 REM   LOOP FRAMES, STEP 3 - ASSIGN ANSWER
400 REM
420      ANSWER = N1 + N2
430      PRINT N1 " + " N2 " = ";
440 REM -----------------------------------------------------
450 REM   LOOP FRAMES, STEP 4 - CHECK REPLY; OK? COUNT IT
460 REM
470      INPUT REPLY
480      IF REPLY = ANSWER THEN CRCT = CRCT + 1 : GOTO 540
490 REM -----------------------------------------------------
500 REM   LOOP FRAMES, STEP 5 - INCORRECT? SHOW ANSWER
510 REM
520      PRINT :  PRINT "THE CORRECT ANSWER IS " ANSWER
530      VTAB 20 : HTAB 30 : INPUT "RETURN => "; Z$
540    NEXT I
550 REM -----------------------------------------------------
560 REM   FINAL FRAME - PERFORMANCE REPORT
570 REM
580      HOME  : VTAB 12
590      PRINT "YOU WERE CORRECT ON " CRCT " OF " NUMBER " PROBLEMS"
600      END
```

For practice and review, RUN PROGRAM 5 from the text disk.

3.4 Statement Pair GOSUB–RETURN

PURPOSE

This statement pair is very useful for programs in which a sequence of statements is repeated several times throughout program execution. Whenever GOSUB is encountered, program execution is transferred to the statement number specified in the GOSUB. Execution continues from that statement until the RETURN *statement* (*not* the RETURN key) is encountered. Execution is then transferred (RETURNed) to the statement number *immediately following the particular GOSUB* statement that caused the transfer in the first place.

A typical example in instructional computing would be an answer-checking sequence for student input in a program containing several questions. Rather than writing an identical answer-checking sequence for each question, we write it only once as a subroutine. GOSUB may then be used after each question to check the answer.

EXAMPLE

```
10 REM          FRAME 1 - TITLE
20 REM ------------------------------------
30 HOME : VTAB 12 : HTAB 8
40 PRINT "Examples of GOSUB-RETURN Use"
50 FOR P = 1 TO 2000 : NEXT P
60 REM ------------------------------------
70 REM          FRAME 2 - 1ST QUESTION/ANSWER ASSIGNMENT
80 QUES$ = "Identify the capital of Texas"
90 ANS$ = "AUSTIN"
100 GOSUB 5000
110 REM ------------------------------------
120 REM          FRAME 3 - NEXT QUESTION/ANSWER ASSIGNMENT
130 QUES$ = "X marks the --?--"
140 ANS$ = "SPOT"
150 GOSUB 5000
160 REM ------------------------------------
170 REM          ADDITIONAL FRAMES MAY BE ADDED
4930 REM ------------------------------------
4940 REM          FINAL FRAME
4950 HOME : VTAB 12 : HTAB 8
4960 PRINT "You answered " C " question(s) correctly."
4970 END
4980 REM ------------------------------------
4990 REM          THE SUBROUTINE
5000 HOME : VTAB 12 : PRINT QUES$
5010 VTAB 14 : HTAB 10 : INPUT REPLY$
5020 IF REPLY$ <> ANS$ THEN 5050
5030 HOME : VTAB 12 : HTAB 18 : PRINT "GREAT!"
5040 C = C + 1 : FOR P = 1 TO 1000 : NEXT P : GOTO 5070
5050 PRINT : PRINT "The correct answer is " ANS$
5060 VTAB 22 : HTAB 30 : INPUT "Return =>";Z$
5070 RETURN
```

Mentally execute this program before entering and RUNning it. Note that the program has room to incorporate other questions between statements 150 and 4930, and that END may come before the subroutine.

3.5   One-Dimensional Arrays and the DIM Statement

For our purposes, a one-dimensional array is just an organized *list* of information stored in a new type of variable. That information could consist of any string or numeric values: student names, states, chemical names, school districts, test scores, ages, weights, years. This list of information may be assigned to variables using any of the methods previously discussed, such as (LET), INPUT, and DATA-READ statements. As you will see, once we have assigned this information to lists, we may apply a variety of uses.

We define the length (dimension) of the list using the DIM statement. For example, the statement

```
DIM N$(4)
```

"reserves" room in the memory of the microcomputer for a list of four string variables. (Actually, the microcomputer automatically reserves room for as many as eleven items in a list (numbered 0–10), but we will always use the DIM statement for lists of any size.)

For example, we can easily make a list of names using one-dimensional arrays in BASIC.

Consider some of the possible BASIC statements we could use. First, there is information (names) that will be used; thus, we might use DATA statements. Of course, if there is data, it will need to be READ. Also, a FOR-NEXT loop could be used to do the READing. Thus:

```
10 DIM N$(4)
20 FOR L = 1 TO 4
30   READ N$(L)
40 NEXT L
50 DATA "Chuck","Mary","Phil","Jeannie"
```

This should appear somewhat familiar, with the exception of statement 30, READ N$(L). N$(L) is an example of another type of variable. This type, however, uses an "internal" variable, (L), to distinguish one value of N$(L) from the others. Remember, the variable L is going to have a value that may be 1, 2, 3, or 4 (FOR L = 1 TO 4). Thus, the variable values in this example are

```
N$(1) = Chuck
N$(2) = Mary
N$(3) = Phil
N$(4) = Jeannie
```

Or, said another way, there is a four-item list (one-dimensional array) of N$(L) values:

L	N$(L)
1	Chuck
2	Mary
3	Phil
4	Jeannie

The name given to these types of variables is *subscripted variables.* The value of N$(1), pronounced "N-string sub 1," is equal to the string Chuck; the value of N$(2) is equal to the string Mary, and so on.

It is quite simple to build a *series* of lists using subscripted variables. Suppose that we wished to make two lists of names and scores. Consider

```
10 DIM N$(4), S(4)
20 FOR L = 1 TO 4
30   READ N$(L),S(L)
40 NEXT L
90 DATA "Chuck",95,"Mary",80,"Phil",95,"Jeannie",35
```

If these statements were to be executed, what would be the value of N$(3)? Of S(4)? If the following statements were added to the preceding statements, what would be the result of execution?

```
50 FOR I = 4 TO 1  STEP -1
60   PRINT N$(I),S$(I)
70 NEXT I
80 END
```

(Mentally trace the execution; then enter and RUN to check your mental interpretation.)

Enter and RUN the following program:

```
10 DIM N$(5)
20 HOME : VTAB 2 : HTAB 8
30 PRINT "Here's a list of 5 names:" : PRINT
40 FOR I = 1 TO 5 : READ N$(I) : PRINT, N$(I) : NEXT I
50 PRINT : PRINT "Let's randomly choose 4 sets of 2 names"
60 VTAB 22 : HTAB 30 : INPUT "RETURN =>";Z$ : HOME
70 FOR I = 1 TO 4
80   FOR J = 1 TO 2 : VTAB I + 1 : HTAB J * 10
90     X = INT(5 * RND(1) + 1)
100    PRINT N$(X)
110  NEXT J
120 NEXT I
130 PRINT : PRINT "And here's the list in reverse" : PRINT
140 FOR I = 5 TO 1 STEP -1 : PRINT, N$(I) : NEXT I
150 DATA "Kay","Buck","Karyn","Tracy","George"
```

As you can see (and will see again), one advantage of using one-dimensional arrays is that, once the values have been assigned to positions in the list, we may pick and choose items from the list at will. Note that the FOR I = 1 TO 4 loop has another loop (FOR J = 1 TO 2) "nested" within it. In this example, the "inner" J loop, which randomly selects and displays 2 names, will be executed 4 times by the "outer" I loop. Thus, a total of 8 names will be randomly selected and displayed. Some will be repeated, of course, since there are only 5 names in the list. Also note how the VTAB and HTAB in statement 80 use the values of I and J, respectively, in positioning the display of the names.

There are many more applications of one-dimensional arrays in instructional computing than just building lists of names and scores. The following program gives an example of some of these uses.

3.5.1   PROGRAM 6: Random Sentences, Questions, and Responses

One use of one-dimensional arrays may be seen in PROGRAM 6. This program demonstrates the use of one-dimensional arrays in forming random sentences. One array will contain the subjects, another the verbs, and another the direct objects. Using random numbers, a subject, verb, and direct object will be selected from each list and printed as a sentence. Since each list will contain five items, a total of 125 (5 × 5 × 5) different sentences is possible. A one-dimensional array is also used to randomly select the "question" to be asked; that is, "Identify the ([SUBJECT]/[VERB]/[DIRECT OBJECT])." Another one-dimensional array will contain the "positive feedback" comments given for a correct answer. This feedback will also be randomly selected from the list. Thus, the use of one-dimensional arrays provides a method of increasing the variety of questions, answers, and feedback in instructional computing programs without extensive programming.

Frame by frame and step by step, the design of this program is as follows:

FRAME 1   Present a title for a moment or two, then size the arrays and assign the lists of subjects, verbs, and direct objects and sentence parts to identify and feedback to their appropriate arrays.

FRAME 2   Present an introduction until the RETURN key is pressed.

FRAME 3   Let the user select the number of sentences to practice (within defined limits).

FRAME 4,   Begin the question loop by randomly selecting each part of the sentence
STEP 1   (subject, verb, and direct object).

FRAME 4,   Assign the randomly selected part to identify as the correct answer.
STEP 2

Very carefully examine the listing of PROGRAM 6 that follows to see how these concepts are translated frame by frame and step by step into BASIC code.

```
10 REM              PROGRAM 6
20 REM
30 REM -------------------------------------------------
40 REM       FRAME 1 - TITLE AND ASSIGNMENTS
50 REM
60      HOME   :   VTAB 12   :   HTAB 8
70      PRINT "RANDOM SENTENCES"
80      FOR P = 1 TO 3000   :   NEXT P
90      DIM SUBJ$(5), VERB$(5), DIROBJ$(5)
100     FOR I = 1 TO 5 : READ SUBJ$(I),VERB$(I),DIROBJ$(I) : NEXT I
110     PART$(1) = "SUBJECT" : PART$(2) = "VERB"
           : PART$(3) = "DIRECT OBJECT"
120     FDBK$(1) = "PERFECT" : FDBK$(2) = "GREAT" : FDBK$(3) ="A-OK"
130 REM -------------------------------------------------
140 REM   FRAME 2 - INTRODUCTION
150 REM
160     HOME   :   VTAB 4
170     PRINT "I'LL GIVE YOU SOME SENTENCES AND YOU" : PRINT
180     PRINT "WILL BE ASKED TO IDENTIFY EITHER THE" : PRINT
190     PRINT "SUBJECT, VERB, OR DIRECT OBJECT. YOU" : PRINT
200     PRINT "MAY SELECT 3-25 SENTENCES TO PRACTICE."
210     VTAB 20 : HTAB 30 : INPUT "RETURN =>"; Z$
220 REM -------------------------------------------------
230 REM   FRAME 3 - NUMBER OF SENTENCES TO PRACTICE
240 REM
250     HOME : VTAB 12
260     INPUT "HOW MANY SENTENCES DO YOU WANT (3-25)? "; NUMBER
270     IF NUMBER < 3 OR NUMBER > 25 THEN 250
280 REM -------------------------------------------------
290 REM   FRAME 4, STEP 1 - RANDOM SELECTIONS
300 REM
310     FOR I = 1 TO NUMBER   :   HOME : VTAB 8
320        PRINT "GIVEN THE SENTENCE: "   :   PRINT
330        SBJ = INT(5 * RND(1) + 1)
340        VRB = INT(5 * RND(1) + 1)
350        DOB = INT(5 * RND(1) + 1)
360        PRT = INT(3 * RND(1) + 1)
370 REM -------------------------------------------------
380 REM   FRAME 4, STEP 2 - ASSIGN PART SELECTED TO ANSWER$
390 REM
400        IF PRT = 1 THEN ANSWER$ = SUBJ$(SBJ)
410        IF PRT = 2 THEN ANSWER$ = VERB$(VRB)
420        IF PRT = 3 THEN ANSWER$ = DIROBJ$(DOB)
```

FRAME 4,   Display the sentence and get a reply from the user.
STEP 3

FRAME 4,   If the reply is correct, assign a random feedback to the correct answer
STEP 4   variable. Otherwise, display the correct answer as feedback. In either
                     case, display the result until the RETURN key is pressed.

FINAL   Display a performance report to the user.
FRAME

DATA LIST   Include a list of DATA for the subjects, verbs, and direct objects at the
                     end of the program.

```
430 REM  ---------------------------------------------------
440 REM    FRAME 4, STEP 3 - DISPLAY SENTENCE;  CHECK REPLY
450 REM
460        PRINT "SUBJ$(SUB) " " VERB$(VRB) " THE "DIROBJ$(DOB) "."
                 : PRINT
470        PRINT "WHAT IS THE " PART$(PRT) ;
480        INPUT REPLY$  :  PRINT
490 REM  ---------------------------------------------------
500 REM   FRAME 4, STEP 4 - CORRECT?  FEEDBACK TO ANSWER$
510 REM
520           IF REPLY$ = ANSWER$ THEN ANSWER$ = FDBK$(PRT)
                    : COUNT = COUNT + 1
530           PRINT "THE ANSWER TO THAT QUESTION IS " ANSWER$ "!"
540           VTAB 20 : HTAB 30 : INPUT "RETURN =>"; Z$
550        NEXT I
560 REM  ---------------------------------------------------
570 REM     FINAL FRAME - PERFORMANCE REPORT
580 REM
590        HOME  :    VTAB 12  :    HTAB 6
600        PRINT "YOU CORRECTLY ANSWERED " COUNT "."
610        END
620 REM  ---------------------------------------------------
630 REM   DATA FOR SUBJECTS,  VERBS,  DIRECT OBJECTS
640 REM
650 DATA "SAM","LIKES","DOG","MARY","LOVES","CAT","TRACY","KISSED"
660 DATA "FISH","HERB","SOLD","BIRD","LISA","BOUGHT","CAR"
```

PROGRAM 6 SAMPLE RUNS— FRAME 4, STEPS 1–4

```
Given the sentence:

SAM SOLD THE CAR.

What is the DIRECT OBJECT? SOLD

The answer to that question is CAR!

--------------------------------- RETURN =>
Given the sentence:

TRACY LIKES THE BIRD.

What is the VERB? LIKES

The answer to that question is A-OK!
```

For practice and review, RUN PROGRAM 6 from the text disk.

3.6 Posers and Problems

1. Correct any errors in the following programs:

```
10 FOR X = 1 TO 10
20     PRINT Y,Y*Y
30 NEXT Y
40 END
```

```
10 DATA "How old is George",50," (in 1988)"
20 READ Q$,A,C
30 PRINT Q$;C;
40 INPUT R
50 IF A$ = R THEN 70
60 PRINT "No...!"
70 PRINT A " is correct!"
80 END
```

2. Following are some student data for a name and test score. Complete the program so that the name and score are assigned to one-dimensional arrays and printed in columnar form.

```
10 DATA "CHUCK", 95, "MARY", 80, "PHIL", 95, "JEANNIE", 35
20 FOR L = 1 TO 4
30 READ ?, ?
  ? ?
```

3. Modify your program from Problem 2 to print the average of the scores after printing the list of names and scores. Hint: review "cumulative total" techniques shown in Section 3.2.3.
4. Enter and RUN the following program. Be prepared to discuss its flow.

```
10 FOR R = 10 TO 1 STEP -1
20     HOME : VTAB 12
30     PRINT R " little rabbit(s)...see the tail(s)!"
40     PRINT,
50       FOR T = 1 TO R
60         PRINT "* ";
70       NEXT T
80     PRINT
90     VTAB 20 : HTAB 12 : PRINT "FRAME " 11 - R
100    VTAB 22 : HTAB 30 : INPUT "RETURN =>"; Z$
110 NEXT R
120 HOME : VTAB 12 : HTAB 10
130 PRINT "And then there were NONE..."
```

In particular, what is the purpose of STEP − 1 in statement 10, the comma in statement 40, the semicolon in statement 60, and PRINT in statement 80? After RUNning the program, delete statements 90–100 and 120. RUN the program again and note the results.
5. Modify PROGRAM 4 to present a drill on multiplication.
6. Modify PROGRAM 4 to present a drill on division. Use random numbers that will *not* have a remainder after division. Note: this task may be accomplished by incorporating the statement

```
410 IF N1/N2 <> INT(N1/N2) THEN 360
```

This will ensure that any quotient derived from dividing N1 by N2 will be a whole number—that is, a positive integer value with no remainder.

4

Think about This (for Fun)
Four strangers meet in a room. How many handshakes are required for all to be introduced to one another?

Think about This (Seriously)
Should *every* student have had an exposure to computers by the time of graduation from high school?

Combining the
BASIC
Ingredients

4.1 Objectives

For the successful completion of this chapter, you should be able to

1. Modify one or more of the example programs in the chapter to contain content of your choosing.
2. Incorporate a "menu" program on your disk and incorporate record keeping into one or more of your modified programs.

4.2 The Purpose of This Chapter

Now that we have discussed some of the fundamental BASIC statements, let us combine them into some simple programming examples. This chapter contains a series of instructional computing programs designed using a top-down, frame-by-frame approach. They may be easily modified or adapted to actual classroom use by anyone with a limited introduction to BASIC and computers in education. The programs provide an introduction to certain strategies and techniques that may be applied to drill, tutorial, testing, and record-keeping applications. Hopefully, they will plant an "imaginative seed" leading to enhanced development and application. Nonetheless, if you do nothing more than just make simple modifications to the examples, you will have a product of instructional computing programs of *your own content.* And, you will have created it in a total of just a few short hours.

In addition, three "utility" programs are provided on the disk that accompanies this text. These programs illustrate how a computer can be used by a teacher as a convenient tool for determining class statistics and creating a personal bibliography.

4.3 The Existing Content of the Example Programs

The content of the example programs is intentionally trivial, because the content is *not* the point to be made. Rather, the programs illustrate some of the simple strategies that may be used in designing instructional computing materials. The content of the modifications is left to you as you use or expand upon these strategies. Generally, these modifications involve little more than changing or adding PRINT and DATA statements to reflect the content you desire.

Although a program design may be evident in its LISTing, it is important that you "see" its action. Therefore, each appropriate program should be executed from the disk before you work with it. Executing the program will give you a point of reference for understanding its design and use.

4.4 Modifying the Example Programs

As mentioned earlier, the examples may be modified by simply changing PRINT and DATA statements to reflect whatever content you want. For example, if you want a different title, you would change the PRINT statement(s) in the **TITLE FRAME** to the title you choose. Similarly, you would change the DATA statements in a **DATA FRAME** if you wanted different questions, answers, hints, and so forth. To make these changes even easier, in each program listing the **minimum** statements that might be changed are shown in an "outline" type face, like this: DATA. Of course, you might want to make other modifications than the minimum shown. Also, each program is designed so that an indefinite number of questions and so forth may be added without having to redo the program. Worksheets are provided for each program to serve as a guide for modifying the programs.

In outline, the modification steps would be

1. **Examine** the listing of the program to determine the statements to change and the strategy sequence.
2. Use the worksheet to **write** out your changes.
3. **LOAD** the program from the disk provided.
4. **Modify** the program.
5. **SAVE** the program using a different but meaningful name.
6. **Test** the program.
7. **Revise** and **SAVE** if needed, using the new name from Step 5.

4.5 "Packaging" Your Products

The final programs in this book illustrate how your programs may be presented as a "menu" of options for a user and how simple record keeping may be used or incorporated into each program. Thus, you can have a relatively complete package of instructional computing applications presenting *your* content in *your* area of interest when you have completed modifying the programs in the book.

4.6 Drill and Practice Applications

Drill and practice programs have wide application in any area in which certain fundamental concepts require practice for mastery, such as multiplication tables, chemical nomenclature, Latin-English word root translations, state capitals, or for general review on any given topic.

Drill and practice programs are generally very straightforward. An introduction, usually including examples, is given; drill questions are presented; answers are entered and checked for accuracy; appropriate feedback is given; the next question is asked; and, at the end of the program, some form of performance report is given.

The four example programs that follow illustrate use of GOSUB-RETURN, FOR-NEXT, and DATA-READ use for both linear and random selection of questions.

4.6.1 LINDRILL-1 Program

Linear drill programs are easy to design using GOSUB-RETURN. In the example shown, PRINT statement(s) are used to ask a question, and the anticipated correct answer is assigned to the variable ANSWER$, followed by a GOSUB 10000 to get the user's response and check it for accuracy. Follow this same sequence to add an indefinite number of questions of your own choosing. Note that, in the subroutine beginning at 10000, the LEN string function is used to display a number of hyphens (-) corresponding to the number of characters in the anticipated answer. The program also includes positive feedback that is assigned to an array for random selection for each question correctly answered.

Again, by following the sequence of PRINT(s) for the question, ANSWER$ = "<correct answer>", and GOSUB 10000, the program may be used to present questions on any topic. (Remember that the **minimum** program statements to change for different content are shown in "outline" type face.)

WORK SHEET FOR LINDRILL-1

Suggested Activities:
· Modify the title and existing questions to five or more of your choosing.
· Modify the PRINT in statement 10000 to display X's.

TITLE FRAME

70 PRINT" _____"

QUESTION FRAMES

130 PRINT" _____"

140 ANSWER$=" _____" : GOSUB 10000

180 PRINT" _____"

190 ANSWER$=" _____" : GOSUB 10000

230 PRINT" _____"

240 ANSWER$=" _____" : GOSUB 10000

(Follow the same sequence for additional questions)

_____

_____

_____

_____

_____

_____

SAVE _____ (your program name)

```
10 REM                    LINDRILL-1 PROGRAM
20 REM
30 REM -------------------------------------------------------
40 REM                FRAME 1 - TITLE AND ASSIGNMENTS
50 REM
60         HOME : VTAB 12 : HTAB 2
70         PRINT "DRILL USING A SUBROUTINE FOR INPUT"
80         FOR P = 1 TO 3000 : NEXT P : HOME : VTAB 12
90         DIM FDBK$(6) : FOR A = 1 TO 6 : READ FDBK$(A) : NEXT A
100 REM -------------------------------------------------------
110 REM             FRAME 2 - FIRST QUESTION SEQUENCE
120 REM
130        PRINT "THE STATE FLOWER OF TEXAS IS THE"
140        ANSWER$ = "BLUEBONNET" : GOSUB 10000
150 REM -------------------------------------------------------
160 REM             FRAME 3 - NEXT QUESTION SEQUENCE
170 REM
180        PRINT "THE LARGEST MUSCLE IN THE BODY IS THE"
190        ANSWER$ = "GLUTEUS MAXIMUS" : GOSUB 10000
200 REM -------------------------------------------------------
210 REM             (FRAMES FOR ADDITIONAL QUESTIONS)
220 REM
9930 REM -------------------------------------------------------
9940 REM             FINAL  FRAME - PERFORMANCE REPORT
9950 REM
9960       SCRE=INT((C*100/Q)*10)/10 : PRINT "YOUR SCORE IS " SCRE"%"
9969 END
9970 REM -------------------------------------------------------
9980 REM             POSITIONING  AND INPUT SUBROUTINE
9990 REM
10000      VTAB 16 : HTAB 12 : FOR  S = 1 TO LEN(ANSWER$) :
           PRINT"-"; : NEXT S: Q=Q+1

10010      VTAB 16 : HTAB 9 : INPUT "=>"; REPLY$ : PRINT
10020      IF  REPLY$ = ANSWER$  THEN  10050
10030      PRINT "THE CORRECT ANSWER IS "   ANSWER$
10040      VTAB 20 : HTAB 30 : INPUT  "RETURN =>"; R$ : HOME :
           VTAB 12 : RETURN

10050      C = C  +1 : HOME :   VTAB 12 :   HTAB 12 :
           PRINT FDBK$(6 * RND(1) + 1) "!"

10060      FOR P = 1 TO 1000 : NEXT P : HOME : VTAB 12 : RETURN
11000 REM -------------------------------------------------------
11010 REM             SIX (6) DATA ELEMENTS FOR FEEDBACK
11020 REM
11030      DATA"RAZZLE-DAZZLE",  "HOT-DOGGIES",  "WONDERFUL"
11040      DATA "SIMPLY SWELL",  "OHH! GREAT",  "THAT'S THE WAY"
```

■ **An Example of a Modification.**   Suppose we wanted to replace *one* of the existing questions (statements 130–140) and *incorporate two* additional questions (after statement 220) in the LINDRILL-1 program. Also, we have decided to name the modified program MUSCLE DRILL. After booting the disk, the typing and entering steps would be (and would appear on the screen as)

```
]LOAD LINDRILL-1
]70 PRINT "A SHORT DRILL ON MUSCLES OF THE BODY"
]130 PRINT "THE PRIMARY MUSCLE THAT FLEXES THE ARM IS THE"

]140 ANSWER$ = "BICEPS" : GOSUB 10000
]230 PRINT "THE  PRIMARY MUSCLE  THAT EXTENDS THE  ARM IS THE"

]240 ANSWER$ = "TRICEPS" : GOSUB 10000
]250 PRINT "THE LARGEST MUSCLE OF THE CHEST IS THE"
]260 ANSWER$ = "PECTORALIS MAJORA" : GOSUB 10000
]SAVE MUSCLE DRILL
```

The disk would now contain a program, MUSCLE DRILL, that asks *four* drill questions about muscles.

4.6.2 LINDRILL-2 Program

The LINDRILL-1 program design was straightforward: we used PRINT(s) to ask a question, we assigned the correct answer to ANSWER$, and we then used a GOSUB 10000 to get a reply, check it for accuracy, and respond accordingly. However, feedback was limited to displaying either a randomly selected comment for correct answers or the anticipated correct answer.

We can expand this design to include presentation of a hint by simple modifications of the general design of LINDRILL-1. We will need to assign a hint to a string variable in each question frame, and we will have to modify the subroutine slightly so that the hint will be presented on the *first* incorrect answer and the correct answer given on the *second* incorrect reply. Our first modification will be to include HNT$ = "<hint>" in each question frame. The other modifications will require some way of determining in the subroutine if a given question is missed on the *first* or the *second* attempt. To do this, the subroutine will begin by assigning a value of 0 (zero) to a numeric variable named MISS. When a question is missed, the value of MISS will be checked. If it is 0, a value of 1 will be assigned to MISS, the hint will be PRINTed, and the question repeated. If the question is missed again, the value of MISS is 1 (from the first miss), so the correct answer will be PRINTed rather than the hint. Examine the listing of LINDRILL-2. Each statement number that was modified or added ends with a 2. Also note that the beginning statement number of the subroutine now assigns the value of 0 to MISS since each question must *begin* with no misses.

Again, however, all you need do to reflect content of your choosing is change or add (a) PRINT(s) for the question, (b) HNT$ = "<a hint>", and (c) ANSWER$ = "<the correct answer>" : **GOSUB** 10000.

WORK SHEET FOR LINDRILL-2

Suggested Activities:

· Modify the title and existing questions to five or more of your choosing. Include a hint for each question.
· Add an introduction to the program.
· Modify the feedback DATA elements to six of your choosing.

TITLE FRAME

70 PRINT" _____ "

INTRODUCTION

91 PRINT" _____ "

92 PRINT" _____ "

93 PRINT" _____ "

.

.

99 VTAB 23 : HTAB 30 : INPUT "RETURN => ";R$: HOME : VTAB 12

QUESTION FRAMES

130 PRINT" _____ "

132 HNT$=" _____ "

140 ANSWER$=" _____ " : GOSUB 10000

180 PRINT" _____ "

182 HNT$=" _____ "

190 ANSWER$=" _____ " : GOSUB 10000

230 PRINT" _____ "

240 HNT$=" _____ "

250 ANSWER$=" _____ " : GOSUB 10000

.

.   (Follow the same sequence for additional questions)

.

11030 DATA "_____", "_____", "_____"

11040 DATA "_____", "_____", "_____"

SAVE _____ <your program name>

```
10 REM                    LINDRILL-2 PROGRAM
20 REM
30 REM --------------------------------------------------------
40 REM               FRAME 1 - TITLE AND ASSIGNMENTS
50 REM
60          HOME : VTAB 12 : HTAB 2
70          PRINT "DRILL USING A SUBROUTINE FOR INPUT"
80          FOR P = 1 TO 3000 : NEXT P : HOME : VTAB 12
90          DIM FDBK$(6) : FOR A = 1 TO 6 : READ FDBK$(A) : NEXT A
100 REM -------------------------------------------------------
110 REM              FRAME 2 - FIRST QUESTION SEQUENCE
120 REM
130          PRINT "THE STATE FLOWER OF TEXAS IS THE"
132          HNT$ = " A BEE IN A BLUE ONE..."
140          ANSWER$ = "BLUEBONNET" : GOSUB 10000
150 REM -------------------------------------------------------
160 REM              FRAME 3 - NEXT QUESTION SEQUENCE
170 REM
180          PRINT "THE LARGEST MUSCLE IN THE BODY IS THE"
182          HNT$ = "THE MAXIMUM OF THE GLUTEALS"
190          ANSWER$ = "GLUTEUS MAXIMUS" : GOSUB 10000
200 REM -------------------------------------------------------
210 REM              (FRAMES FOR ADDITIONAL QUESTIONS)
220 REM
9930 REM -------------------------------------------------------
9940 REM          FINAL   FRAME -     PERFORMANCE REPORT
9950 REM
9960         SCRE = INT((C*100/Q)*10)/10  : PRINT "YOUR SCORE   IS    "SCRE "%"
9969 END
9970 REM -------------------------------------------------------
9980 REM           POSITIONING   AND      INPUT  SUBROUTINE
9990 REM
10000        MISS = 0 : Q = Q + 1
10002        VTAB 16  :  HTAB 12  :  FOR S = 1 TO LEN(ANSWER$) :
             PRINT "-"; : NEXT S
10010        VTAB 16 : HTAB 9 : INPUT "=>"; REPLY$ : PRINT

10020        IF  REPLY$ = ANSWER$  THEN  10050
10022        IF  MISS = 0  THEN  MISS = 1 : PRINT "HINT:   " HNT$ :
             GOTO 10002
10030        PRINT "THE CORRECT ANSWER IS "   ANSWER$
10040        VTAB 20 : HTAB 30 : INPUT  "RETURN =>"; R$ :     HOME:
             VTAB 12 : RETURN

10050        C = C  +1 : HOME :    VTAB 12 :    HTAB 12 :
             PRINT FDBK$(6 * RND(1) + 1) "!"

10060        FOR P = 1 TO 1000 : NEXT P : HOME : VTAB 12 : RETURN
```

```
11000 REM  ------------------------------------------------
11010 REM           SIX (6) DATA ELEMENTS FOR FEEDBACK
11020 REM
11030      DATA "RAZZLE-DAZZLE", "HOT-DOGGIES", "WONDERFUL"
11040      DATA "SIMPLY SWELL", "OHH! GREAT", "THAT'S THE WAY"
```

4.6.3 LINDRILL-3 Program

Linear drill programs also can be easily constructed with FOR-NEXT and DATA-READ statements. The DATA consists of question-answer pairs on any chosen topic that are READ as part of a FOR-NEXT question sequence. Hints may also be included as DATA to be READ. This example program READs *two* hints for each question-answer sequence. The first hint will be given if a question is missed once, the second hint will be given on the next incorrect attempt, and the correct answer will be given after the third incorrect reply. The program may be used for drill on any topic by changing the PRINT statements in the title and introduction frames and the DATA statements accordingly.

Let's review the format we will follow for DATA statements, since this program is our first example in which questions, answers, and so forth are included as DATA elements.

The following format will be consistent for all of the remaining example programs that allow you to modify DATA statements to present content of your choosing:

1. The *first* DATA element will be a numeric value that represents the *number* of possible questions to be presented. This value will be assigned to a numeric variable named ITEMS. Thus, if you were going to modify a program to contain ten questions, this particular statement would be changed to DATA 10.
2. The next sequence of DATA elements will be the content for the number of questions, answers, hints, and so forth. If the program has the sequence

   DATA "Question", "Answer", "Hint1", "Hint2"

(as does LINDRILL-3), you *must* follow that same sequence, unless you redesign the program. In other words, you *cannot* change the sequence to

   DATA "Question", "Hint1", "Hint2", "Answer"

or

   DATA "Answer", "Question", "Hint1", "Hint2"

**WORK
SHEET
FOR
LINDRILL-
3**

Suggested Activities:
· Modify the title and existing questions, answers, and hints in the
  DATA statements to five or more of your choosing.
· Add an introduction to your program.

TITLE FRAME

70 PRINT" _____ "

INTRODUCTION FRAME

140 PRINT" _____ "

150 PRINT" _____ "

.

.

159 PRINT" _____ "

DATA FRAMES

10000 DATA _____

10040 DATA "_____"," _____"," _____"," _____"

10050 DATA "_____"," _____"," _____"," _____"

10060 DATA "_____"," _____"," _____"," _____"

10070 DATA "_____"," _____"," _____"," _____"

10080 DATA "_____"," _____"," _____"," _____"

10090 DATA "_____"," _____"," _____"," _____"

.

.

SAVE _____ <your program name>

```
10 REM              LINDRILL-3 PROGRAM
20 REM
30 REM -----------------------------------------------------
40 REM          FRAME 1 - TITLE AND ASSIGNMENTS
50 REM
60        HOME : VTAB 12 : HTAB 8
70        PRINT   "S T A T E    C A P I T A L S"
80        FOR P = 1 TO 2000 :   NEXT P
90        READ ITEMS
```

```
100 REM -------------------------------------------------------
110 REM                 FRAME  2  -  INTRODUCTION
120 REM
130        HOME : VTAB 4
140        PRINT "YOU WILL BE GIVEN " ITEMS " STATES." : PRINT
150        PRINT "PLEASE ENTER THE CAPITAL OF EACH STATE."
160        VTAB 20 : HTAB 30 : INPUT "RETURN =>"; R$
170 REM -------------------------------------------------------
180 REM       LOOP FRAMES, STEP 1 - READ DATA; ASK QUESTION
190 REM
200        FOR Q = 1 TO ITEMS
210     READ QUES$,  ANS$,  FSTHNT$,  SECHNT$
220     HOME : VTAB 4 : HTAB 8 : MISS = 0
230     PRINT : PRINT QUES$;
240          INPUT "? => "; REPLY$
250     IF REPLY$ = ANS$  THEN  C = C + 1 : GOTO 350
260 REM --------------------------------
270 REM       LOOP FRAMES, STEP 2 - FEEDBACK IF MISSED
280 REM
290     MISS = MISS + 1
300     ON MISS GOTO  310,  320,  330
310     PRINT "FIRST HINT: " : PRINT FSTHNT$ : GOTO 230
320     PRINT "SECOND HINT: " : PRINT SECHNT$ : GOTO 230
330     PRINT "THE CORRECT ANSWER IS: "; : INVERSE : PRINT   ANS$
340     VTAB 23 : HTAB 30 : INPUT "RETURN =>"; R$ : NORMAL
350        NEXT Q
360 REM -------------------------------------------------------
370 REM             FINAL FRAME - PERFORMANCE REPORT
380 REM
390        HOME : VTAB 12 : HTAB 8
400        SCRE = INT((C*100/ITEMS)*10)/10 : PRINT "YOUR SCORE IS  "SCRE "%"
9969 END
9970 REM -------------------------------------------------------
9980 REM          DATA FOR THE NUMBER OF ITEMS
9990 REM
10000       DATA   3
10010 REM -------------------------------------------------------
10020 REM        DATA FOR EACH QUESTION, ANSWER,  AND HINTS
10030 REM
10040       DATA "TEXAS", "AUSTIN", "IT'S IN CENTRAL TEXAS", "AUS---"
10050       DATA "NEW MEXICO", "SANTA FE", "A RAILROAD", "NOT SANTA CLAUS..."
10060       DATA "MISSISSIPPI", "JACKSON", "OFFSPRING OF A GIANT KILLER", "JACK---"
```

4.6.4 RANDRILL-1 Program

The preceding programs illustrated two strategies for linear drill programs. They are linear because the sequence of questions will always be the same for each RUN of the program. If questions are to be randomly selected, the list of questions, answers, and hints (if desired) can be READ from DATA and assigned to lists (one-dimensional arrays). Once assigned, questions may be randomly selected without repetition of any previously selected item. The following program is one example of how this may be accomplished.

In addition, a list is also made of a user's *last* incorrect response to any given question. Missed questions, including the question, the user's last incorrect response, and the correct response, are reviewed at the conclusion of the program.

From a programming standpoint, this example is a bit more complicated in technique than our previous programs. As before, however, this program may be modified to present questions on any topic by simply changing the PRINT and DATA statements accordingly.

**WORK
SHEET
FOR
RANDRILL
-1**

Suggested Activities:
- Modify the title and add an introduction for a different topic of your choosing.
- Modify the existing questions, answers, and hints in the DATA statements to ten or more of your choosing.
- Modify the feedback DATA to five (5) *pairs* of your choosing.

TITLE FRAME

70 PRINT "_____"

INTRODUCTION FRAME

200 HOME : VTAB 2 : HTAB 10 : PRINT"_____"

210 VTAB _____ : PRINT"_____"

220 PRINT : PRINT"_____"

229 PRINT : PRINT"_____"

DATA FRAMES

10000 DATA _____

10040 DATA "_____", "_____", "_____"

10050 DATA "_____", "_____", "_____"

10060 DATA "_____", "_____", "_____"

10070 DATA "_____", "_____", "_____"

10080 DATA "_____", "_____", "_____"

    .

15030 DATA "_____", "_____", "_____", "_____", "_____"

15040 DATA "_____", "_____", "_____", "_____", "_____"

SAVE _____ <your program name>

```
10 REM                  RANDRILL-1 PROGRAM
20 REM
30 REM -----------------------------------------------------
40 REM              FRAME 1, STEP 1 - TITLE
50 REM
60        HOME : VTAB 12 : HTAB 4
70        PRINT "RANDOM QUESTIONS WITH FEEDBACK AND REVIEW"
80        FOR P = 1 TO 2000 : NEXT P
90 REM - ----------------------------------
100 REM             FRAME 1, STEP 2 - DATA ASSIGNMENTS
110 REM
120       READ ITEMS
130          DIM    QUES$(ITEMS),      ANS$(ITEMS),      HNT$(ITEMS),MISSED$(ITEMS)
140       DIM ASKED(ITEMS), RGHTFDBK$(5), WRNGFDBK$(5)
150       FOR A =  1 TO ITEMS :    READ   QUES$(A),ANS$(A),HNT$(A):   NEXT A
160       FOR A = 1 TO 5 : READ RGHTFDBK$(A),   WRNGFDBK$(A) : NEXT A
170 REM -----------------------------------------------------
180 REM             FRAME 2 - INTRODUCTION WITH USER OPTION
190 REM
200       HOME : VTAB 2 : HTAB 10 : PRINT "TRIVIAL QUESTIONS"
210       VTAB 6 : PRINT "SO YOU THINK YOU KNOW TRIVIA...WELL,"
220       PRINT : PRINT "THERE ARE " ITEMS " QUESTIONS AVAILABLE."
230       PRINT : INPUT "HOW MANY WOULD YOU LIKE? ";   TRY
240       IF TRY < 1 OR TRY > ITEMS THEN 220
```

```
250 REM -------------------------------------------------------
260 REM     LOOP FRAMES, STEP 1 - POSITION; INITIALIZE MISS FLAG
270 REM
280         FOR Q = 1 TO TRY
290     HOME : VTAB 4 : MISS = 0
300 REM - ------------------------------------
310 REM    LOOP FRAMES, STEP 2 - SELECT FEEDBACK & QUESTION
320 REM
330     FDBK = INT (5 * RND (1) + 1)
340     RANQ = INT (ITEMS * RND (1) + 1)
350     IF ASKED (RANQ) = 1 THEN 340
360     ASKED (RANQ) = 1
370     PRINT : PRINT  QUES$ (RANQ) : VTAB 8   : INPUT "=>     "; REPLY$ :
        PRINT

380 REM - ------------------------------------
390 REM   LOOP FRAMES, STEP 3 - FEEDBACK  BASED UPON REPLY & MISS VALUE
400 REM
410     IF  REPLY$ = ANS$ (RANQ)   THEN   500
420     MISSED$ (RANQ) = REPLY$
430     IF MISS = 1  THEN   450
440     MISS = 1 : PRINT WRNGFDBK$ (FDBK) : PRINT HNT$ (RANQ)  : GOTO 370
450     VTAB 18 : PRINT "THE CORRECT ANSWER IS "; : INVERSE :
        PRINT  ANS$ (RANQ)

460     VTAB 22 : HTAB 30 : INPUT "RETURN =>"; R$ :   NORMAL : GOTO 540
470 REM -------------------------------
480 REM   LOOP FRAMES, STEP 4 - PROCESSES FOR CORRECT ANSWER
490 REM
500     HOME : VTAB 12 : HTAB 12 : PRINT RGHTFDBK (FDBK) "!"
510     FOR P = 1 TO 1000 : NEXT P
520     IF MISS = 0 THEN FRSTCNT = FRSTCNT + 1
530     IF MISS = 1 THEN SCNDCNT = SCNDCNT + 1
540        NEXT Q
550 REM -------------------------------------------------------
560 REM           NEXT FRAME - PERFORMANCE REPORT
570 REM
580     HOME : VTAB 4 : HTAB 8 : PRINT "HERE ARE  YOUR SCORES: "
590     VTAB 6 :     PRINT "CORRECT ON FIRST  TRY = "     FRSTCNT : PRINT
600     PRINT "CORRECT ON SECOND TRY = "  SCNDCNT : PRINT
610     PRINT "TOTAL CORRECT = " FRSTCNT + SCNDCNT : PRINT
620     IF FRSTCNT = TRY  THEN   PRINT, "EXCELLENT! " :    GOTO640
630     PRINT "HERE ARE QUESTIONS YOU MISSED AT LEAST ONCE: "
640     VTAB 20 : HTAB 30 : INPUT "RETURN =>"; R$
```

```
650 REM ----------------------------------------------------
660 REM              LOOP FRAMES - REVIEW OF MISSED QUESTIONS
670 REM
680      FOR L = 1 TO ITEMS
690      IF MISSED$(L) = ""  THEN  750
700      HOME : VTAB 4
710      PRINT "THE QUESTION WAS:" : PRINT QUES$(L) : PRINT
720      PRINT "YOUR  ANSWER  WAS:"   :    PRINT MISSED$(L)      : PRINT
730      PRINT "THE CORRECT ANSWER IS:" : PRINT ANS$(L)
740      VTAB 20 : HTAB 30 : INPUT "RETURN =>";  R$
750        NEXT L
760 REM ----------------------------------------------------
770 REM              FINAL FRAME - PERCENTAGE SCORE
780 REM
790       HOME : VTAB 12
800       SCRE = INT ((FRSTCNT * 100 / TRY) * 10) / 10
810       PRINT "YOUR 'FIRST TRY' SCORE IS "  SCRE  " PERCENT."
9969        END
9970 REM ----------------------------------------------------
9980 REM             DATA FOR NUMBER OF QUESTION ITEMS
9990 REM
10000       DATA 5
10010 REM ----------------------------------------------------
10020 REM            DATA FOR QUESTIONS, ANSWERS, AND HINTS
10030 REM
10040       DATA "THE LARGEST RIVER IN THE WORLD", "AMAZON","BIG-MOMMA!"

10050       DATA "THE LAST NAME OF 'BOLERO'S COMPOSER",
            "RAVEL","SWEATERS CAN UN-"

10060       DATA "THE NUMBER  OF CRANIAL  NERVES IS",
            "12",    "A BAKER'S DOZEN MINUS 1"

10070       DATA "THE LAST NAME OF THE PLAYER WHO HIT 61 HOME RUNS",
            "MARIS"

10080       DATA "COLTS' MOTHERS ARE", "THE PILGRIMS' YEAR",
            "1620", "...4, 8, 12..."
15000 REM ----------------------------------------------------
15010 REM            DATA FOR FIVE (5) CORRECT, INCORRECT FEEDBACK
15020 REM
15030    DATA "GREAT","NO...CONSIDER THIS","FINE","HOLD IT","PERFECT",
         "NO...NOT YET"

15040    DATA "HOT-DOGGIES","LET ME HELP","MARVELOUS","THIS MAY HELP"
```

4.7 Tutorial Applications

The previous programs have presented examples that may be easily modified to present content of your choosing. However, any form of tutorial feedback has consisted of hints for an incorrect response. Programs may be developed that search a user's input for anticipated key words or key phrases. More specific feedback can be presented if a match is found with any of these anticipated responses. If a match does not occur, a hint or some other form of feedback may be given at that point. The next example illustrates one method of expanding the type of feedback that may be presented.

4.7.1 TUTORIAL-1 Program

This example incorporates a key word or key phrase subroutine that allows specific feedback for a variable number of *anticipated* correct or incorrect answers. The program is arbitrarily designed to allow as many attempts for a given question as there are anticipated answers, and it credits correct answers only if they occur on the first attempt.

As seen previously in the LINDRILL-2 program, PRINT statements are used to present a question, and a hint is assigned to HNT$. However, the sequence of elements in DATA statements is slightly different than it was before. Anticipated answers, appropriate feedback for each answer, and a number (1 if the answer is correct, 0 if incorrect) are included as *elements* in each DATA statement. The *number* of anticipated answers for the question is assigned to the variable CHK, which is followed by a GOSUB 10000. Each question sequence consists of

1. PRINT statement(s) to present the question.
2. Assignment of a hint to HNT$.
3. DATA statements containing the elements of
   a. An anticipated answer.
   b. The response for that answer if matched.
   c. The number 1 if the answer is correct or a 0 if incorrect.
4. Assignment of the *number* of anticipated answers to the variable CHK, followed by GOSUB 10000.

By modifying the PRINT, DATA, and assignment statements shown in the example, the program may be used to present content of your choosing. However, the sequence shown above *must* be followed for each question.

**WORK
SHEET
FOR
TUTORIAL-
1**

Suggested Activities:
- Modify the title and add an introduction for a different topic of your choosing.
- Modify the existing questions, answers, and hints to five or more of your choosing.

TITLE FRAME

70 PRINT "_____"

QUESTION FRAMES

130 PRINT "_____"

140 HNT$="_____"

150 DATA "_____", "_____", _____

160 DATA "_____", "_____", _____

170 CHK = _____ : GOSUB 10000

210 PRINT "_____"

220 PRINT "_____"

230 HNT$="_____"

240 DATA "_____", "_____", _____

250 DATA "_____", "_____", _____

260 DATA "_____", "_____", _____

270 DATA "_____", "_____", _____

280 CHK = _____ : GOSUB 10000

.
.
.

SAVE _____<your program name>

```
10 REM            TUTORIAL-1 PROGRAM
20 REM
30 REM ----------------------------------------------------
40 REM     FRAME 1, STEP 1 - TITLE AND ASSIGNMENTS
50 REM
60         HOME : VTAB 12
70         PRINT "VARIABLE ANSWER MATCHING WITH FEEDBACK"
80         FOR P = 1 TO 2000 : NEXT P : HOME : VTAB 2
90     DIM ANSWER$(10),FDBK$(10),CRT(10) : CHK = 0 : MISS = 0
100 REM ----------------------------------------------------
110 REM    FRAME  2 - FIRST QUESTION, DATA, & ASSIGNMENT SEQUENCE
120 REM
130    PRINT "THE FIRST PRESIDENT OF THE USA WAS"
140    HNT$ = "GEO. CLEANING 2K LBS."
150    DATA "GEORGE WASHINGTON","YES, I CANNOT TELL A LIE. YOU'RE RIGHT",1
160    DATA "WASHINGTON","THE LAST NAME MATCHES; INCLUDE HIS FIRST",0
170    CHK = 2 : GOSUB 10000
180 REM ----------------------------------------------------
190 REM     FRAME 3 - SIMILAR SEQUENCE FOR NEXT QUESTION
200 REM
210    PRINT "NAME A STATE THAT BORDERS TEXAS AND"
220    PRINT "ALSO HAS CONSIDERABLE OIL RESERVES."
230    HNT$ = "SOONER ALLIGATORS"
240    DATA "ARKANSAS",  "ARKANSAS? THAT STATE HAS NOTHING",0
250    DATA "LOUISIANA","LOTS OF SWAMPS, BUT OK",1
260    DATA "OKLAHOMA","THAT'S TEXAS' BULL PASTURE, BUT IT'S OK",1
270    DATA "NEW MEXICO","IT HAS SOME, BUT NOT CONSIDERABLE",0
280    CHK = 4 : GOSUB 10000
290 REM ----------------------------------------------------
300 REM      (FRAMES FOR ADDITIONAL QUESTIONS)
310 REM
9930 REM ----------------------------------------------------
9940 REM     FINAL FRAME - PERFORMANCE REPORT
9950 REM
9960       VTAB 12 : SCRE = INT(((C * 100)/ Q )*10)/10 :
           PRINT "YOUR SCORE IS "SCRE "%"
9969       END
9970 REM ----------------------------------------------------
9980 REM     INPUT AND REPLY CHECKING SUBROUTINE
9990 REM
10000      MISS = 0 : Q = Q + 1 : POKE 34,6
10010      FOR I = 1 TO CHK : READ ANSWER$(I),FDBK$(I),CRT(I) : NEXT I
10020      VTAB 12 : HTAB 7 : INPUT "=> "; REPLY$ : PRINT
10030      FOR I = 1 TO CHK
10040    L = LEN(ANSWER$(I))
10050      FOR A = 1 TO (LEN(REPLY$) - L + 1)
10060          IF MID$(REPLY$,A,L) <>  ANSWER$(I) THEN 10090
10070          PRINT FDBK$(I) : IF CRT(I) = 0 THEN 10110
10080          GOTO 10140
10090      NEXT A
```

```
10100        NEXT I
10110        MISS = MISS + 1
10120        IF MISS < CHK   THEN PRINT : PRINT "HERE'S MY HINT: "HNT$
10130        IF MISS = CHK THEN GOSUB 15000
10140        VTAB 23 : HTAB 30 : INPUT "RETURN => "; R$
10150        IF MISS < CHK AND CRT(I) = 0 THEN HOME : GOTO 10020
10160        IF CRT(I) = 1 AND MISS = 0 THEN  C = C + 1
10170        POKE 34,0 : HOME : RETURN
14970 REM ----------------------------------------------------
14980 REM          SUBROUTINE TO DISPLAY ALL CORRECT ANSWERS
14990 REM
15000        PRINT : HTAB 10 : PRINT "ACCEPTABLE ANSWER(S) ARE: " : PRINT
15010        FOR I = 1 TO CHK
15020     IF CRT(I) = 1 THEN PRINT ANSWER$(I) "      ";
15030        NEXT I
15040        RETURN
```

4.8   Testing Applications

Testing is an application similar to drill. A question is presented, the user's response is entered, feedback may be given, and the user's performance is indicated at the conclusion of the program. In testing applications, feedback for incorrect answers is usually limited to presenting the correct answer or giving some explanation of why the user's answer was not acceptable. The next two examples illustrate forms of these techniques.

4.8.1   TEST-1 Program

This program tests the naming of the seven dwarfs of Snow White fame. The names are READ into a list, and then a question loop asks for any one of those names. An internal loop checks the user's response for a match with a name in the list. If a match occurs, it is then checked for being previously named (FLAGged). Feedback occurs if the user's response has been previously entered or does not match one of the names in the list. The user is presented response opportunities equal only to the number of items in the list, since this program is a "testing" example. At the conclusion of the program, the complete list is presented, and any name not entered by the user is starred (*****).

Although this program tests naming the dwarfs, it may be used as a general test program. By simply changing the title PRINT and the DATA statements accordingly, it will test naming from any given list.

**WORK
SHEET
FOR
TEST-1**

Suggested Activities:
· Modify the program to present a list of your choosing.
· Add a more complete introduction to the program.

TITLE FRAME

70 PRINT "_____"

INTRODUCTION FRAME

180 HOME : VTAB ____

181 PRINT "_____"

182 PRINT "_____"

183 PRINT "_____"

184 PRINT "_____"

.

.

DATA FRAME

10000 DATA ____

10010 DATA "_____", "_____", "_____"

10020 DATA "_____", "_____", "_____"

10030 DATA "_____", "_____", "_____"

.

.

SAVE _____ <your program name>

```
10  REM            TEST-1 PROGRAM
20  REM
30  REM ---------------------------------------------------
40  REM            FRAME 1, STEP 1 - TITLE
50  REM
60         HOME : VTAB 12 : HTAB 5
70         PRINT "SNOW WHITE AND THE 7 DWARFS"
80         FOR P = 1 TO 2000 : NEXT P
90  REM - --------------------------------
100 REM     FRAME 1, STEP 2 - DATA   ASSIGNMENTS
110 REM
120        READ ITEMS
130        DIM NAME$(ITEMS),  FLAG(ITEMS)
140        FOR A = 1 TO ITEMS : READ  NAME$(A) : NEXT A
```

```
150 REM --------------------------------------------------
160 REM              FRAME  2  -  INTRODUCTION
170 REM
180          HOME : VTAB 12
190          PRINT "LET'S SEE IF YOU CAN NAME THEM..."
200          VTAB 20 : HTAB 30 : INPUT "RETURN =>";  R$
210 REM --------------------------------------------------
220 REM      LOOP FRAMES, STEP 1 - GET A NAME INPUT
230 REM
240          FOR L = 1 TO ITEMS
250            HOME : VTAB 12
260            PRINT "ANSWER NUMBER "  L  " IS";
270            INPUT REPLY$ : PRINT
280 REM - --------------------------------
290 REM      LOOP FRAMES, STEP 2 - CHECK LIST FOR A MATCH
300 REM
310            FOR CHECK = 1 TO ITEMS
320            IF REPLY$ <> NAME$(CHECK)   THEN   360
330            IF FLAG(CHECK) = 0   THEN   C = C + 1 : FLAG(CHECK) = 1 :
               GOTO 380

340          PRINT "THAT'S BEEN PREVIOUSLY NAMED!"
350          VTAB 20 : HTAB 30 : INPUT "RETURN =>";  R$ : GOTO380
360          NEXT CHECK
370            PRINT "THAT IS NOT IN MY LIST!" : VTAB 20 : HTAB 30 :
               INPUT "RETURN =>"; R$

380          NEXT L
390 REM --------------------------------------------------
400 REM      FINAL FRAME - SHOW COMPLETE LIST & PERFORMANCE
410 REM
420          HOME : HTAB 10
430          PRINT "THE COMPLETE LIST IS: " : PRINT
440          FOR L = 1 TO ITEMS
450            PRINT TAB(12) NAME$(L);
460                  IF FLAG(L) = 0   THEN   PRINT " *****";
470            PRINT
480          NEXT L
490          PRINT
500          IF C <> ITEMS   THEN PRINT TAB(10) "(ITEMS MISSED ARE STARRED)"
510          PRINT
520          SCRE =  INT(((C * 100) / ITEMS) * 10) / 10
530          PRINT TAB(10) "YOUR SCORE IS "  SCRE  " PERCENT."
9969         END
9970 REM --------------------------------------------------
9980 REM          DATA FOR NUMBER OF ITEMS AND NAMES IN LIST
9990 REM
10000          DATA 7
10010          DATA "BASHFUL", "DOC", "DOPEY", "GRUMPY"
10020          DATA "HAPPY", "SLEEPY", "SNEEZY"
```

4.8.2 TEST-2 Program

The TEST-2 program is another example of a testing technique. This example illustrates how multiple-choice questions may be presented. However, it goes beyond simply saying "CORRECT" or "INCORRECT" following the user's selection. Appropriate feedback is presented for *every* choice possible with a given question. Thus the user gains information from all possible choice selections.

PRINT statements are used to present a given question. DATA statements provide the choices and their appropriate responses. The number of possible choices and the correct choice are assigned to the numeric variables CHOICES and RGHT, respectively. A GOSUB 10000 then transfers execution to a subroutine that displays the choices and evaluates the user's response. This sequence of PRINT(s) (for the question), DATA (for each choice and its response), CHOICES = <the number of possible choices>, RGHT = <the correct number choice>, and GOSUB 10000 may be repeated for an indefinite number of multiple-choice questions in the program.

Note: A maximum of five choices are possible for each question. If more choices are desired, it will be necessary to change the 5's in statement 90 to the new maximum number.

**WORK
SHEET
FOR
TEST-2**

Suggested Activities:
- Add an introduction to a multiple-choice test on a topic of your choosing.
- Modify the program to present questions of your choosing. Vary the number of choices among the questions.

TITLE FRAME

70 PRINT "_____"

INTRODUCTION

91 PRINT "_____"

92 PRINT "_____"

.

.

99 VTAB 23 : HTAB 30 : INPUT "RETURN=> ";R$

QUESTION SEQUENCE FRAMES

130 PRINT "_____"

.

.

```
160 DATA "_____", "_____"
    .
    .
210 CHOICES= _____ : RGHT= _____ : GOSUB 10000
250 PRINT "_____"
    .
    .
260 DATA " _____", "_____"
    .
    .
290 CHOICES= _____ : RGHT= _____ : GOSUB 10000
    .
    .
```

SAVE _____<your program name>

```
10 REM              TEST-2 PROGRAM
20 REM
30 REM ----------------------------------------------------
40 REM          FRAME 1 - TITLE AND ASSIGNMENTS
50 REM
60        HOME : VTAB 12 : HTAB 4
70        PRINT "LINEAR MULTIPLE-CHOICE WITH FEEDBACK"
80        FOR P = 1 TO 2000 : NEXT P : HOME
90        DIM CHOICE$(5), FEEDBK$(5)
100 REM ----------------------------------------------------
110 REM          FRAME 2 - FIRST QUESTION SEQUENCE
120 REM
130       PRINT "WHICH OF THE FOLLOWING IS AN"
140       PRINT "EXAMPLE OF A COMPUTER OUTPUT"
150       PRINT "DEVICE?"
160       DATA "CPU", "NO, THAT'S THE CENTRAL PROCESSING UNIT"
170       DATA "A PRINTER", "YES, BUT THERE IS A BETTER CHOICE"
180       DATA "THE TERMINAL KEYBOARD", "THAT'S AN INPUT DEVICE"
190       DATA "A MONITOR SCREEN", "YES, BUT SO IS A PRINTER"
200       DATA "BOTH 2 AND 4 ABOVE", "YES, THAT'S THE BEST ANSWER"
210       CHOICES = 5 : RGHT = 5 : GOSUB 10000
220 REM ----------------------------------------------------
230 REM          FRAME 3 - NEXT QUESTION SEQUENCE
240 REM
250       PRINT "THE LARGEST RIVER IN THE WORLD IS THE"
260       DATA "AMAZON", "YES, THAT IS THE LARGEST RIVER"
270       DATA "NILE", "NO, THAT IS THE L O N G E S T  RIVER"
280       DATA "MISSISSIPPI", "THAT'S THE LARGEST IN THE USA"
290       CHOICES = 3 : RGHT = 1 : GOSUB 10000
```

```
300 REM -----------------------------------------------------
310 REM       (FRAMES FOR ADDITIONAL QUESTION SEQUENCES)
320 REM
9910 REM ----------------------------------------------------
9920 REM            FINAL FRAME - PERFORMANCE REPORT
9930 REM
9940          HOME : VTAB 12 : HTAB 5
9950          SCRE = INT((C*100/Q)*10)/10 : PRINT "YOUR SCORE IS "SCRE "%"
9969          END
9970 REM ----------------------------------------------------
9980 REM        CHOICE DISPLAY, INPUT, & FEEDBACK SUBROUTINE
9990 REM
10000     PRINT : FOR A = 1 TO CHOICES
10010            READ CHOICE$(A), FEEDBK$(A) : PRINT  A" - "CHOICE$(A)
10020               NEXT A : PRINT : Q = Q + 1
10030     PRINT "YOUR CHOICE IS (1-"  CHOICES  ")" ; : INPUT REPLY : PRINT
10040     IF REPLY < 1  OR  REPLY > CHOICES   THEN   10030
10050     PRINT CHOICE$(REPLY) : PRINT FEEDBK$(REPLY) "."
10060     PRINT : IF REPLY = RGHT   THEN   C = C + 1 : GOTO 10090
10070     PRINT "THE CORRECT CHOICE IS "  RGHT   ":"
10080     PRINT CHOICE$(RGHT) "."
10090     VTAB 20  :  HTAB 30  :  INPUT "RETURN =>";  R$  :  HOME :   RETURN
```

4.9 Displaying Your Program Selections

By now, you are aware of several BASIC commands, such as LOAD, LIST, and RUN. Many of these commands may be incorporated as *statements* within the body of a BASIC program. When one of these statements is executed it could, for example, execute (RUN) another program from the disk. This example is particularly useful in that one program can "command" another program to RUN, which, at its conclusion, could command another program to RUN, and so on. Thus, programs may be linked together in a "chain" fashion.

A common use of this feature in instructional computing is to design one program as a "menu" of available programs on the disk. When this menu program is executed, a selection of programs is displayed, and the user may enter the choice desired. Based upon the user's input, another program is retrieved from the disk and executed.

4.9.1 MENU Program

The MENU program that follows illustrates how the example programs with this booklet are incorporated into a menu for selection. As in previous program examples, the *first* DATA element contains the **number** of items possible—in this case, the number of programs available on the menu. The remaining DATA elements contain the *name* of the program as it is stored on the disk and its *description* to be displayed on the menu. By simply replacing these DATA statements with the elements that correspond to the number, name, and description of your programs, MENU will present your descriptions and execute the appropriate program selected by a user.

   Note: It is important that you SAVE your modifications using a different program name before testing the program. When this program is successfully executed, another program is loaded into memory.

**WORK
SHEET
FOR
MENU**

Suggested Activities:
- Modify the title of the menu to reflect the content of your program selections.
- Change the DATA elements to present your selection of programs.
- Modify the appropriate programs you have created to return to your menu program at their conclusion (see Section 5.2).

FRAME 1

80 PRINT "_____" : PRINT

NOTE: Delete the Existing DATA statements by entering:

DEL 290,420

DATA

290 DATA _____

300 DATA "_____","_____"

310 DATA "_____","_____"

320 DATA "_____","_____"

330 DATA "_____","_____"

.
.

(REMEMBER: The *last* DATA statement must be elements for any dummy name and the description you wish displayed for the "STOP" option.)

SAVE _____ <your menu program name>

```
10 REM                    MENU PROGRAM
20 REM
30 REM -------------------------------------------------------
40 REM              FRAME 1 - ASSIGNMENTS, DISPLAY AND POSITIONING
50 REM
60    DIM P$(20),D$(20)
70    HOME : LM = 6 : RM = LM + 1 : VTAB 1 : HTAB LM
80    PRINT "EXAMPLE PROGRAM SELECTIONS" : PRINT
90    FR = 3 : READ ITEMS : FOR I = 1 TO ITEMS
100        READ P$(I),D$(I) : PRINT TAB(LM) D$(I)
110   NEXT I
120   VTAB 22 : HTAB 5
130   PRINT "PRESS ANY KEY TO MOVE SELECTION OR"
140   PRINT TAB(10) "PRESS RETURN TO SELECT. "
150   ROW=FR : FOR CNT = 1 TO ITEMS : COL=(LEN(D$(CNT))) + RM :
      INVERSE

160        VTAB ROW : HTAB(LM-3) : PRINT "=>"
170        VTAB ROW : HTAB COL : PRINT "<="; : GET K$ : NORMAL
180        VTAB ROW : HTAB(LM-3) : PRINT " " : VTAB ROW :
           HTAB COL : PRINT "  "

190        IF K$ = CHR$(13) THEN 240
200        ROW = ROW + 1 : NEXT CNT : GOTO 150
210 REM -------------------------------
220 REM      FRAME 2 - END PROGRAM OR EXECUTE SELECTION
230 REM
240    IF CNT = ITEMS THE HOME : NEW
250    PRINT CHR$(4)   "RUN "  P$(CNT)
260 REM -------------------------------------------------------
270 REM    DATA ELEMENTS: ITEM NUMBER, FILE NAME, DESCRIPTION DISPLAY
280 REM      (LAST ITEM MUST BE DUMMY NAME AND STOP DESCRIPTION)
290    DATA 13
300    DATA "LINDRILL-1", "LINEAR DRILL - EXAMPLE 1"
310    DATA "LINDRILL-2", "LINEAR DRILL - EXAMPLE 2"
320    DATA "LINDRILL-3", "LINEAR DRILL - EXAMPLE 3"
330    DATA "RANDRILL-1","RANDOM TRIVIA  QUESTIONS"
340    DATA "TUTORIAL-1", "EXAMPLE OF TUTORIAL FEEDBACK"
350    DATA "TEST-1", "TEST ON NAMING A LIST"
360    DATA "TEST-2", "MULTIPLE-CHOICE WITH FEEDBACK"
370    DATA "WRITE-RECORDS", "RECORD STORING EXAMPLE"
380    DATA "READ-RECORDS", "RECORD RETRIEVAL EXAMPLE"
390    DATA "STATISTICS", "CLASS SCORE STATISTICS"
400    DATA "BIBLWRITE", "BIBLIOGRAPHIC FILE UPDATE"
410    DATA "BIBLREAD", "BIBLIOGRAPHIC FILE RETRIEVAL"
420    DATA "STOP","STOP THE INTERACTION"
```

4.9.2 Completing the Cycle

Your menu program allows selection and execution of programs from the disk. However, when execution of the selected program is completed, a return to the MENU will *not* occur. To accomplish a return to your menu program, it will be necessary to make the following modification to each of the programs available through your menu.

Replace the **END** statement with the following statement:

```
9969 VTAB 23 : HTAB 30 : INPUT "RETURN =>"; R$ : PRINT CHR$(4)
"RUN <your menu name>"
```

Your menu program will then be executed when the RETURN key is pressed.

4.9.3 Automatic Execution of Your Menu Program

You may have your menu program automatically displayed when the disk is booted by doing the following:

1. **LOAD** <your menu name>
2. **SAVE HELLO**

Henceforth, your menu program will be displayed every time the system is booted with the disk.

Note: The example MENU program shown above was SAVEd on the disk both as HELLO and MENU. Thus, it appeared when the system was booted, since the HELLO program is the program automatically loaded and executed. You replace only the booklet version of HELLO on the disk with your version when you do the two steps above. Both the original booklet version of MENU and your version (<your menu name>) remain on the disk.

4.10 Simple Record-Keeping Applications

Up to this point, we have presented programs that may be easily modified to present content of your choosing. As you recall, this involved LOADing a given program, *modifying* certain statements (generally, PRINT and DATA), then SAV(E)ing the program using a different name. Now we will present two programs that may be used directly for student record storing and retrieval applications. These programs "stand alone;" that is, they may be used without any modifications.

Each of these programs uses *text files* for storing information on the disk. You will get to name these files during the execution of each of the programs. Thus, you could use the name PERIOD1 to store information about your first-period class, PERIOD2 for your second-period class, and so on. Naming the files logically is important. Use names that have meaning to you, since each program will prompt you for the name of the text file you wish to access. The text file names will be preceded by a *T* when a CATALOG of the disk is displayed.

In the simplest sense, text files contain information in a form similar to DATA statements in a program. However, the information in text files may be modified automatically in program execution. DATA statements, on the other hand, would have to be reentered in the program and SAVEd.

4.10.1 WRITE-RECORDS Program

This program allows you to enter a student's name, test name, and score. As many as 200 names and scores may be entered during any one RUN of the program. You must specify the text file name to which the information is to be written, so use logical names that have meaning to you. The program may be used directly without modification.

The disk contains a text file named **SAMPLE** that contains sample information. Use this name and **QUIZ 1** for a test name in a trial RUN.

```
10  REM                      WRITE-RECORDS PROGRAM
20  REM
30  REM --------------------------------------------------------
40  REM           FRAME 1   -    TITLE AND ASSIGNMENTS
50  REM
60    HOME : VTAB 12 : HTAB 12
70    PRINT "RECORD KEEPING:" : PRINT
80    PRINT TAB(2)   "STUDENT NAME, TEST NAME, AND SCORE"
90    FOR P = 1 TO 4000 : NEXT P
100   DIM STUDNT$(200),  TSTNAME$(200),   SCRE(200)
110 REM --------------------------------------------------------
120 REM           FRAME 2 - INTRODUCTION
130 REM
140   HOME : VTAB 4
150   PRINT "UP TO 200 STUDENT NAMES, TEST NAMES," : PRINT
160   PRINT "AND SCORES MAY BE ENTERED DURING ONE" : PRINT
170   PRINT " 'RUN' OF THIS PROGRAM."
180   VTAB 20 : HTAB 30 : INPUT "RETURN =>"; R$
190 REM --------------------------------------------------------
200 REM           FRAME 3 - TEXT FILE NAME FOR STORING INFO
210 REM
220   HOME : VTAB 10
230   PRINT "WHAT IS THE NAME OF THE FILE TO WHICH" : PRINT
240   PRINT "YOU WILL ADD INFORMATION?" : PRINT
250   INPUT " (MAY BE A NEW OR EXISTING FILE)  => "; F$ : PRINT
260   PRINT "THE NAME YOU ENTERED IS " F$ : PRINT
```

```
270   HTAB 8 : INPUT "IS THIS CORRECT? ";  Z$ :
      IF   LEFT$(Z$,1) <> "Y"  THEN  220


280 REM ----------------------------------------------------
290 REM            FRAME 4 - INFORMATION TO BE FILED
300 REM
310   HOME
320   FOR A = 1 TO  200
330         INPUT "STUDENT NAME  (OR STOP)? "; STUDNT$(A)
340         IF STUDNT$(A) =  "STOP"  THEN  390
350         INPUT "TEST NAME? "; TSTNAME$(A)
360         INPUT "SCORE?   "; SCRE(A)
370         PRINT
380   NEXT A
390         ENTRIES  =  A - 1
400 REM ----------------------------------------------------
410 REM           FRAME 5 - DISK FILE WRITING SEQUENCE
420 REM
430   HOME : VTAB 12 : HTAB 4
440   PRINT "UPDATING RECORDS IN FILE "  F$
450   D$  =  CHR$(4)
460   PRINT D$  "APPEND  "  F$
470   PRINT D$  "WRITE  "  F$
480   FOR A = 1 TO ENTRIES
490         PRINT  STUDNT$(A) : PRINT TSTNAME$(A) : PRINT SCRE(A)

500   NEXT A
510   PRINT D$  "CLOSE  "  F$
520 REM ----------------------------------------------------
530 REM           FRAME 6 - CONCLUSION
540 REM
550   HOME : VTAB 12 : HTAB 6 : PRINT "FILE RECORDS HAVE BEEN ADDED."
560   VTAB 23  :  HTAB 30  :  INPUT "RETURN =>"; R$ :
      PRINT CHR$(4) "RUN MENU" : END
```

4.10.2 READ-RECORDS Program

This program allows you to retrieve information either by student name or test name from the text file name you specify. An average of the scores is displayed and an option to edit names or scores is provided. Thus, you may retrieve from the file *all* scores for either a given *student* or a given *test* using this program.

The program may be used directly without any modifications. However, you will be prompted for the name of the text file, so we mention again that it is important to use logical, meaningful names for your files.

RUN this program using SAMPLE as the text file name. Retrieve information by test name using QUIZ 1 or by student name, using one of the names you entered when you did a trial RUN of the WRITE-RECORDS program.

   Note: Both the WRITE-RECORDS and READ-RECORDS programs include the "return to the menu" statement discussed in Section 5.2.

```
10 REM              READ-RECORDS PROGRAM
20 REM
30 REM --------------------------------------------------
40 REM           FRAME 1 - TITLE AND ASSIGNMENTS
50 REM
60   HOME : VTAB 12 : HTAB 12
70   PRINT "RECORD RETRIEVAL: " : PRINT
80   PRINT TAB(2) "STUDENT NAME, TEST NAME, AND SCORE"
90   FOR P = 1 TO 4000 : NEXT P
100  DIM STUDNT$(600), TSTNAME$(600), SCRE(600) : FLAG = 0 : LINE = 0

110 REM --------------------------------------------------
120 REM         FRAME 2 - TEXT FILE NAME FOR RETRIEVING INFO
130 REM
140  HOME : VTAB 10
150  PRINT "WHAT IS THE NAME OF THE FILE FROM" : PRINT
160  PRINT "YOU WISH TO RETRIEVE INFORMATION? => "; F$ : PRINT
170  PRINT "THE NAME YOU ENTERED IS  " F$ : PRINT
180  HTAB 8 : INPUT "IS THIS CORRECT?  "; Z$
190  IF  LEFT$(Z$,1)  <>  "Y"  THEN  140
200 REM --------------------------------------------------
210 REM         FRAME 3 - DISK FILE READING SEQUENCE
220 REM
230  D$  =  CHR$(4)
240  PRINT D$  "OPEN  "  F$
250  PRINT D$  "READ  "  F$
260  ONERR GOTO 300
270  FOR  RECRD = 1 TO 600
280      INPUT  STUDNT$(RECRD) : TSTNAME$(RECRD) : SCRE(RECRD)
290  NEXT RECRD
300  ENTRIES  =  RECRD - 1
310  PRINT D$ "CLOSE  "  F$
320 REM --------------------------------------------------
330 REM         FRAME 4 - SEARCH OPTIONS
340 REM
350  HOME : VTAB 4 : HTAB 10
360  PRINT "FILE SEARCH" : PRINT
370  PRINT "DO YOU WISH TO SEARCH BY: " : PRINT
380  PRINT TAB(8) "1. STUDENT NAME"
390  PRINT TAB(8) "2. TEST NAME" : PRINT
400  INPUT "ENTER 1 OR 2 => "; CHOICE
410  IF CHOICE < 1  OR  CHOICE > 2  THEN  400
```

```
420   IF CHOICE = 1   THEN   SRCH$ = "STUDENT"
430   IF CHOICE = 2   THEN   SRCH$ = "TEST"
440 REM -------------------------------------------------
450 REM               FRAME 5,  STEP 1 - SEARCH PROCEDURE
460 REM
470   PRINT : PRINT   SRCH$   "  NAME SOUGHT IS => ";  :  INPUT NAME$
480   HOME :  SUM  =  0 :  CNT  =  0 :  LINE = 0
490   PRINT "RECORD # "  TAB (10)  "STUDENT"  TAB (26)  "TEST"  TAB (35)  "SCORE"
500   FOR P = 1 TO 39 : PRINT "-"; : NEXT P  : PRINT
510   FOR L = 1 TO ENTRIES
520       IF NAME$  <>  STUDNT$ (L)   AND  NAME$  <>  TSTNAME$ (L) THEN   560
530       PRINT TAB (5) L   TAB (10)   STUDNT$ (L)
          TAB (26)  TSTNAME$ (L)  TAB (36)  SCRE (L)

540       SUM = SUM + SCRE (L) :  CNT = CNT + 1 :  LINE = LINE + 1
550       IF LINE = 20   THEN   VTAB 23 :  HTAB 30 :  INPUT "MORE =>"; R$ :
          LINE = 0

560   NEXT L
570   IF CNT  =  0  THEN   PRINT "NO SCORES FOUND FOR  "  NAME$ :  GOTO 850
580   PRINT : PRINT TAB (10) "AVERAGE SCORE IS  "   INT ( (SUM/CNT) *10) /10
590   PRINT
600 REM -------------------------------- -
610 REM           FRAME 5,  STEP 2 - OPTION TO EDIT
620 REM
630   INPUT "DO YOU WISH TO EDIT ANY RECORD?   "; R$
640   IF LEFT$ (R$, 1)   <>  "Y"  THEN   840
650   INPUT "RECORD NUMBER TO EDIT IS  => "; RECRD :  FLAG  = 1
660   IF RECRD < 1   OR   RECRD  >   ENTRIES THEN PRINT "* OUT OF RANGE *" :
      GOTO 650
670 REM ------------------------------------------------
680 REM           FRAME 6 - EDITING OPTIONS & PROCEDURE
690 REM
700   HOME :  HTAB 10
710   PRINT "RECORD # "   RECRD
720   PRINT : PRINT "STUDENT = "   STUDNT$ (RECRD)
730   INPUT "EDIT? "; R$ :  IF LEFT$ (R$, 1)  <>  "Y" THEN   750
740   INPUT "REVISED STUDENT NAME IS => ";   STUDNT$ (RECRD)
750   PRINT : PRINT "TEST NAME = "   TSTNAME$ (RECRD)
760   INPUT "EDIT? "; R$ :  IF LEFT$ (R$, 1)   <>   "Y" THEN   780
770   INPUT "REVISED TEST NAME IS => ";   TSTNAME$ (RECRD)
780   PRINT : PRINT "SCORE = "   SCRE (RECRD)
790   INPUT "EDIT? "; R$ :  IF LEFT$ (R$, 1)   <>  "Y" THEN   480
800   INPUT "REVISED SCORE IS => "; SCRE (RECRD) :  GOTO  480
810 REM ------------------------------------------------
820 REM           FRAME 7 - OPTION FOR ANOTHER SEARCH
830 REM
840   HOME :  VTAB 12 :  HTAB 12
850   PRINT : INPUT "DO YOU WANT ANOTHER SEARCH? "; R$
860   IF LEFT$ (R$, 1)  =  "Y"   THEN   350
```

```
870  REM -------------------------------------------------
880  REM            FRAME 8 - UPDATE OF RECORDS IF EDITED
890  REM
900   IF FLAG = 0   THEN   1020
910   HOME : VTAB 12 : HTAB 4
920   PRINT "UPDATING RECORDS IN FILE  "  F$
930   PRINT D$  "OPEN  "  F$
940   PRINT D$  "WRITE  "  F$
950   FOR A = 1 TO ENTRIES
960        PRINT STUDNT$(A) : PRINT  TSTNAME$(A) : PRINT SCRE(A)
970   NEXT A
980   PRINT D$  "CLOSE  "  F$
990  REM -------------------------------------------------
1000 REM            FRAME 9 - CONCLUSION
1010 REM
1020 HOME : VTAB 12 : HTAB 12
1030 PRINT "*** DONE   ***"
1040 VTAB 23 : HTAB 30 : INPUT "RETURN => "; R$ :
     PRINT CHR$(4) "RUN MENU" : END
```

4.10.3 Adding Record Keeping to Your Programs

The two programs just listed illustrate how records may be entered from the keyboard using the WRITE-RECORDS program and retrieved by student or test name using the READ-RECORDS program. It is also possible to have any of your programs automatically *write* record information to a file. This information also may be *retrieved* using the READ-RECORDS program.

As you recall, four items of information are needed:

1. The text file name (the file where records will be kept).
2. The student name.
3. The test (or program) name.
4. The score.

By simple modification of your programs, this information may be added and written to a file.

Make the following modifications to any of your programs in which you wish to add record keeping:

1. In the introduction frame, add

```
51 HOME : VTAB 12 : INPUT "PLEASE ENTER YOUR FULL NAME => "; STUDNT$
52 TSTNAME$ = "<your program name (or) a logical name of your choice>"
53 F$ = "<a logical text file name of your choice>"
```

2. In the final frame, add

```
9962 D$ = CHR$(4)
9963 PRINT D$ "APPEND " F$
9964 PRINT D$ "WRITE " F$
9965 PRINT STUDNT$ : PRINT TSTNAME$ : PRINT SCRE
9966 PRINT D$ "CLOSE " F$
```

Information may then be retrieved using the READ-RECORDS program from the file you assigned to F$ either by student name or by the name you assigned to TSTNAME$.

4.11   Three Teacher Utility Programs

The next three programs are stand-alone programs provided for your convenience. They require no modification and may be used directly. Listings of the programs are not included in this book. However, they may be accessed directly from the disk or from the MENU program. Note that these programs automatically transfer back to the MENU when execution is completed.

4.11.1   Class Statistics (STATISTICS Program)

The STATISTICS program computes standard statistics for a set of entered scores. The mean, variance, standard deviation, z-score, and percentile ranking (assuming normal distribution of scores) are determined. RUN the program to see its options and output.

4.11.2   Bibliographic Files (BIBLWRITE and BIBLREAD Programs)

Teachers often keep card files containing reference information on items such as journal articles, books, audiovisual materials, and so forth. The BIBLWRITE program allows you to enter information of this type. The program prompts for the name of the author, the reference title, a brief abstract, and three descriptors that may be used later in retrieving information. These descriptors may be considered as consistent "key words" you would use with a given reference. Thus, you might use the descriptor DRILL for all references related to drill programs.

The BIBLREAD program allows you to retrieve information by the name of the author, a descriptor, or the complete list of references on file. All references found in a given search are sorted alphabetically by the author's name.

Both BIBLWRITE and BIBLREAD use the text file BIBLIO on the disk. This file has one reference item stored as an example. The descriptors are BASIC, CAI, and TEACH.

TWO

AppleWorks®:
A Tool for
Educators

Introduction

One of the primary uses of computers in education is the management of information. Teachers and administrators use computers to prepare written communications, keep attendance records, calculate student grades, monitor school equipment, develop class materials, and many other tasks.

There are five major applications in the management of information with computers: word processing, electronic spreadsheet, data base, presentation graphics, and telecommunications. Word processing software allows the user to enter, edit, and print text. Spreadsheet software is used to manipulate numbers, make estimates, track budgets, and perform hypothetical "what if" analyses. Data base software acts like an electronic filing cabinet, organizing and retrieving information and printing reports. Graphics software gives the user designing tools to prepare overhead transparencies, posters, charts, graphs, and other visual representations of information. Telecommunications software connects your microcomputer with another microcomputer, minicomputer, or mainframe computer via telephone lines in order to share information or access remote data bases.

Until recently, an educator wanting to use all five of these applications would need to purchase five separate programs on at least five diskettes, would need to learn five different sets of commands and instructions from five manuals, and would still not be able to share data easily between programs. In the past few years, however, *integrated* programs were introduced to combine several of these applications into one software package. One of the first and still most popular integrated packages is Lotus 1-2-3 for the IBM Personal Computer. It combines spreadsheet, data base, and graphics. Lotus Symphony for the IBM PC and Lotus Jazz for the Apple Macintosh combine all five applications into one program.

AppleWorks is an integrated package that combines word processing, spreadsheet, and data base applications into one program for the Apple IIe, Apple IIc, and Apple IIgs computers. Like other integrated packages, it has the advantages of having only one set of commands and one manual for reference. It is less expensive to purchase than three separate programs, and data from all three applications can be stored on one diskette and can be shared by all three applications. For example, a proposed budget can be electronically "cut" from the spreadsheet and "pasted" into a grant proposal in the word processor. AppleWorks is the most widely used integrated package in education.

The following three chapters will provide an introduction to AppleWorks. Chapter 5 explains what is needed to use the program and how to get started in word processing. Chapter 6 explains spreadsheets using common educational applications. And Chapter 7 describes the data base capabilities of AppleWorks. The chapters are organized to develop the student's skills from easy concepts to more difficult ones. The authors suggest that the chapters be read in order, as each builds on skills learned in previous sections. The student needs to have the appropriate computer hardware as described in Chapter 5 and the AppleWorks program to complete the hands-on exercises included in these chapters. It should be noted that the AppleWorks program is not on the supplemental diskette accompanying this book and must be acquired from your instructor or purchased from an Apple dealer.

5

Think about This (for Fun)

There are fourteen punctuation marks in English grammar. How many can you name? (Nine is average.)

Think about This (Seriously)

Can the use of word processing improve one's writing?

"Many books require no thought from those who read them, and for a very simple reason; they made no such demand upon those who wrote them."
Charles Caleb Colton

"There is no such thing as a moral or immoral book. Books are well written, or badly written. That is all."
Oscar Wilde

"One man's letter is another man's literature."
anonymous

I Can't Type . . .
Don't Make Me

5.1 Objectives

For the successful completion of this chapter, you should be able to

1. Boot the Apple computer and load the AppleWorks program (Section 5.2.3).
2. Format a blank data diskette using the AppleWorks Desktop (Section 5.3.1).
3. Enter and edit text in the AppleWorks word processor (Section 5.3.3).
4. Use the AppleWorks Desktop menus to save, list, and delete files on a data diskette (Section 5.3.4, 5.3.5, and 5.3.6).
5. Find specific text anywhere in a document and replace that text with new text (Section 5.4.2).
6. Delete, move, and copy blocks of text within a word processing document (Section 5.4.3).
7. Print the AppleWorks screen and print a word processing file (Section 5.4.4).

5.2 Getting Started with Word Processing

Word processing is one of the most practical applications of computers in education. It can be used by administrators for preparing memos, letters, and reports; by teachers for producing lesson plans, tests, and handouts; and by students for improving their writing skills and learning about computers.

The first word processing systems were dedicated computers. In other words, they were microcomputers whose sole function was word processing. These machines were developed primarily by typewriter companies and sold for thousands to tens of thousands of dollars. Such systems are still available but used primarily by businesses having large word processing needs, such as in the legal profession. Today, word processing is available to anyone having access to a general-purpose microcomputer and appropriate word processing software. A word processing program can be purchased for almost any computer for as little as $50 or as much as $700.

5.2.1 Advantages of Word Processing

Basically, word processing software does what a typewriter does: puts text on a page. The main advantage of word processing software is that the text on the page can be easily modified. Writing is not just collecting your ideas and putting them down on paper. It involves editing, correcting, and rewriting. If it meant retyping the page, most students (and their teachers) would not take the time to rewrite a sentence or paragraph, even when they knew it would read better. Using word processing, you put your ideas into words on the computer's screen. Corrections, insertions, and deletions of a single letter, a word, a sentence, or a whole paragraph are as simple as moving the cursor to the desired location and entering and deleting the appropriate material. After rewriting and correcting are complete, a simple command transfers the written material to the computer's printer.

In addition to changing letters, words, sentences, and para-graphs, other major advantages of word processing are replacing and moving text.

■ **Find and replace.**   These features of word processing software allow the user to search the entire document quickly to *find* the next occur-rence of a word or phrase. Once the text is found, the user may *replace* the located text with new text. Let's suppose that Pam Banker is a teacher at San Clemente School and that she has prepared her class handouts using word processing software. She takes a new position at La Jolla School. With the find-and-replace feature of her software, she can easily change every occurrence of *San Clemente* to *La Jolla* in her handouts using only one command.

■ **Deleting, moving, and copying text.**   Text can be *deleted* one let-ter at a time by using the DELETE key. Special functions will delete one word at a time, or one line, or even an entire paragraph. Other special functions allow the user to *move* a word, sentence or paragraph from one location in a document to somewhere else. *Copy* features allow you to duplicate text anywhere in the same document or store the text to be inserted into other documents at a later time. These electronic cut-and-paste features could be used to prepare customized letters to parents from a standard list of paragraphs describing student progress and behavior.

5.2.2   What You Need to Process Words

In order to use word processing effectively you will need access to a suitable microcomputer, a printer, appropriate word processing soft-ware, and some blank floppy diskettes. The rest of this chapter will assume that you will be using the AppleWorks software (see the Intro-duction to Part Two).

In order to use AppleWorks for word processing you will also need an Apple IIe or Apple IIc computer system. The older Apple II and Apple II+ computer systems will *not* run AppleWorks. If you will be using an Apple IIe, you will also need to have what is called an "80-Column Text Card" or, even better, an "Extended 80-Column Text Card." A text card fits inside the Apple IIe (see Tip 1) and allows for 80 char-acters to be printed on each line of the screen. The Extended 80-Col-umn Text Card also doubles the Apple IIe's memory. This extended memory will let you write and edit larger word processing documents. The Apple IIc comes with the Extended 80-Column Text Card built in.

In addition to the computer, you will need a monitor capable of displaying 80 characters per line, such as Apple's Monitor II, and at least one disk drive. A second disk drive is highly recommended although not required. If you are planning to do a lot of word processing, the second disk drive will eliminate the need to change diskettes frequently and help eliminate file-saving errors. This text assumes that you will have two disk drives.

You will need a printer and the appropriate interface card and cable in order to print your creative activities. A variety of printers can be used with AppleWorks. Tip 1 will provide a general description of printers if you aren't familiar with using one. Part Two of this text assumes that you will be using an Apple Imagewriter printer. Even though it is a dot matrix printer, the Imagewriter is the most popular printer among AppleWorks users because it can print different sizes of characters, special foreign language characters, boldface text, underlined text, and proportionally spaced text.

It is also recommended that you have at least one blank floppy diskette to be used to store the examples from the text and eventually your own documents.

5.2.3 Starting AppleWorks

In order to load the AppleWorks program follow these instructions:

1. Using the diskette labeled "AppleWorks Startup," boot up the system following the directions in Tip 1. If done properly, the AppleWorks title should appear on the screen (Figure 5.1).
2. Remove the AppleWorks Startup diskette and place the AppleWorks Program Disk (usually on the reverse side of the AppleWorks Startup disk) in Drive 1 and press the RETURN key.
3. Enter today's date in the form month/day/year (10/28/85 would be October 28, 1985) and press the RETURN key. If the date shown on

```
          ┌─────────────────────────────────┐
          │                                 │
          │        AppleWorks®              │
          │                                 │
          │      Integrated Software        │
          │                                 │
          └─────────────────────────────────┘




          By Robert Lissner and Apple Computer, Inc.
          Copyright Apple Computer 1983   V1.1   USA
--------------------------------------------------------------------------
Place the AppleWorks PROGRAM disk in Drive 1 and Press Return.    10K Avail.
```

Figure 5.1

the screen is the current date, you do not need to enter the date; simply press the RETURN key.

4. After a few seconds, the MAIN MENU should appear on the screen (Figure 5.2). You are ready to begin.

5.3 The AppleWorks Desktop

If you correctly followed the directions in the previous section for starting AppleWorks, you now see displayed on the computer's screen what is referred to as AppleWork's Desktop (Figure 5.2). The Desktop is a series of menus that allow the user to perform a variety of functions such as formatting diskettes, loading a file from your diskette, or saving a file on your diskette. A knowledge of the use of the Desktop is essential to learning to do word processing with AppleWorks.

5.3.1 Formatting a Diskette

In order to permanently save your word processing files, you will need to prepare a data diskette. Newly purchased blank diskettes are just that . . . blank. There is absolutely no information stored on them, and they can be used with many computer systems. A blank diskette can be formatted for use with AppleWorks as follows:

1. From the MAIN MENU on the Desktop, press the DOWN ARROW key four times to highlight option "5. Other Activities" and press the RETURN key.

Disk: Drive 2   MAIN MENU
_____

```
  ┌──────────────────┐
  │  Main Menu       │
  └──────────────────┴──────────────────────────────────┐
  │                                                      │
  │                                                      │
  │    1. Add files to the Desktop                       │
  │                                                      │
  │    2. Work with one of the files on the Desktop      │
  │                                                      │
  │    3. Save Desktop files to disk                     │
  │                                                      │
  │    4. Remove files from the Desktop                  │
  │                                                      │
  │    5. Other Activities                               │
  │                                                      │
  │    6. Quit                                            │
  │                                                      │
  └──────────────────────────────────────────────────────┘
```

_____
Type number, or use arrows, then press RETURN key   @ – ? for Help

Figure 5.2

2. The OTHER ACTIVITIES menu should now appear on the screen. Again, press the DOWN ARROW key four times to highlight option "5. Format a blank disk" and press the RETURN key.

3. The DISK FORMATTER instructions should now appear on the screen (Figure 5.3). The formatter will use the disk drive shown on the top line of the screen, usually Drive 2. Type in a name for your data disk. You may use as many as fifteen letters, numbers, and periods, but the first character in the name must be a letter. For example, Fred Stone might want to name his disk "FREDS.FILES." After typing in your disk name, press the RETURN key.

4. Insert the blank diskette into the disk drive shown on the top line of the screen. Press the SPACE BAR to begin formatting. When the process is complete (about one minute), the screen will display "Successfully formatted."

5. To return to the MAIN MENU, press the ESCAPE key three times.

Note: If at any time in AppleWorks you make a mistake or are confused, you can press the ESCAPE key as many times as necessary to return to the MAIN MENU to start over. The ESCAPE key erases the previous option that you selected and lets you back up one step at a time.

5.3.2 Adding Files to the Desktop

In order to use the AppleWorks word processor, you need to add the file you want to use to the Desktop. Think of your diskette as a filing cabinet and the computer's memory as the top of a desk. Just as you find a student folder in your filing cabinet and place it on your desk to use

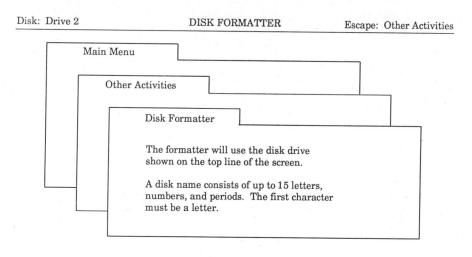

| Disk: Drive 2 | DISK FORMATTER | Escape: Other Activities |

Main Menu

Other Activities

Disk Formatter

The formatter will use the disk drive shown on the top line of the screen.

A disk name consists of up to 15 letters, numbers, and periods. The first character must be a letter.

Type a disk name: 10K Avail.

Figure 5.3

it, you need to tell the computer which files you want to be placed on the computer's Desktop. You can have several files on your Desktop if you have sufficient memory to store them (if you have a big enough desk).

Follow the steps below to add the file PEAS to your Desktop. We will use this file in Section 5.3.3.

1. From the MAIN MENU of the Desktop, select option "1. Add files to the Desktop" and press the RETURN key.
2. The ADD FILES menu should appear on the screen. Press the DOWN ARROW key two times to select the option "3. Make a new file for the Word Processor" and press the RETURN key.
3. The WORD PROCESSOR menu should appear on the screen. Press the RETURN key to select the option "1. Make a new file from scratch."
4. Type the name for this new file, PEAS, and press the RETURN key. A new file named PEAS will be added to the Desktop, and you will automatically enter the word processor. Your screen should look like Figure 5.4.

```
File: PEAS                  REVIEW/ADD/CHANGE              Escape: Main Menu
=====|====|====|====|====|====|====|====|====|====|====|====|====|====|====|===
```

```
-------------------------------------------------------------------------------
Type entry or use @ commands          Line 1   Column  1       @-? for Help
```

Figure 5.4

5.3.3 Entering Text (A PEASful Example)

Entering text in the AppleWorks word processor is as simple as typing the keys on a typewriter. Here are a few features of the word processor that will simplify the task:

■ **RETURN and ESCAPE Keys.** The RETURN key is not used at the end of each line as it is on a typewriter. The RETURN key in the word processor is used to indicate the end of a block of text. This means that normally you do not press the RETURN key until the end of a paragraph. However, if you are entering text that must appear on a line by itself, such as a line in a poem or a title, you press the RETURN key at the end of each complete line.

The ESCAPE key will take you out of the word processor and back to the MAIN MENU of the Desktop. To return to the word processor from the MAIN MENU press the ESCAPE key again. Try it.

■ **ARROW Keys.** In the lower right corner of the Apple keyboard are four keys with arrows that point left, right, down, and up. These keys control the screen location of the cursor (the flashing bar on the screen that indicates where to type). Try pressing the ARROW keys and see how they move the cursor on the screen. You can type letters anywhere on the screen beginning at the location of the cursor. If there is already text at the cursor location, the new text typed will be inserted into the line, and the other characters will slide to the right.

■ **DELETE Key.** This key deletes the character to the left of the cursor. Type in the word *Apples.* Press the DELETE key six times slowly and watch how each letter of the word *Apples* disappears. You can use the ARROW keys to move the cursor to the right of a letter that you want to correct and the DELETE key to erase the letter. Then you can type in the correct letter. For example, type *PEACE.* Press the DELETE key twice and type the letter *S.* You have just corrected the title of our example poem from *PEACE* to *PEAS.*

■ **CAPS LOCK.** The CAPS LOCK key locks the alphabetic keys in uppercase mode. This eliminates the need for typing the SHIFT key repeatedly if you desire all capitals. CAPS LOCK is active when the key is in the down position. When it is in the up position, the keyboard functions normally. The numeric and punctuation keys are not affected by the CAPS LOCK key.

■ **OPEN APPLE.** The OPEN APPLE key is located immediately to the left of the SPACE BAR. It is used in conjunction with other keys to initiate special AppleWorks commands (see HELP.)

■ **HELP.**   If you forget the function of these keys or any of the other commands that we will learn later in this chapter you can get HELP on your screen by holding down the OPEN-APPLE key (to the left of the SPACE BAR) and pressing the ? key. A list of all the AppleWorks word processor commands will appear on the screen (see also Tip 11). To return to the word processor, press the ESCAPE key.

Using the hints provided above, enter the following poem (your screen should resemble Figure 5.5 when you are finished):

> Peas
> I eat my peas with honey,
> I've done it all my life.
> It makes the peas taste funny,
> But it keeps them on my knife.
> —anonymous

5.3.4 Saving Your Poem

At this point in time the file named PEAS contains a poem (we hope one that resembles Figure 5.5) on the Desktop only. You must SAVE your file if you want to store it permanently on your diskette; otherwise,

```
File: PEAS                     REVIEW/ADD/CHANGE                 Escape: Main Menu
=====|====|====|====|====|====|====|====|====|====|====|====|====|====|====|===
Peas

I eat my peas with honey,
I've done it all my life.
It makes the peas taste funny,
but it keeps them on my knife.


        --anonymous




----------------------------------------------------------------------------
Type entry or use @ commands          Line 8  Column 29         @-? for Help
```

Figure 5.5

when you quit AppleWorks and turn off the computer, your file will be lost! To save your file:

1. Press the ESCAPE key to go to the MAIN MENU.
2. Press the DOWN ARROW key twice to select the option "3. Save Desktop files to disk" and press the RETURN key.
3. Press the RIGHT ARROW key to choose the file PEAS (Figure 5.6) and press the RETURN key.
4. Press the RETURN key to select the option "1. Save the file on the current disk." The computer will indicate that it is "Carefully saving the file." When it has been saved, the MAIN MENU will appear on the screen.

There is another way to save the file that you are currently working on. Return to the word processor by pressing the ESCAPE key. The poem PEAS should appear on the screen. Hold down the OPEN-APPLE key and press the S key simultaneously. Watch the screen go through each of the steps that you did above—and you only had to press two keys!

5.3.5 Listing Files on a Diskette

The Desktop also allows you to list all the files currently stored on your data diskette. Press the ESCAPE key until you get to the MAIN MENU of the Desktop and follow these directions:

1. Press the DOWN ARROW key four times to select the option "5. Other Activities" and press the RETURN key.

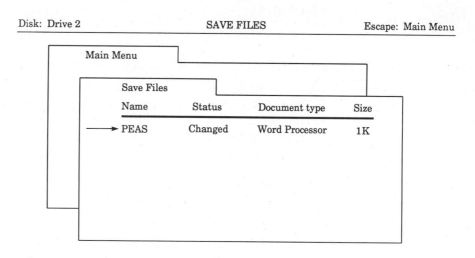

Disk: Drive 2   SAVE FILES   Escape: Main Menu

Main Menu

Save Files

Name	Status	Document type	Size
→ PEAS	Changed	Word Processor	1K

Use RIGHT ARROW key to choose files, LEFT ARROW key to undo   9K Avail.

Figure 5.6

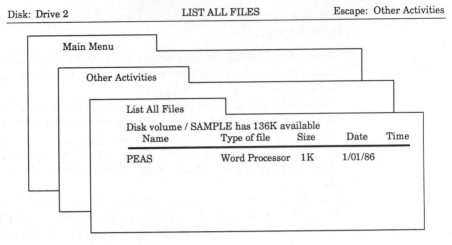

Use up/down arrows to move through list   9K Avail.

Figure 5.7

2. Press the DOWN ARROW key once to select the option "2. List all files on the current disk drive" and press the RETURN key. A listing of all the files on your diskette should appear on the screen (Figure 5.7).

5.3.6 Removing Files from the Desktop and Deleting Files from a Diskette

It is possible that you may not have enough room on your Desktop to hold several files, especially if they are long documents. You can remove a file from the Desktop (but first be sure that you have saved the most recent version) as follows:

1. From the MAIN MENU of the Desktop, press the DOWN ARROW key three times to select the option "4. Remove files from the Desktop" and press the RETURN key.

2. Use the ARROW keys to select the file to remove and press the RETURN key.

Deleting a file from a diskette is a serious consideration. Once a file has been deleted from a diskette it cannot be recovered except by retyping the entire file. Some reasons for deleting a file from the diskette are that the file is no longer of value to you, or the file is a draft version of a document, or you have two copies of the same file on a diskette. To delete a file from a diskette, follow these directions, but remember that it is *irreversible:*

1. From the MAIN MENU of the Desktop, press the DOWN ARROW key four times to select the option "5. Other Activities" and press the RETURN key.
2. The OTHER ACTIVITIES menu should appear on the screen. Press the DOWN ARROW key three times to select the option "4. Delete files from disk" and press the RETURN key.
3. A list of files on the diskette will be displayed on the screen. Use the ARROW keys to select the file you want to delete and press the RETURN key.
4. AppleWorks will warn you that what you are about to do is permanent. If you really want to delete the file, press the RIGHT ARROW key to select "Yes" and press the RETURN key. The file will be deleted.

5.3.7 Quitting AppleWorks

Now that you have been introduced to the word processor of Apple-Works, you need to know how to quit the program properly:

1. From the MAIN MENU of the Desktop, press the DOWN ARROW key five times to select the option "6. Quit" and press the RETURN key.
2. AppleWorks will ask if you really want to quit. Press the RIGHT ARROW key once and press the RETURN key.
3. You may now remove your diskettes and turn off the computer.

5.4 Getting Fancy: Word Processing Commands

The previous section introduced you to the AppleWorks word processor. This section will provide a more detailed look at how some of the special features work, like finding specific text in your document, moving blocks of text, and printing a document. In order to practice the commands necessary to execute these features, enter the example letter in Figure 5.8. Let's review the necessary steps (see the previous section for detailed instructions if you are unsure):

1. Boot the Apple and load the AppleWorks program (Section 5.2.3).
2. Add a new word processor file named LETTERHOME to the desktop (Section 5.3.2).
3. Enter the text in Figure 5.8 (Section 5.3.3). Remember to use the RETURN key only at the end of each paragraph.
4. Save the file on your data diskette (Section 5.3.4).

February 7, 1985

Mrs. Peter Johnson
123 Main Street
Los Angeles, CA 90001

Dear Mrs. Johnson:

I wanted to take this opportunity to let you know how much
Johnny has improved in his academic work and in his
behavior. Since our last conference, he seems to have
settled down, keeping his hands to himself, and controlling
his disruptive comments.

I wish to thank you for your support in helping him obtain
better study habits. Your efforts have obviously paid off
as you can see by the improvement in his grades:

          Spelling   C+
          Reading   C
          Arithmetic   D+
          Social Studies   C
          Science   C-

If he keeps up the good work, I am sure that he will achieve
some "B" grades by the semester.

Yours truly,

Linda Simpson

Figure 5.8

5.4.1 Other Ways to Move the Cursor

In addition to using the ARROW keys, the cursor can be moved around
the screen with some other commands. Try these using the LETTER-
HOME file.

■ **Tabulation.**   The AppleWorks word processor has tab stops just like
a typewriter. The second line at the top of the screen indicates the
location of each tab stop with a vertical line. Each time you press the
TAB key, the cursor will move to the next tab stop. If you hold down
the OPEN-APPLE key while pressing the TAB key, the cursor will move
backward to the previous tab stop.

■ **Setting Tab Stops.**   To change the tab stops from their current settings, hold down the OPEN-APPLE key and simultaneously press the T key. The cursor will be placed at the beginning of the tab stop line (the second line on the screen). Using the RIGHT and LEFT ARROW keys, move the cursor to the desired tab stop location. Then choose one of the following options by pressing the appropriate key:

S	Sets a tab stop at the cursor location.
C	Clears the tab stop at the cursor location.
R	Removes all tab stops.
ESC	Exits tab setting mode and returns to the word processor.

Practice using the TAB key and setting tab stops in the LETTERHOME file. A practical application for tabbing can be found in the second paragraph, listing Johnny's grades.

■ **Jumping One Word at a Time.**   You can move the cursor forward one word at a time by using the OPEN-APPLE and the RIGHT ARROW keys in unison. You can jump backward one word at a time by using the OPEN-APPLE and the LEFT ARROW keys.

■ **Jumping One Screen at a Time.**   You can move the cursor to the bottom of the screen by using the OPEN-APPLE and the DOWN ARROW keys in unison. If you type this command again, the next twenty lines of text will appear on the screen. Using this feature repeatedly allows you to scroll through the entire document in twenty-line segments.

Similarly, the OPEN-APPLE and UP ARROW keys will move the cursor to the top of the screen. This feature used repeatedly will scroll backward twenty lines at a time until you eventually reach the beginning of the document.

5.4.2 Searching for Information

You can find specific text anywhere in your document with the OPEN-APPLE and F keys. The search will begin from the present location of the cursor and continue to the end of the document. Each time the text is located, AppleWorks asks you if you want to find the next occurrence of the text. Let's try an example using the LETTERHOME file.

1. Move the cursor to the beginning of the document (under the *F* in *February* in the first line).
2. Hold down the OPEN-APPLE key and simultaneously press the F key.
3. The prompt at the bottom of the screen asks, "Find:". Press the RETURN key to choose "Text."

4. After the prompt "Find what text?" type *Johnny* and press the RETURN key. The word *Johnny* in the first line of the first paragraph should be highlighted.
5. The prompt at the bottom of the screen now asks, "Find next occurrence?" Press the Y key to answer Yes. The computer will beep and a message at the bottom of the screen says, "Not found, press Space Bar to continue." The word *Johnny* did not appear anywhere else in the document.
6. Press the SPACE BAR. The cursor is now located after the last text found (in this case, *Johnny*).

AppleWorks will also allow you to find text and then replace it with new text by using the OPEN-APPLE and R keys. For example, to change *Johnny* to *Mary* you would do the following:

1. Move the cursor to the beginning of the document (under the *F* in *February* in the first line).
2. Hold down the OPEN-APPLE key and simultaneously press the R key.
3. The prompt at the bottom of the screen asks, "Replace:". Press the RETURN key to choose "Text."
4. After the prompt "Replace what?" *Johnny* should be printed on the screen. AppleWorks will automatically print the last text that you searched for. Press the RETURN key to replace *Johnny*.
5. After the prompt "Replace with what?" type *Mary* and press the RETURN key.
6. The next prompt asks whether you want to replace "One at a time" or "All." Press the RETURN key to select one at a time. The word *Johnny* in the first line of the first paragraph should be highlighted.
7. The prompt at the bottom of the screen now asks, "Replace this one?" Press the Y key to answer Yes. *Johnny* has just been changed to *Mary* on the screen.
8. The prompt at the bottom of the screen now asks, "Find next occurrence?" Press the Y key to answer Yes. The computer will beep and a message at the bottom of the screen says, "Not found, press Space Bar to continue." The word *Johnny* did not appear anywhere else in the document.
9. Press the SPACE BAR. The cursor is now located after the last text replaced (in this case, *Mary*).

You have successfully changed *Johnny* to *Mary*, but now the pronouns *he, his,* and *him* need to be replaced with *she, hers,* and *her.* Try to replace these on your own using the nine steps above. Hint: in step six, use the "All" option to replace automatically every occurrence, but be careful to change only whole words. (If you need help, see Tip 11.)

5.4.3 Dealing with Blocks of Text

AppleWorks provides some very powerful features that allow blocks of text—words, sentences, or paragraphs—to be deleted from the document, moved from one place to another within the document, or to be copied (duplicated) within the document or to another document. All three functions are performed in similar fashion in that they require the user to identify the block of text.

■ **Deleting Blocks of Text.**   The OPEN-APPLE and D keys will command AppleWorks to delete a block of text. First you must indicate what text is to be included in the block, and then you must confirm that it is to be deleted. In the LETTERHOME example, the following steps will remove the formal name and address at the top of the letter:

1. Move the cursor to the beginning of the block of text to be deleted. In our example, the cursor should be under the *M* in *Mrs. Peter Johnson.*
2. Hold down the OPEN-APPLE key and simultaneously press the D key.
3. Use the cursor keys to highlight the entire block of text to be deleted. In our example, press the DOWN ARROW key three times (see Figure 5.9). Press the RETURN key, and the block of text will be deleted.

```
File: LETTERHOME                    DELETE TEXT           Escape: Review/Add/Change
=====|====|====|====|====|====|====|====|====|====|====|====|====|====|====|===
February 7, 1985



Mrs. Peter Johnson
123 Main Street
Los Angeles, CA 90001

Dear Mrs. Johnson:

I wanted to take this opportunity to let you know how much
Johnny has improved in his academic work and in his
behavior.  Since our last conference, he seems to have
settled down, keeping his hands to himself, and controlling
his disruptive comments.

I wish to thank you for your support in helping him obtain
better study habits.  Your efforts have obviously paid off
as you can see by the improvement in his grades:

     Spelling            C+
--------------------------------------------------------------------------
Use cursor moves to highlight block, then press Return          8K Avail.
```

Figure 5.9

■ **Moving Blocks of Text.**   The OPEN-APPLE and M keys move text in AppleWorks. This is a cut-and-paste operation in which the highlighted block of text is deleted (cut) from its original location and inserted (pasted) into a new location. Let's see how to move the last sentence in LETTERHOME below the signature line as a P.S.:

1. Move the cursor to the beginning of the block of text to be deleted. In our example, the cursor should be under the *I* in *If he keeps up.*
2. Hold down the OPEN-APPLE key and simultaneously press the M key.
3. The prompt at the bottom of the screen asks whether you want to move text within the document, to the clipboard, or from the clipboard. Since the clipboard is used to move text between documents, you want press the RETURN key to select the move-within-the-document option.
4. Use the cursor keys to highlight the entire block of text to be deleted. In our example, press the DOWN ARROW key two times and press the RETURN key.
5. Use the cursor keys to move to the new location for the text. In our example, press the DOWN ARROW key six times and press the RETURN key. The block of text is deleted from its original location and inserted in the new location.

■ **Copying Blocks of Text.**   The OPEN-APPLE and C keys command AppleWorks to copy text from one location to a new location. The difference between copy and move is that copy does not delete the original text; it makes a duplicate. This feature is usually used when copying text from one document to another using the clipboard. To use the copy feature, follow the instructions for moving text, substituting the OPEN-APPLE and C keys.

5.4.4 Printing

There are two methods of printing in AppleWorks: you can print the screen or you can print a document. Before you print, it is a good practice to save any changes that you have made to your file. In the example, you changed the LETTERHOME file considerably. Not only did you delete the formal name and address, but you changed *Johnny* to *Mary* and moved the last paragraph. Therefore, it would be a good idea to save your edited version of LETTERHOME under another name. To change the name of your document and save it on the data diskette, follow these steps:

1. Hold down the OPEN-APPLE key and simultaneously press the N key.

2. Edit the filename LETTERHOME at the bottom of the screen to read MARY.LETTER and press the RETURN key. Note that the filename in the upper left-hand corner of the screen has been changed.

3. Save this file by holding down the OPEN-APPLE key and simultaneously pressing the S key.

■ **Printing the Screen.**   To print an exact copy of the screen, including the AppleWorks prompt lines at the top and bottom of the screen, use the OPEN-APPLE and H keys. Be sure that the power on your imagewriter printer is turned on and that the printer is selected (see Tip 1 if you need help).

■ **Printing a Document.**   AppleWorks contains many special options that allow you to format your documents precisely the way you want. There are options to set the left and right margins, to choose single, double, or triple spacing, to specify page numbering, and many, many more. To describe all of these features is beyond the scope of this text. The curious reader is referred to Chapter 8 in the *AppleWorks Reference Manual* by Apple Computer, Inc.

To print a document using the standard AppleWorks format (which is acceptable for most applications like letters, memos, and class handouts), follow these steps:

1. Check to see that the Imagewriter's power light and select light are on, and adjust the paper to your liking.

2. Hold down the OPEN-APPLE key and simultaneously press the P key.

3. Answer the prompt "Print from?" by pressing the RETURN key to select from the "Beginning."

4. Answer the question "Where do you want to print the file?" by pressing the RETURN key to choose the "Imagewriter" option.

5. Answer the prompt "How many copies?" by typing in the desired number of copies (one, in our example) and press the RETURN key. Your letter will be printed after a few seconds (Figure 5.10).

February 7, 1985

Dear Mrs. Johnson:

I want to take this opportunity to let you know how much
Mary has improved in her academic work and in her behavior.
Since our last conference, she seems to have settled down,
Keeping her hands to herself, and controlling her disruptive
comments.

I wish to thank you for your support in helping her obtain
better study habits.   Your efforts have obviously paid off
as you can see by the improvement in her grades:

        Spelling   C+
        Reading   C
        Arithmetic   D+
        Social Studies   C
        Science   C-

Yours truly,

Linda Simpson

P.S.   If she keeps up the good work, I am sure that she will
achieve some "B" grades by the semester.

Figure 5.10

5.5 Posers and Problems

1. Using AppleWorks, create a reading passage for your students with intentional mistakes in spelling, grammar, verb tense, and so forth. Create mistakes that are appropriate to what the students are currently studying. Save the file and print it. (In a classroom situation, you can have the students make the corrections using AppleWorks and print out their homework to be turned in.)

2. Exchange the file that you created in Problem 1 with another person in your class. You correct their file and have them correct your file using AppleWorks. Save the corrected file and print it.

3. Create a reading passage for your students with synonyms for your current vocabulary list. Save the file and print it.

4. Use the find-and-replace features of AppleWorks to locate the synonyms and change them to the vocabulary words. Save this file under a different name and print it.

5. Write a poem that is formatted in a way meaningful to its content. For example, a poem about the colorful California folk hero Zorro might be formatted in the shape of a Z. (Hint: use the ARROW and TAB keys.)

6

Figures Won't Lie, but Spreadsheets Will Figure

6.1 Objectives

For the successful completion of this chapter, you should be able to

1. Start up the AppleWorks program and create a new spreadsheet file from scratch (Section 6.2.2).
2. Enter labels, values, and formulas into a spreadsheet (Section 6.3.2).
3. Edit a spreadsheet by blanking cell contents, inserting rows or columns, and deleting rows or columns (Section 6.3.3).
4. Modify the spreadsheet layout by centering labels, changing the width of a column, or changing the value format (Section 6.3.4).
5. Save a spreadsheet on a data diskette and print a spreadsheet report (Section 6.3.5).
6. Use the @AVG, @SUM, @COUNT, and @SQRT functions in formulas (Section 6.4.2).
7. Use a table look-up function in a spreadsheet (Section 6.4.3).

6.2 Getting Started with Spreadsheets

An electronic spreadsheet is a computer program that turns the computer's screen into a video columnar pad. For years, accountants have been using large paper worksheets containing many columns for entering financial data by hand. The numbers in each column and row are added, averaged, or otherwise manipulated to provide the accountant with the desired calculations or projections. Today's personal computers can provide an electronic means of doing the same functions with spreadsheet software.

6.2.1 Advantages of Electronic Spreadsheets

Any accounting, budgeting, projection, or tabulation problem that can be solved by pencil and paper can be solved faster and more easily using a computerized spreadsheet. The spreadsheet program allows the user to define each entry in its appropriate row and column. The entry could be a label (such as TEACHER'S SALARIES, TEXTBOOKS, or EQUIP-MENT), a numeric value (like $99.95, 250, or 3.14159), or a formula or calculation (B1 + B2 + B3 − A5). Instead of your manually calculating a row or column of figures, the spreadsheet automatically solves all calculations. If a numeric entry is changed, all the calculations in the spreadsheet are refigured. (An example spreadsheet can be seen in Figure 6.1.)

In a large spreadsheet, once a calculation is defined for a particular row or column, it can be easily reproduced to apply to as many rows or columns as desired. This feature saves the experienced user time when designing their spreadsheet. Spreadsheet programs also have features for editing entries, saving and loading worksheets on floppy diskettes, and printing reports.

MY GRADE BOOK

STUDENT'S NAME	TEST 1	TEST 2	TEST 3	TEST 4	AVERAGE
JOHN SMITH	75	80	78		77.67
MARY JONES	95	90	97		94.00
DAVID GREEN		73	83		78.00
SALLY SMART	99	99	98		98.67
CLASS AVERAGE	89.67	85.50	89.00		87.08

Figure 6.1

In education, spreadsheets have obvious administrative applications in budgeting and financial modeling. But classroom teachers also use spreadsheets for a variety of purposes such as calculating student grades, keeping track of band uniforms and equipment, and analyzing football game scores. Figure 6.1 shows an example spreadsheet for a teacher's gradebook. It is abbreviated to fit the limitations of the printed pages of this text but could be expanded to include more scores and more students.

In figure 6.1, TEST 4 has not yet been administered. After the exam is scored, the teacher will enter each student's score. The CLASS AVERAGE for that exam will automatically be calculated, and each student's AVERAGE will be recalculated to include the new test score. Notice that DAVID GREEN missed the first test. If he makes up this test, his score can be entered, and the CLASS AVERAGE for TEST 1 will be recalculated along with David's overall AVERAGE. The automatic calculation feature of electronic spreadsheets can save hours of manual work.

6.2.2 Using the AppleWorks Spreadsheet

The AppleWorks program contains an electronic spreadsheet in addition to the word processor and the data base applications. The remainder of this chapter will assume that you are already familiar with the basic functioning of AppleWorks and have a data diskette formatted to store the examples. If you have not read Chapter 5 or you feel that you need a review of basic AppleWorks, it is suggested that you study the following sections:

1. Section 5.2.2, hardware needed to use AppleWorks.
2. Section 5.2.3, how to start AppleWorks.
3. Section 5.3, using the AppleWorks Desktop.
4. Section 5.3.1, how to format a data diskette.
5. Section 5.3.2, how to add files to the Desktop.

The following sections of this chapter will explain how to use the features of the AppleWorks spreadsheet through the design and development of two example spreadsheets. To gain maximum benefit from this chapter, the reader should work the examples on a computer while following the instructions in the text.

6.3 Spreading the Wealth (A Budgeting Example)

In this example, you will design and develop a simple school budget using AppleWorks. You will learn how to enter data, calculate projected expenses, edit data, customize the layout, save the spreadsheet on diskette, and print a budget report. To begin, start up AppleWorks following the directions in Chapter 5 (section 5.2.3). The MAIN MENU should appear on your screen (figure 5.2). Insert your data diskette (the one that you formatted in section 5.3.1) into the disk drive indicated in the top left corner of the screen. (If you have previously been using AppleWorks, you do not need to restart AppleWorks. Just press the ESCAPE key until the MAIN MENU appears.)

Follow these steps to add the file BUDGET to your Desktop:

1. From the MAIN MENU of the Desktop, select option "1. Add files to the Desktop" and press the RETURN key.
2. The ADD FILES menu should appear on the screen. Press the DOWN ARROW key four times to select the option "5. Make a new file for the Spreadsheet" and press the RETURN key.
3. The SPREADSHEET menu should appear on the screen. Press the RETURN key to select the option "1. Make a new file from scratch."
4. Type the name for this new file, BUDGET, and press the RETURN key. A new file named BUDGET will be added to the Desktop, and you will automatically enter the spreadsheet.

6.3.1 Moving around the Spreadsheet

The AppleWorks spreadsheet is comprised of 127 columns labeled from "A" to "DW" across the top of the screen and 999 rows labeled down the left side of the screen. Each entry in the spreadsheet is placed in what is called a cell, and the cells are identified by their column-row coordinates. For example, the cell in the upper left corner of the spreadsheet is identified as A1 because it is in column A, row 1. Likewise, the cell in the lower right corner of the screen is H18 (column H, row 18).

The active cell is the cell that you are currently working in and is identified by a large white rectangle on the screen. Press the RIGHT ARROW key several times to move the active cell. If you keep pressing the RIGHT ARROW key, the screen will scroll to the right. Try using the LEFT ARROW, DOWN ARROW, and UP ARROW keys, and discover how to move the active cell around the spreadsheet. Also notice that the active cell is identified by its column-row coordinates just below the dashed line at the bottom of the screen. After you have experimented with these keys, move the active cell so that A1 is located at the top left of the spreadsheet (see figure 6.2).

6.3.2 Entering Data

Entering data into the spreadsheet is as simple as entering text into the word processor. However, before entering data, you must choose the appropriate active cell and determine which type of data that you will be entering: a label, value, or formula. To enter data:

1. Move the active cell to the desired location using the ARROW keys.
2. Type the data. Use the DELETE key to erase mistakes.
3. Press RETURN, TAB, or an ARROW key.

Figure 6.2

■ **Labels.** Labels are alphabetic letters and numbers that help describe the data but are not used in any formulas. Examples of labels are titles, column and row headings, and footnotes. For our BUDGET example, move to cell B4, type *JAN.* and press the RIGHT ARROW key. You have just entered *JAN.* into cell B4 and are ready to enter the next label into C4. Type *FEB.* and press the RIGHT ARROW key again. Continue with this procedure entering *MAR.* in cell D4 and *TOTAL* into cell E4. You have just entered the column headings for our budget. Now move the active cell to A5 and enter the following row headings:

A5	PAPER
A6	PENCILS
A7	CHALK
A8	BUS TRIPS
A9	TOTAL

Finally, move to cell B2 and enter the name of your school and the word *BUDGET* (for example, *MAGNOLIA SCHOOL BUDGET*). Your screen should now look like figure 6.3.

```
File: BUDGET                  REVIEW/ADD/CHANGE              Escape: Main Menu
========A========B========C========D========E========F========G========H====
   1|
   2|        MAGNOLIA SCHOOL BUDGET
   3|
   4|        JAN.     FEB.     MAR.     TOTAL
   5|PAPER
   6|PENCILS
   7|CHALK
   8|BUS TRIPS
   9|TOTAL
  10|
  11|
  12|
  13|
  14|
  15|
  16|
  17|
  18|
------------------------------------------------------------------------------
A9: (Label) TOTAL

Type entry or use @ commands                              @-? for Help
```

Figure 6.3

■ **Values.** This type of entry includes any numeric data entered into a cell. In our example, we need to budget some values for each month and expense category. Move to cell B5 and enter *200* for January paper expenses. Do not enter a dollar sign ($) and do not be alarmed that the *200* does not align with the January heading. Techniques for formatting your layout will be discussed later. Continue entering values for the remainder of the months and expenses using figure 6.4 as an example. *Do not* enter the totals, as you will program the spreadsheet to calculate them automatically.

■ **Formulas.** You can enter a formula into a cell to program the spreadsheet to perform automatic calculations. In our school budget, we need to sum the expenses for each month and sum the expenses for each item. Move to cell B9 and enter the formula *+B5+B6+B7+B8* and press the RETURN key. This formula says to add the values in cells B5, B6, B7, and B8 together. The value *230* should now appear in B9. Move to cell C9 and enter the formula for the February total (Hint: *+C5+C6+C7+C8*). Now on your own enter the formula for the March total expenses.

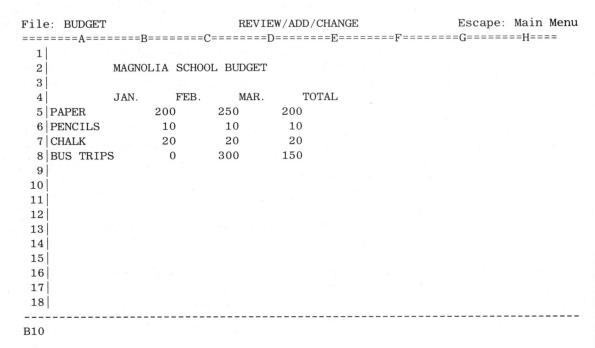

```
File: BUDGET                    REVIEW/ADD/CHANGE              Escape: Main Menu
=======A=======B=======C=======D=======E=======F=======G=======H====
   1|
   2|        MAGNOLIA  SCHOOL  BUDGET
   3|
   4|        JAN.      FEB.      MAR.      TOTAL
   5|PAPER            200       250       200
   6|PENCILS           10        10        10
   7|CHALK             20        20        20
   8|BUS  TRIPS         0       300       150
   9|
  10|
  11|
  12|
  13|
  14|
  15|
  16|
  17|
  18|
------------------------------------------------------------------------
B10

Type  entry  or  use  @  commands                        @-? for Help
```

Figure 6.4

■ **Built-In Functions and Copying Formulas.** In our example we have only a few columns and a few rows. But what if we had dozens of columns and hundreds of rows? It would seem to take forever to enter the formulas; however, several shortcuts exist. One of these shortcuts is the use of the SUM function to sum a long column or row of values. Use these directions to calculate the three-month total expenses for paper in our example:

1. Move the active cell to the desired location (in our example, E5).
2. Type *@SUM(*
3. Type the first cell to be summed in the row or column (in our example, B5).
4. Type a period (.)
5. Type the last cell to be summed in the row or column (in our example, D5) and a right parenthesis ")".
6. Press the RETURN key.

This technique greatly reduces the amount of typing necessary to enter the formula for summing a long row or column of numbers.

Now that you have entered the formula to calculate the total expenses for paper, you can copy that formula into the cells for the totals of the other expense categories. Follow these general directions for copying formulas to complete your example:

1. Move the active cell to the cell that contains the formula that needs to be copied if it is not already there (in our example, E5).
2. Hold down the OPEN-APPLE key and simultaneously press the C key.
3. The prompt at the bottom of the screen asks "Copy?" and gives you three choices. Press the RETURN key to choose "Within worksheet."
4. Press the RETURN key to choose the active cell as the "Source."
5. Press the DOWN ARROW key once. Press the period (.) key. Press the DOWN ARROW key three more times. This sequence has defined the "Destination" for the copy operation. (In our example, the cells E6, E7, E8, and E9 should be highlighted.) Press the RETURN key.
6. For each cell reference in the source formula, you will be asked "No change" or "Relative." A relative reference means that the spreadsheet should use the appropriate cells in the same row as the copied formula. Since that is what we want, press the R key twice, once for cell B5 and once for cell D5.

You have completed entering the data for our school budget example. Your screen should look like the example in figure 6.5.

```
File: BUDGET                    REVIEW/ADD/CHANGE            Escape: Main Menu
========A========B========C========D========E========F========G========H====
  1|
  2|          MAGNOLIA  SCHOOL  BUDGET
  3|
  4|          JAN.      FEB.      MAR.       TOTAL
  5|PAPER        200       250       200        650
  6|PENCILS       10        10        10         30
  7|CHALK         20        20        20         60
  8|BUS TRIPS      0       300       150        450
  9|TOTAL        230       580       380       1190
 10|
 11|
 12|
 13|
 14|
 15|
 16|
 17|
 18|
------------------------------------------------------------------------------
E5:  (Value) @SUM(B5...D5)

Type entry or use @ commands                              @-? for Help
```

Figure 6.5

6.3.3 Editing the Spreadsheet

Any cell can be edited at any time by moving the active cell to the desired
location, entering the new data, and pressing the RETURN key. If there
are any formulas that use the edited value, they will automatically be
recalculated. For example, move the active cell to B8, the cost of January bus trips. The current value in cell B8 is *0.* Enter the value *200*
and press the RETURN key. Watch carefully to see the spreadsheet
change the value of E8, total for all bus trips, to *650;* the value of B9,
January total, to *430;* and the value of E9, total of totals, to *1390.* In
actual practice, the budgeted amounts in the spreadsheet can be replaced
monthly with the actual expenditures, and you can track how closely
you stay within your budget.

■ **Blanking Cells.**   Sometimes you need to erase the entire contents
of a cell or groups of cells. Move the active cell to the desired location. Hold down the OPEN-APPLE key and simultaneously press the
B key. You may then choose to blank the entry, a row, a column, or a
block of cells. Use RIGHT ARROW key to make your choice and press the
RETURN key.

■ **Inserting Rows or Columns.** If you wish to add one or more rows or columns between adjacent rows or columns, use the OPEN-APPLE I (insert) command. In the school budget example, move the active cell anywhere in row 5 (e.g., A5). Hold down the OPEN-APPLE and press the I key. You will be given the choice to insert rows or columns; type R to insert rows. Now you must enter how many rows to insert. Since we want to add just one row, type *1* and press the RETURN key. A new row was inserted immediately above the active cell. On your own, insert another row between BUS TRIPS and TOTAL.

To make your budget example easier to read, you can add horizontal lines. Move the active cell to A5, type a quotation mark ("), and hold down the hyphen key (-) until a line is drawn across columns A through E. Now move the active cell to A10, type a quotation mark ("), and hold down the equal sign key until a double line is drawn across columns A through E. Check your work against figure 6.6.

```
File: BUDGET                  REVIEW/ADD/CHANGE              Escape: Main Menu
========A========B========C========D========E========F========G========H====
  2|         MAGNOLIA  SCHOOL  BUDGET
  3|
  4|         JAN.      FEB.      MAR.      TOTAL
  5|--------------------------------------------------
  6|PAPER        200       250       200        650
  7|PENCILS       10        10        10         30
  8|CHALK         20        20        20         60
  9|BUS TRIPS      0       300       150        450
 10|==================================================
 11|TOTAL        230       580       380       1190
 12|
 13|
 14|
 15|
 16|
 17|
 18|
--------------------------------------------------------------------------------
E6:  (Value) @SUM(B6...D6)

Type entry or use @ commands                              @-? for Help
```

Figure 6.6

■ **Deleting Rows or Columns.**   One or more rows or columns can be deleted by moving the active cell to the row or column you wish to delete, holding down the OPEN-APPLE key and pressing the D key. Follow the directions at the bottom of the screen to select rows or columns and the number of rows or columns to delete. OPEN-APPLE D (for delete) removes the entire row or column and brings the adjacent rows or columns together. OPEN-APPLE B (for blank) erases the contents of a row or column and leaves the empty row or column in the spreadsheet.

6.3.4 Changing the Layout

By now, you probably have noticed that there seem to be some limitations on the formatting of data entered into the spreadsheet. For example, all columns are nine characters wide, values are printed as real numbers, labels are left-justified, values are right-justified, and so on. You can override these defaults by using the OPEN-APPLE L (for layout) command.

■ **Changing the Value Layout.**   To demonstrate how to change the format of cell values let us change all the values in our budget example to dollars and cents:

1. Move the active cell to B6, hold down the OPEN-APPLE key and simultaneously press the L key.
2. Choose the "Block" option by typing the B key.
3. Move the active cell to E11 by pressing the DOWN ARROW key five times and the RIGHT ARROW key three times. Press the RETURN key. A block of cells with our budget values should be highlighted.
4. Now choose the "Value format" option by typing the V key.
5. Choose the "Dollars" format by typing the D key.
6. Finally, type the number of decimal places desired, which in our example is two, and press the RETURN key.

If done properly, all of the values within the highlighted cells now appear with two decimal places and are preceded by a dollar sign. Notice that the grand total in cell E11 appears as "#########". This indicates that the cell width is too small for the value to be printed. The OPEN-APPLE L command will also let us widen columns—read on.

■ **Changing Column Width.**   Follow these steps to widen a column:

1. Move the active cell to any cell in the column (E6, in our example).
2. Hold down the OPEN-APPLE key and simultaneously press the L key.
3. Choose the "Columns" option by typing the C key.

4. If you want to widen more than one column, use the ARROW keys to select the columns and press the RETURN key. In our example, just press RETURN.
5. Choose the "Column width" option by pressing the C key.
6. Hold down the OPEN-APPLE key and press the RIGHT ARROW (about two times) to adjust the column width to fit our total of $1,190.00. Press the RETURN key when you're pleased with the width.

■ **Changing the Label Layout.**   To complete our budget example, you need to move the column labels (*JAN., FEB., MAR.,* and *TOTAL*) to be centered in their respective columns. To change the label layout follow these instructions:

1. Move the active cell to B4, hold down the OPEN-APPLE key and simultaneously press the L key.
2. Choose the "Row" option by typing the R key.
3. Press the RETURN key to select row 4.
4. Now choose the "Label format" option by typing the L key.
5. Choose the "Center" option by typing the C key.

Figure 6.7 shows how your completed school budget should look.

```
File: BUDGET                    REVIEW/ADD/CHANGE                  Escape: Main Menu
========A========B========C========D========E========F========G========H====
   2|          MAGNOLIA  SCHOOL  BUDGET
   3|
   4|            JAN.      FEB.      MAR.        TOTAL
   5|-------------------------------------------------
   6|PAPER      $200.00   $250.00   $200.00     $650.00
   7|PENCILS     $10.00    $10.00    $10.00      $30.00
   8|CHALK       $20.00    $20.00    $20.00      $60.00
   9|BUS TRIPS    $0.00   $300.00   $150.00     $450.00
  10|=================================================
  11|TOTAL      $230.00   $580.00   $380.00   $1.190.00
  12|
  13|
  14|
  15|
  16|
  17|
  18|
-------------------------------------------------------------------------------
B4:  (Label, Layout-C) JAN.

Type entry or use @ commands                                    @-? for Help
```

Figure 6.7

6.3.5 Saving and Printing a Spreadsheet

Before printing a spreadsheet, it is always recommended that you save the spreadsheet on your data diskette just in case something goes wrong during the printing process. Section 5.3.4 describes one way to save a file. Another technique is to hold down the OPEN-APPLE key while simultaneously pressing the S key. Your spreadsheet will be saved on your data diskette, using the file name in the upper left corner of the screen.

To print your spreadsheet follow these simple directions:

1. Hold down the OPEN-APPLE key and simultaneously press the P key.
2. Press the RETURN key to select the "All" option.
3. Choose the appropriate printer from the printer menu. If you are using an Apple Imagewriter, simple press the RETURN key.
4. Optionally you may enter a report date, or press the RETURN key to skip the date.
5. Enter the number of copies or press the RETURN key for one copy.

Your printed output should resemble the report in Figure 6.8. Congratulations! You have designed, entered, saved, and printed your first electronic spreadsheet. If you are up for a more complicated example, continue with the next section.

```
File: BUDGET


                  MAGNOLIA SCHOOL BUDGET

                    JAN.      FEB.      MAR.       TOTAL
          --------------------------------------------------
PAPER             $200.00   $250.00   $200.00    $650.00
PENCILS            $10.00    $10.00    $10.00     $30.00
CHALK              $20.00    $20.00    $20.00     $60.00
BUS TRIPS           $0.00   $300.00   $150.00    $450.00
          ==================================================
TOTAL             $230.00   $580.00   $380.00  $1,190.00
```

Figure 6.8

6.4 Test Statistics (A More Advanced Example)

In this section, some additional features of the spreadsheet will be explored, including mathematical functions and table look-ups. The example spreadsheet will take a set of student test scores and calculate the following information: mean, standard deviation, and sample size. In addition, the z-score will be calculated for each student, and the percentile rank will be looked up in table and printed next to the student's score. Instructions for functions previously discussed in the text will be abbreviated, but complete instructions will be given for new commands.

6.4.1 The Basics

It is best to begin designing a spreadsheet around the basic information that is known, then add the calculations later. The formatting and layout can be modified as you feel the need to perfect the appearance of your spreadsheet. Start up AppleWorks or, if you were already using AppleWorks, press the ESCAPE key until the MAIN MENU appears on the screen. Choose the option to add files to the Desktop. Make a new spreadsheet file from scratch called TEST SCORES. (If you have difficulty doing this, you should review Section 6.2.2.)

Figure 6.9 presents the basic labels and values that need to be entered into the spreadsheet. Use the skills you learned in the prior sections to replicate this spreadsheet on your screen. If you have trouble, review the previous example before continuing. Your spreadsheet must match Figure 6.9 exactly in order for you to proceed with this exercise. (Note: all the column widths are the standard nine characters.)

6.4.2 Calculated Risks (More Functions)

The AppleWorks spreadsheet contains many arithmetic functions that can be used in formulas. In the previous example on the school budget, you used the @SUM function to sum the columns and rows of the spreadsheet. Some of the other useful mathematical functions are

@ABS(value)	Calculates the absolute value of the value or cell in parentheses.
@AVG(list)	Calculates the arithmetic mean of the list of values or cells.
@COUNT(list)	Counts the number of non-blank cells in the list.
@INT(value)	Calculates the integer value of the value or cell.
@MAX(list)	Returns the largest value in the cells in the list.
@MIN(list)	Returns the smallest value in the cells in the list.
@SQRT(value)	Calculates the square root of the value.
@SUM(list)	Calculates the sum of the values in the cells in the list.

```
File: TEST SCORES              REVIEW/ADD/CHANGE              Escape: Main Menu
========A========B========C========D========E========F========G========H====
   1|
   2|    Test Score Analysis
   3|--------------------------
   4|Mean
   5|Standard Dev.
   6|Sample Size
   7|
   8|Name                    Score  z-Score   Pctile
   9|------------------------------------------------
  10|Jones, Mary              98
  11|Spade, Sam               77
  12|McMahan, Joe             91
  13|Davis, Jane              62
  14|Banker, Pam              83
  15|
  16|
  17|
  18|
   -------------------------------------------------------------------------
A1

Type entry or use @ commands                                  @-? for Help
```

Figure 6.9

In our example, you will want to calculate the mean, the standard deviation, and the number of the test scores. To simplify this process, break it down into steps:

STEP 1—CALCULATE THE MEAN.

1. Move the active cell to C4.
2. Enter the formula @AVG(C10...C14) and press the RETURN key.
3. Use the OPEN-APPLE L command to set the value format of this entry to a fixed number with two decimal points.

STEP 2—CALCULATE THE SAMPLE SIZE

1. Move the active cell to C6.
2. Enter the formula @COUNT(C10...C14) and press the RETURN key.

STEP 3—CALCULATE THE STANDARD DEVIATION

In order to calculate the standard deviation you must calculate the difference between each score and the mean, the square of each of the differences, and the sum of the squares. To do this, you must use a work area outside of the basic spreadsheet. In the example, you can use columns G and H for these calculations, since they are not used for any other values.

File: TEST SCORES   REVIEW/ADD/CHANGE   Escape: Main Menu

	A	B	C	D	E	F	G	H
1								
2	Test Score Analysis							
3			_step 1_					
4	Mean		82.20 ↙					
5	Standard Dev.		12.35 ←step 3.10					
6	Sample Size		5 ↖ step 2					
7								
8	Name		Score	z-Score	Pctile		step 3.3	step 3.6
9							↓	↓
10	Jones, Mary		98	1.28			15.8	249.64
11	Spade, Sam		77	–.42			–5.2	27.04
12	McMahan, Joe		91	.71			8.8	77.44
13	Davis, Jane		62	–1.64			–20.2	408.04
14	Banker, Pam		83	.06			.8	.64
15								762.8
16				↑				
17				step 4				↑
18								step 3.8

A1

Type entry or use @ commands   @ – ? for Help

Figure 6.10

1. Move the active cell to G10.
2. Enter the formula $+C10-C4$ and press the RETURN key. This formula calculates the difference between Mary Jones' score (C10) and the test mean (C4).
3. Enter the corresponding formulas for the other students' scores in cells G11 through G14 ($+C11-C4$, $+C12-C4$, and so on). A fast way of doing this is with the OPEN-APPLE C command. Check your work with the results in figure 6.10.
4. Move the active cell to H10.
5. Enter the formula $+G10*G10$ and press the RETURN key. This formula squares the difference calculated in step 2.
6. Enter the corresponding formulas for the other students' differences in cells H11 through H14 ($+G11*G11$, $+G12*G12$, and so on). Again, the fastest way of doing this is with the OPEN-APPLE C command. Check your work with the results in figure 6.10.
7. Move the active cell to H15.
8. Enter the formula $@SUM(H10...H14)$ and press the RETURN key. This formula calculates the sum of the squares.
9. Move the active cell to C5.
10. Enter the formula $@SQRT(H15/C6)$ and press the RETURN key. This formula calculates the standard deviation.
11. Use the OPEN-APPLE L command to set the value format of this entry to a fixed number with two decimal points.

Although these directions look lengthy and complicated, once you have become accustomed to designing spreadsheets, the process becomes second-nature. Check your work with Figure 6.10 before continuing with the next step.

STEP 4—CALCULATING THE z-SCORE

1. Move the active cell to D10.
2. Enter the formula $+G10/C5$ and press the RETURN key. This formula divides the difference between the score and the mean (G10) by the standard deviation (C5).
3. Use the OPEN-APPLE L command to set the value format of this entry to a fixed number with two decimal points.
4. Enter the corresponding formulas for the other students' z-scores in cells D11 through D14 ($+G11/C5$, $+G12/C5$, and so on). Again, the fastest way of doing this is with the OPEN-APPLE C command.

This completes the mathematical calculations for the example. You now should be quite comfortable with using mathematical functions in formulas. Check your work against Figure 6.10 one more time before continuing.

6.4.3 Table Look-Up

Another built-in function in the AppleWorks spreadsheet program is the @LOOKUP function. This function searches a table in the spreadsheet for the largest value equal to or less than the value in a cell that you specify. Once the table value is located, the value in the adjacent column of the table is displayed in the cell containing the @LOOKUP function. In the test score analysis example, z-scores need to be converted to percentiles. There is no easy formula to do this (unless you are a whiz at calculus), but a table can be entered into the spreadsheet to give the corresponding percentiles for specific z-scores. Tables for such conversions can be found in most educational statistics texts. A simplified table follows:

z-Score	Percentile
−3	.1
−2	2.0
−1	16.0
0	50.0
1	84.0
2	98.0
3	99.9

Suppose this table were entered into your spreadsheet in columns G and H, with the first entry (-3) in cell G2. The formula *@LOOKUP(D10,G2...G8)* would tell the computer to look in the table beginning at G2 and ending at G8 for the value equal to or less than the value in D10. If D10 were 1.28, then the @LOOKUP function would scan the table and display the value 84. Probably the best way to understand the functioning of a lookup table is to program one in a spreadsheet.

1. Move the active cell to G2 and enter the z-score-to-percentile-conversion table into columns J and K. Compare your table to figure 6.11.
2. Move the active cell to E10.
3. Enter the following *@LOOKUP(D10,G2...G8)* and press the RETURN key.
4. Enter the corresponding function for the other students' z-scores in cells E11 through E14, *@LOOKUP(D11,G2...G8)* and so on. Again, the fastest way of doing this is with the OPEN-APPLE C command.

This completes the test score analysis example. Figure 6.11 shows the finished spreadsheet. Save and print this spreadsheet to use for review.

File: TEST SCORES   REVIEW/ADD/CHANGE   Escape: Main Menu

	A	B	C	D	E	F	G	H
1								
2	Test Score Analysis						−3	.1
3							−2	2
4	Mean		82.20		*Conversion*		−1	16
5	Standard Dev.		12.35		*Table* →		0	50
6	Sample Size		5				1	84
7							2	98
8	Name		Score	z-Score	Pctile		3	99.1
9								
10	Jones, Mary		98	1.28	84		15.8	249.64
11	Spade, Sam		77	−.42	16		−5.2	27.04
12	McMahan, Joe		91	.71	50		8.8	77.44
13	Davis, Jane		62	−1.64	2		−20.2	408.04
14	Banker, Pam		83	.06	50		.8	.64
15								762.8
16								
17					*Lookup results*			
18								

A1

Type entry or use @ commands   @ − ? for Help

Figure 6.11

6.5 On Your Own

Understanding spreadsheets is not a simple task. It takes patience, practice, and experimentation. Experiment with the following commands to discover how they function:

OPEN-APPLE O	Controls printer options
OPEN-APPLE A	Arranges (sorts) rows into alphabetic or numerical order
OPEN-APPLE M	Moves rows or columns around in the spreadsheet
OPEN-APPLE Z	Zooms to show formulas or values

6.6 Posers and Problems

1. Using AppleWorks, create a spreadsheet to budget your own personal finances. Include entries for each of the twelve months and for items such as rent, auto expenses, utilities, and your other expenses. Enter your monthly income and calculate how much you put into saving each month. Calculate the yearly totals.
2. Create a spreadsheet to calculate the cost per mile to operate your automobile. For each month, include your car payment, gasoline expenses, maintenance and repair cost, insurance, license fees, and any other expenses. Enter your monthly mileage. Calculate the annual costs for all items and calculate the cost per mile.
3. Create a spreadsheet to keep student grades. Use the printout on the opposite page as a model to develop your own grade book:

STUDENT'S GRADE BOOK

STUDENT NAMES	TEST 1	TEST 2	TEST 3	TEST 4	TEST 5	TEST 6	TEST 7	TEST 8	AVERAGE
AVONDALE, R	98	95	89	78	98	98	95	89	92.5
BETTINGTON, H	82	95	87	68	92	82	95	87	86.0
COLLINS, C	77	60	86	98	95	77	60	86	79.9
CVERSKI, T	99	78	98	82	95	99	78	98	90.9
EDWARDS, T	70	68	92	77	60	70	68	92	74.6
FARMINGTON, E	50	97	94	99	78	98	78	98	86.5
HEYDEN, S	80	99	87	70	68	92	68	92	82.0
JAMIESON, D	90	76	98	68	92	77	60	70	78.9
LAWRENCE, R	77	87	85	97	94	99	78	98	89.4
LOFTEN, A	66	69	95	99	87	70	68	92	80.8
CLASS AVG	78.9	82.4	91.1	83.6	85.9	86.2	74.8	90.2	84.1

7

Think about This (for Fun)
Read the following sentence once, slowly, counting the number of *F*'s. "Final files are the result of years of scientific study with the experience of years." How many *F*'s did you find?

Think about This (Seriously)
How would our lives be different if today's society had no computer data bases?

"When to the sessions of sweet silent thought
I summon up remembrances of things past,
I sigh the lack of many a thing I sought,
And with old woes new wail my dear time's waste." *William Shakespeare*

"Things that live in memory have no visible means of support." *anonymous*

"If I do not remember thee, let my tongue cleave to the roof of my mouth . . ." *Psalms, 137:6*

I Know It's Here Somewhere!

7.1 Objectives

For the successful completion of this chapter, you should be able to

1. Start up the AppleWorks program and open a new data base file from scratch (Section 7.2.2).
2. Design a data base file and enter categories (Section 7.3.1).
3. Enter, edit, and save records in the data base file (Section 7.3.2 and 7.3.3).
4. Modify the screen layout by changing the width of categories, deleting categories, or inserting categories (Section 7.4).
5. Use the find and select commands to locate specific information in the data base file (Section 7.4.1).
6. Use the ARRANGE function to sort a data base file (Section 7.4.2).
7. Design and save a report format and print a report (Section 7.5).

7.2 What Is a Data Base?

A computer application that is designed to store and retrieve information, much as you or I would use a filing cabinet, is called a data base program. These programs are also referred to as electronic filing programs. They allow the user to *define* what information is to be stored in the *datafile* on the diskette, *input* the information from the keyboard, *edit* or correct the information as necessary, and *print* the information out on a printer. When printing out the information, the user has the options to use a stored REPORT format, to SORT the information alphabetically or numerically, and to SELECT only a portion of the data, based on specific criteria. Anyone who has the need to store information, manipulate it, and print lists, can probably benefit from a data base program.

A variety of data base software is available for the Apple II family of computers. Some are inexpensive programs costing under $50. These are usually slow, have limited storage capacity, and have the minimum of report printing capabilities. The most practical data base program for educators is AppleWorks because of its flexibility. It can be used for many different data base applications and by several teachers in the same school because each datafile can be stored on a separate diskette. The most expensive data base programs are complete systems costing $500 or more. These are too complex for the average instructional application but are being used by schools for applications such as attendance-record-keeping.

7.2.1 What Can You Do with a Data Base?

Outlined here are a few examples of actual data base applications being used by teachers today.

■ **Mailing Lists.**   The creation of mailing lists is one of the major uses of data base programs. Names and addresses of your students, booster club members, or community advisory council members can be easily entered and updated. Pressure-sensitive labels can be used in a printer, and mailing labels can be printed ready for applying to your mailer. For longer lists, the entries can be sorted in ZIP code order for bulk mailings, or subsets of lists can be selected for printing (for example, just the names and addresses of 16-year-old girls could be selected).

■ **Reading Lists.**   Bibliographies can be stored on diskette and can be printed out as reading lists, selected by author, subject matter, grade level, or call number.

■ **Overdue Library Books.**   Some librarians are using data base programs to keep track of overdue books. Individual lists of students with overdue books can be printed for each teacher in the school, and a master list of books in circulation can be maintained for reference.

■ **Sport Statistics.**   Physical education departments are using computers more frequently in their competitive sports programs. Statistics on opposing teams can be kept and retrieved when needed, even during an important game. Also, statistics on individual athletes can be kept and updated rapidly. (Have you ever tried to keep up weekly batting averages on fifty ball players?)

■ **Textbook or Resource Inventories.**   Many schools are using data base programs to keep track of quantities of each textbook and to which classroom or student they are assigned. A California school for severely emotionally disturbed children has catalogued every resource (over 3000 items) in the school: books, playthings, games, manuals, films, and so forth. The teachers can locate a resource by its age level, subject matter, type of material, and appropriateness for specific handicaps.

■ **Band and Orchestra Record Keeping.**   Several school band instructors are using data base applications to keep track of which students have what size uniforms, school-owned instruments, and sheet music. They are also using computers to help with coordinating half-time shows.

■ **Master Catalog of Software.**   Many schools are using data base programs to catalog the available computer software in the school. Teachers and students can then retrieve lists of software that fits their needs.

7.2.2 Using AppleWorks Data Base

The AppleWorks program contains a data base program in addition to the word processor and the spreadsheet applications. The remainder of this chapter will assume that you are already familiar with the basic functioning of AppleWorks and have a data diskette formatted to store the examples. If you have not read Chapter 5 or you feel that you need a review of basic AppleWorks, it is suggested that you study the following sections:

1. Section 5.2.2, hardware needed to use AppleWorks.
2. Section 5.2.3, how to start AppleWorks.
3. Section 5.3, using the AppleWorks Desktop.
4. Section 5.3.1, how to format a data diskette.
5. Section 5.3.2, how to add files to the Desktop.

The following sections of this chapter will explain how to use the features of the AppleWorks data base program through the design and development of an example data base. To gain maximum benefit from this chapter, the reader should work the examples on a computer while following the instructions in the text.

7.3 Creating a Data Base

Creating a data base takes patience and practice, but most of all planning. It is important to identify all of the items of information and consider how you will sort or select the data before you actually enter the data. Otherwise, you may have to reenter data, or, in the worst case, start over. The items of information are called *fields* or *categories*. For a mailing list, your categories would be name, street address, city, state, and ZIP code. A *record* is comprised of the data on each category for a single unit in the data base. For a mailing list, each person's data would be a record. A *file* stored on the data diskette contains all the records in a data base. In summary, a data base *file* is composed of *records* which in turn are composed of *categories*.

The example in this chapter will teach you to design and develop a simple data base using AppleWorks. The data base will be a student's personal dictionary. A student can enter a new and unfamiliar word, its definition, a synonym, and an antonym. This technique is commonly used in education, but usually with 3 × 5 index cards. The computer data base adds a new dimension of quick retrieval, sorting, and reorganizing the words. Through this example, you will learn how to create the data base, enter data, edit data, customize the layout, save the file on diskette, and print a report. To begin, start up AppleWorks following the directions in Chapter 5 (Section 5.2.3). The MAIN MENU should appear on your screen (Figure 5.2). Insert your data diskette (the one that you formatted in Section 5.3.1) into the disk drive indicated in the top left corner of the screen. (If you have previously been using AppleWorks, you do not need to restart AppleWorks. Just press the ESCAPE key until the MAIN MENU appears.)

Follow these steps to add the file DICTIONARY to your Desktop:

1. From the MAIN MENU of the Desktop, select option "1. Add files to the Desktop" and press the RETURN key.
2. The ADD FILES menu should appear on the screen. Press the DOWN ARROW key three times to select the option "4. Make a new file for the Data Base" and press the RETURN key.
3. The DATA BASE menu should appear on the screen. Press the RETURN key to select the option "1. Make a new file from scratch."
4. Type the name for this new file, DICTIONARY, and press the RETURN key. A new file named DICTIONARY will be added to the Desktop, and you will automatically enter the data base.

7.3.1 Creating Categories

If you followed the previous instructions, the CHANGE NAME/CATE-GORY screen should appear (see Figure 7.1). The cursor is flashing beneath the word *Category 1*. You need to replace this name with the first category in your data base, and then list the remaining categories in the order that you will be entering the data. In your DICTIONARY file, you will want the following categories: NewWord, Definition, Synonym, Antonym. Category names cannot exceed twenty characters in length, but they can contain uppercase or lowercase letters or any combination of the two. Follow these instructions to enter your first category:

1. Hold down the OPEN-APPLE key while simultaneously pressing the E key. This will change the cursor from a bar under a letter (the insert cursor) to a rectangular box over a letter (the overstrike cursor). This cursor will let you type over the word *Category 1*.
2. Type *NewWord*, press the SPACE BAR twice, and press the RETURN key.

```
File: DICTIONARY                CHANGE NAME/CATEGORY      Escape: Review/Add/Change


Category names
===============================================================================
Category 1                           |
                                     | Options:
                                     |
                                     | Change category name
                                     | Up arrow   Go to filename
                                     | Down Arrow Go to next category
                                     | @-I            Insert new category
                                     |
                                     |
                                     |
                                     |
                                     |
                                     |
                                     |
-------------------------------------------------------------------------------
Type entry or use @ commands                                        55K Avail.
```

Figure 7.1

You can now enter the remaining category names: Definition, Antonym, Synonym. If you make a mistake before you press the RETURN key, you can correct the error by using the BACKSPACE key. If you discover an error in a previously entered category name, you can use the UP ARROW or DOWN ARROW keys to move to that category and retype the name. If you leave out a category, you can insert the category by using the ARROW keys to move to the category just following the one you wish to insert. Press the OPEN-APPLE and I keys simultaneously to make room for your new category. To delete a category, use the ARROW keys to move to the category you wish to delete and press the OPEN-APPLE and D keys simultaneously. Try these various editing options until you are comfortable with this process.

When you finish defining your categories, your screen should match the screen in Figure 7.2. Press the ESCAPE key. The screen will inform you that the DICTIONARY file does not yet contain any information. Press the SPACE BAR to create the first record.

```
File: DICTIONARY              CHANGE NAME/CATEGORY      Escape: Review/Add/Change


Category names
===============================================================================
New Word                             |
Definition                           | Options:
Synonym                              |
Antonym                              | Type category name
                                     | Up arrow   Go to previous category
                                     |
                                     |
                                     |
                                     |
                                     |
                                     |
                                     |
                                     |
                                     |
                                     |
------------------------------------------------------------------------------
Type entry or use @ commands                              55K Avail.
```

Figure 7.2

7.3.2 Creating Records

You are now ready to enter data for the first record. Each of the category names you defined now appears on the screen (see Figure 7.3). Type the data for each category for each word in your dictionary. Press the RETURN key after each entry. If you make a mistake, use the UP and DOWN ARROW keys to move from one category to the next and use the DELETE key to erase. Enter the following data for the first record:

> Record 1:
>   New Word: Love
>   Definition: To feel affection for
>   Synonym: Like
>   Antonym: Hate

After you have entered the last category (*Hate,* in this example) and pressed the RETURN key, the screen will move to the next record. Continue entering the following data:

> Record 2:
>   New Word: Keen
>   Definition: Having a fine edge or point
>   Synonym: Sharp
>   Antonym: Dull

```
File: DICTIONARY          INSERT NEW RECORDS      Escape: Review/Add/Change


Record 1 of 1
================================================================================
New Word: -
Definition: -
Synonym: -
Antonym: -
```

```
-------------------------------------------------------------------------------
Type entry or use @ commands                                      55K Avail.
```

Figure 7.3

Record 3:
    New Word: Cherish
    Definition: To hold dear
    Synonym: Like
    Antonym: Hate

Record 4:
    New Word: Mobile
    Definition: Capable of moving from one place to
        another
    Synonym: Movable
    Antonym: Immovable

Record 5:
    New Word: Enjoy
    Definition: To have a good time
    Synonym: Like
    Antonym: Hate

Record 6:
    New Word: Coarse
    Definition: Composed of relatively large particles
    Synonym: Rough
    Antonym: Fine

Record 7:
New Word: Hate
Definition: To have a strong aversion to
Synonym: Detest
Antonym: Love

Record 8:
New Word: Rough
Definition: Not smooth or plane
Synonym: Coarse
Antonym: Smooth

Record 9:
New Word: Like
Definition: To feel attraction toward
Synonym: Love
Antonym: Hate

Record 10:
New Word: Merry
Definition: Full of gaiety or high spirits
Synonym: Cheerful
Antonym: Unhappy

The UP ARROW and DOWN ARROW keys can be used to review the records. If the UP ARROW key is pressed when the cursor is on the first category in a record, the screen will display the previous record. If the DOWN ARROW key is pressed when the cursor is on the last category in a record, the screen will display the following record. When all the data is correct, press the ESCAPE key. Your screen will change to display all ten records on the screen. Notice that the complete definition for each word is not printed. You will change the layout to show the entire definition later. Save your file on your data diskette by holding down the OPEN-APPLE key and simultaneously pressing the S key.

7.3.3 Editing Records

AppleWorks allows two ways of viewing data: multiple record layout and single record layout. When you entered your data the screen only showed one record at a time—single record layout. After you pressed the ESCAPE key, the screen displayed several records in a list—multiple record layout. You can jump back and forth between these two layouts by holding down the OPEN-APPLE key and simultaneously pressing the Z key. You already learned how to edit data in the single record layout. The following keys can be used to edit data in the multiple record layout:

DELETE	Erases character to left of cursor.
UP ARROW	Moves the cursor up one record.
DOWN ARROW	Moves the cursor down one record.
LEFT ARROW	Moves the cursor one character to the left in a category.
RIGHT ARROW	Moves the cursor one character to the right in a category.
TAB	Moves the cursor to the next category.
OPEN-APPLE/TAB	Moves the cursor to the previous category.
OPEN-APPLE/I	Inserts a new record just before the record at which the cursor is located. The screen will change to single record layout to enter the new record.
OPEN-APPLE/D	Deletes the record that the cursor is on.
OPEN-APPLE/E	Changes the cursor from the insert cursor to the over-strike cursor and vice versa.
OPEN-APPLE/UP ARROW	Displays the previous screen's records and moves the cursor to the first record on the screen.
OPEN-APPLE/DOWN ARROW	Displays the next screen's records and moves the cursor to the last record on the screen.
OPEN-APPLE/C	Makes a duplicate copy or several copies of a record immediately following the original. Used to save time entering data when two records are almost identical. Copy the original record and then edit the copy.
OPEN-APPLE/M	The move command cuts a record or records from the file to a clipboard and pastes them back from the clipboard to a new location in the file.

Note: After you edit data in any category, the RETURN key must be pressed before moving to another category or record.

7.4 Changing How Data Is Displayed

The way in which data is displayed in the multiple record layout can be modified using the OPEN-APPLE L command. In our example, you need to widen the "Definition" column so that the entire definition shows on the screen. Follow these directions:

1. If the multiple record layout is not displayed, hold down the OPEN-APPLE key and simultaneously press the Z key.
2. Hold down the OPEN-APPLE key and simultaneously press the L key.
3. The CHANGE RECORD LAYOUT menu appears on the screen with three sample records at the bottom. Use the RIGHT ARROW and LEFT ARROW keys to move the cursor to the "Definition" column.
4. Hold down the OPEN-APPLE key and press the RIGHT ARROW key. This widens the column by one character. While holding the OPEN-

APPLE key down, press the RIGHT ARROW the required number of times to show the entire definition on the screen.

5. Press the ESCAPE key followed by the RETURN key.

Practice this procedure by adjusting each column until the screen resembles the layout in Figure 7.4.

The CHANGE RECORD LAYOUT menu also lets you rearrange category positions by using the OPEN-APPLE and > or OPEN-APPLE and < keys. The OPEN-APPLE and the D keys will delete a category, and the OPEN-APPLE and I keys will let you insert a category previously deleted from the layout.

Note: a category deleted in this manner is only deleted from the screen layout. It is *not* permanently deleted from the file. Unless the file is saved (OPEN-APPLE and S keys) after the record layout is changed, the changed layout will be thrown out.

```
File: DICTIONARY              REVIEW/ADD/CHANGE              Escape: Main Menu

Selection: All records


New Word    Definition                                      Synonym    Antonym
==============================================================================
Love        To feel affection for                           Like       Hate
Keen        Having a fine edge or point                     Sharp      Dull
Cherish     To hold dear                                    Like       Hate
Mobile      Capable of moving from one place to another     Movable    Immovable
Enjoy       To have a good time                             Like       Hate
Coarse      Composed of relatively large particles          Rough      Fine
Hate        To have a strong aversion to                    Detest     Love
Rough       Not smooth or plane                             Coarse     Smooth
Like        To feel attraction toward                       Love       Hate
Merry       Full of gaiety or high spirits                  Cheerful   Unhappy




-------------------------------------------------------------------------------
Type entry or use @ commands                                  @-? for Help
```

Figure 7.4

7.4.1 Searching for Information

To search all the records in a file for any occurrence of a word, phrase, or any combination of letters and numbers, use the find command (OPEN-APPLE and F keys). In our example, find every entry in your dictionary that contains the word *Hate.* It could be in the New Word, the Definition, the Synonym, or the Antonym categories.

1. Hold down the OPEN-APPLE key and simultaneously press the F key.
2. Type in the comparison information. In the example, type *Hate* and press the RETURN key.

The screen now displays only the entries that contain the word *Hate* in any category (see Figure 7.5). To display the entire file, press the ESCAPE key.

```
File: DICTIONARY              FIND RECORDS          Escape: Review/Add/Change

Find all records that contain HATE
Press @-F to change Find.

New Word     Definition                          Synonym    Antonym
=====================================================================
Love         To feel affection for               Like       Hate
Cherish      To hold dear                        Like       Hate
Enjoy        To have a good time                 Like       Hate
Hate         To have a strong aversion to        Detest     Love
Like         To feel attraction toward           Love       Hate




----------------------------------------------------------------------
Type entry or use @ commands                             @-? for Help
```

Figure 7.5

Another way to search for information is to select records based on certain criteria in specific categories. In your dictionary, suppose that you want to locate just the records with the word *Hate* in the Antonym category. Follow these directions:

1. Hold down the OPEN-APPLE key and simultaneously press the R key.
2. Use the UP and DOWN ARROW keys to highlight the Antonym category and press the RETURN key.
3. Use the UP and DOWN ARROW keys to highlight the "7. contains" option and press the RETURN key.
4. Type the comparison information *Hate* and press the RETURN key.
5. Press the ESCAPE key.

Figure 7.6 shows the results on the screen. Only those dictionary entries with Hate as an antonym were listed. After viewing these entries, you can display all of your records by holding down the OPEN-APPLE and pressing the R key. Answer the question "Select all records?" by pressing the Y key.

```
File: DICTIONARY            REVIEW/ADD/CHANGE            Escape: Main Menu


Selection: Antonym contains HATE



New Word     Definition                              Synonym    Antonym
=======================================================================
Cherish      To hold dear                            Like       Hate
Enjoy        To have a good time                     Like       Hate
Like         To feel attraction toward               Love       Hate
Love         To feel affection for                   Like       Hate










------------------------------------------------------------------------
Type entry or use @ commands                            @-? for Help
```

Figure 7.6

7.4.2 Sorting Records

The OPEN-APPLE and A keys are used to arrange (sort) records. In the dictionary example, you probably want to alphabetize the new words. To do this,

1. Hold down the OPEN-APPLE key and press the A key.
2. Use the UP and DOWN ARROW keys to choose the order that you want the file arranged by and press the RETURN key. In the example, choose option "1. From A to Z."

Your file is now sorted alphabetically, and your screen should resemble Figure 7.7.

```
File: DICTIONARY              REVIEW/ADD/CHANGE              Escape: Main Menu

Selection: All records


New Word    Definition                                     Synonym   Antonym
=============================================================================
Cherish     To hold dear                                   Like      Hate
Coarse      Composed of relatively large particles         Rough     Fine
Enjoy       To have a good time                            Like      Hate
Hate        To have a strong aversion to                   Detest    Love
Keen        Having a fine edge or point                    Sharp     Dull
Like        To feel attraction toward                      Love      Hate
Love        To feel affection for                          Like      Hate
Merry       Full of gaiety or high spirits                 Cheerful  Unhappy
Mobile      Capable of moving from one place to another    Movable   Immovable
Rough       Not smooth or plane                            Coarse    Smooth



---------------------------------------------------------------------------
Type entry or use @ commands                                   @-? for Help
```

Figure 7.7

7.5 Printing a Report

Since it is very likely that the data base user would want to print different reports from the same data base, AppleWorks lets you define and save multiple report formats on your data diskette. For example, you might want to print your dictionary sorted alphabetically by new word and another list sorted alphabetically by antonym. Setting up a report format can be tricky, since there are a lot of customizing options. Follow these directions to print an alphabetical dictionary listing:

1. Hold down the OPEN-APPLE key and simultaneously press the P key.
2. Use the UP and DOWN ARROW keys to choose option "2. Create new tables format" and press the RETURN key.
3. Type in the report name *Dictionary Listing* and press the RETURN key.
4. The REPORT FORMAT menu will appear on the screen. You can use any of the commands listed to customize your printout. Most of these commands we have previously discussed. For a complete description of each option, refer to the *AppleWorks Reference Manual.*
5. When the sample layout at the bottom of the screen resembles your desired output, hold down the OPEN-APPLE key and simultaneously press the P key.
6. Use the UP and DOWN ARROW keys to choose the printer (normally "1. Imagewriter") and press the RETURN key.
7. If you want a date printed on your report, enter the date and press the RETURN key. Otherwise, just press the RETURN key.
8. Type the number of copies desired and press the RETURN key.

The report in Figure 7.8 was generated using this procedure. When you are finished printing, you can return to the multiple record layout by pressing the ESCAPE key two times. On your own, try printing a report for just those records with the synonym *Like.*

```
File:    DICTIONARY                                                  Page   1
Report:  Dictionary List
New Word    Definition                                Synonym    Antonym
----------  ---------------------------------------   ---------  ---------
Cherish     To hold dear                              Like       Hate
Coarse      Composed of relatively large particles    Rough      Fine
Enjoy       To have a good time                       Like       Hate
Hate        To have a strong aversion to              Detest     Love
Keen        Having a fine edge or point               Sharp      Dull
Like        To feel attraction toward                 Love       Hate
Love        To feel affection for                     Like       Hate
Merry       Full of gaiety or high spirits            Cheerful   Unhappy
Mobile      Capable of moving from one place to another Movable  Immovable
Rough       Not smooth or plane                       Coarse     Smooth
```

Figure 7.8

7.6 Posers and Problems

1. Using AppleWorks, design a data base using one of the examples listed in Section 7.2.1 Enter at least twenty records. Rearrange the data to your liking and print a report.
2. Using AppleWorks, design a data base for your own application. (The best way to learn a computer application is to do something practical and of immediate value.)
3. Using AppleWorks, design a data base to store your personal address book. Enter the data and print out mailing labels.

THREE

Logo, a Language for Learning

Introduction

Why Should I Read This?

Logo is a very popular computer programming language and the centerpiece of a particular philosophy of educational computing. Since the first commercial copies of Logo were made available, it has been a popular language for introducing young students to computers and computer programming. Logo continues to be popular. Teacher magazines on educational computing contain regular columns on Logo. There is a national and there is an international Logo users' group; educators gather annually at national and regional conferences devoted to the Logo language. Not many programming languages can boast of such an organized and faithful following. Even if you never use Logo or you find yourself in disagreement with the Logo philosophy, you are obliged to know what you're missing.

What Is Logo?

Most languages, such as Fortran, BASIC, and Cobol, were built to deal with computations. Logo is derived from LISP, a language which is particularly good at processing words and lists. (The name Logo comes from the Greek word *logos,* which means *word.*) The Logo language was created at the Artificial Intelligence Laboratory at M.I.T. in the late 1960s. Dr. Seymour Papert, an M.I.T. mathematics professor, is generally recognized as the "father of Logo." His motivation for creating Logo and his outlook on educational computing are clearly documented in his well-known book *Mindstorms: Children, Computers, and Powerful Ideas* (1980).

Logo is an easy language to learn because it uses English words that essentially mean the same thing in Logo that they do in English. Programming in Logo is done by writing small units of instructions, called *procedures.* These procedures are small programs that accomplish a specific task. More complex Logo programs are built by stacking little procedures in a particular order. This modular approach to programming simplifies the "debugging" process of finding and eradicating programming errors. Because procedures are self-contained modules, each one can be tested and perfected separately.

Logo is best known for its graphics programming, in which the programmer creates patterns and shapes by directing a small triangular cursor around the screen. This cursor is called a *turtle.* The turtle world is easy to gain access to and yet allows for the discovery of some very important mathematical concepts, such as variables, symmetry, and properties of circles, polygons, and angles. Unfortunately, Logo's "user friendliness" has led many uninformed people to the belief that Logo is a "little kids" language. These critics often oppose Logo on the grounds that students need to learn to program in one of the commercially used languages like BASIC, FORTRAN, COBOL, or Pascal.

Although Logo was created with young children in mind, it is not limited by that audience. In fact, Logo is a very powerful language because of its simple syntax. (The syntax of a programming language is analogous to the "grammar" of natural language; it is the rules for writing acceptable lines of programming instructions.) A simple syntax allows the programmer to focus on the content of the program, instead of on the rules for communicating it. For novice programmers, frustration with syntax can make programming an unpleasant struggle. But its simple syntax doesn't mean that Logo is a "wimpy" language. Logo's LISP heritage allows the creation of complex programs, such as *expert systems.* (Expert systems are programs that model the knowledge of an expert in a particular field, such as epidemiology or geology. These programs make decisions, predictions, or recommendations based upon a data base of rules describing relationships among objects and characteristics.)

Logo and Learning

The ease of learning Logo has made it a popular language for introducing young children to computers and programming. However, Logo was not developed to provide children with employment skills in the computer job market or to fill the "computer literacy" niche in the school curriculum. Logo creators had a particular educational philosophy that they hoped to translate into practice through Logo.

The Logo working group at M.I.T. had a different sort of learning experience in mind than the one usually associated with classroom computing. They wanted students to become "masterful" computer users by taking charge of the computer rather than by having the computer take charge of them through computer-assisted instruction and programming exercises. They believed that they could create a programming language that was simple enough for children to explore with little direction and yet powerful enough to lead children toward some very important insights about mathematics, logic, and their own thinking processes.

Drawing upon Piaget's theory of intellectual development, Papert asserts that children learn best without formal teaching from adults. This learning is the result of children's unfettered, socially contexted interaction with the world. Some experiences refine understanding by expanding the range of "examples" for a given concept. Other experiences that are not readily assimilated by current knowledge require the child to modify understandings to accomodate the new information. In these ways, Papert believes, children operate as "epistemologists," validating and revising their knowledge as they interact with their natural world.

Papert further proposes that particular characteristics of the environment better support this developmental process than do others. Learners need free access to a small world that offers interesting phenomena of varying sophistication, and a means to interact with the elements and properties associated with those phenomena. Papert describes his childhood fascination with a set of gears from a car transmission. These gears comprise a model world of proportion and ratio. Yet, the pleasure of discovery and manipulation resulted in unforced learning of powerful ideas that later transferred to mathematics learning. The gears system is a nonelectronic example of the same kind of "microworld" learning environment that Logo is intended to provide.

Microworlds

A microworld is a closed environment or system that contains manipulatable objects whose relationship to one another is governed by a consistent set of deducible (testable) principles. In other words, a microworld is a working model. As such, it invites experimentation, invention, simulation, and problem-solving analysis. Microworlds contain familiar elements, making them at once accessible and intriguing. By virtue of their manipulatable objects, microworlds invite symbolic reasoning and provide a "language" for talking about abstract ideas, problems, and possible solutions. The fact that microworlds model real and constant relationships means that the system can be explored on a variety of levels of complexity and sophistication.

Dr. Papert's first microworld was a set of gears from a car transmission. The gears were manipulatable, familiar, real objects. The objects worked in a system that obeyed certain rules of proportion, and the consistency of the system allowed these rules to be deduced from various manipulations (experiments) carried out by the child, Papert. Logo was intended to be an electronic microworld, a place with tools and objects that students could use to explore mathematical, physical, and logical relationships. Some of those tools are Logo language features; as the student programmer masters these tools, they can be used to create new tools. The main object is the cursor graphics, but student programmers are able to create and manipulate objects of their own making.

Powerful Ideas

Microworlds are compelling teaching tools because of the nature of the ideas that learners can encounter there. Papert refers to these ideas as *powerful ideas* because they empower their owners. Powerful ideas are transferrable to other contexts; they are heuristics, analogies, metaphors, strategies, insights, principles. Children in possession of powerful ideas can use those ideas to extend their learning and to gain further control over the world they live in and independence from others as sources of information and solutions.

There are a number of powerful mathematics and physics concepts that Logo users can experience through illustration and manipulation in Logo graphics—for example, the properties of angles or circles, the concepts of symmetry and recursion. In Dr. Papert's world of gears, ratio was a powerful idea that served him well in later formal mathematics instruction. Not all the powerful ideas that emerge from Logo programming are mathematical. In these chapters you will be introduced to powerful problem-solving ideas: modularity and debugging. These ideas have been validated as elements of the problem-solving processes that arise in a number of different settings, including essay writing and logical reasoning.

Working in the Logo Learning Environment

Although Logo allows and encourages its users to think and work in these ways, it does not assure it. It is possible to reduce Logo graphics to an expensive "etch-a-sketch" or another set of rules and terms to memorize and exercises to carry out. This happens when teachers try to "teach Logo" rather than use it to learn about other concepts or the learning process itself. When this occurs, the motivational and instructional power of Logo is greatly diminished. Logo in and of itself is nothing more than an elegant programming language. The context and purpose for Logo use in the classroom are the key to effecting its microworld properties.

There are a few important elements of the Logo learning experience that you should try to create for yourself (and your students). They will affect what sense you make of your Logo programming experience.

First, do a little planning. Have some sort of goal in mind when you begin. Imagine what you are trying to accomplish. Part of the common misunderstanding about Logo learning (and Piagetian theory) is that learning just happens. As it turns out, learning occurs when plans go awry, expectations are not met, and the learner searches for solutions to the problems.

Second, keep pencil and paper handy at the computer, and take notes on the commands you enter and the effects they produce. The catalyst for "discovery" in Logo is reflection on your work.

Third, don't be embarrassed to stand up and act out turtle commands. It is always easier to relate to your own body than to a two-dimensional object you cannot touch. Or, ask a friend to act out the commands you have written.

Fourth, work with a buddy. You need not share computers to do this, although scarce resources may require sharing computers. Sharing problems, ideas, and discoveries is a second key to the Logo learning environment. Logo was created to give people words for talking about mathematics problems. And an important part of any problem-solving activity is the ability to describe the problem to someone else.

Your experiences, notes, and conversations with your buddies are all key elements of the Logo learning environment. They raise the programming experience to an intellectual activity that provides opportunities for acquiring powerful ideas.

The Three Faces of Logo

There are three parts to Logo software: Logo graphics (turtle graphics), Logo text (list processing), and the editor. The graphics screen is where you will find the turtle and where Logo can display the pictures and patterns you program. The text screen is where you can write orders to Logo using words and numbers, and where Logo can write back to you. The editor is not really part of the Logo language; it is a little word processor whose main function is to make it easier for you to compose and revise your Logo programs. You will learn about the editor in the next chapter.

Whether you are in the turtle graphics or text programming mode, you can *execute* (run) one line of Logo code at a time, or you can write programs that will control the execution of many lines of code. The one-at-a-time approach, called the *interactive* mode, is a good place to start learning Logo. Because you immediately see the consequences of each line you enter, it is easier to spot and correct mistakes. In this chapter you will be introduced to both graphics and text in the inter-active mode.

The Floor Turtle

In Logo's graphics mode, the cursor is called a *turtle*. That name originated with the introduction of a dome-shaped robotic device called a *floor turtle*. The turtle is a mechanical, motorized device attached to the computer by a long cord. The cord length limits the roaming range of the turtle, and the size of the turtle (about one foot in diameter) limits the finesse of its movements. Floor turtles have pen holders for marking pens that can be raised or lowered to leave a visible "trail" as the turtle runs across the floor (or paper). The floor robot allows young children or partially disabled children to program turtle movements and immediately see the effects of each command in a three-dimensional, real world. Young minds often find it easier to identify with and direct this large physical object than the small blinking symbol of the on-screen turtle. Unfortunately, floor turtles are fairly expensive. Many teachers have taken to using small programmable robot toys with their students. Although not connected to the computer, and hence not programmable in the Logo language, these substitute devices still allow children to plan and carry out a sequence of commands and to observe the consequences of those commands.

The On-Screen Turtle

The Logo graphics mode also has a turtle. Here the turtle is a triangular cursor that can be directed to move about on the screen leaving a "pen" trail behind it. It is probably easier to start learning Logo by working in turtle graphics, because the turtle movements help you track what is going on in your programming. Turtle graphics does provide a gentle introduction for learning programming principles, but that was not the main purpose for its creation. Turtle graphics was intended to operate as a microworld for exploring geometric principles through the creation and manipulation of shapes and angles.

List Processing

Most published materials on Logo and most Logo workshops you might attend focus on turtle graphics. The emphasis has lead to a wide-spread misunderstanding of Logo. In fact, many people believe Logo is only about programming turtles to draw pictures. There is a Logo world that is not inhabited by turtles; this non-graphics mode is usually, incorrectly, referred to as *list processing*. In this mode, Logo really makes use of its powerful LISP inheritance. Those who have heard of Logo's other side are often afraid of it, largely because it seems a lot more like "real programming." As you will see, list processing arises in the graphics mode also.

Dialects

L.C.S.I. and M.I.T. are the two main dialects of the Logo language available for a variety of microcomputers. Logo Computer Systems Incorporated (L.C.S.I.) offers Apple Logo for the Apple II+ and IIe, and Apple Logo II for the enhanced (128K, ProDOS) IIe and the IIc. M.I.T. versions of Logo are available from Terrapin or Krell, for Apples. At the time of this writing, L.C.S.I. has just released a new and very different version of Logo called *LogoWriter.* This package offers the power of Logo combined with expanded word processor capabilities for the editing functions. L.C.S.I. will be marketing this product, rather than the Apple Corporation. You are urged to see a demonstration of LogoWriter; it is a wonderful expansion of Logo with excellent support materials for the classroom teacher.

These chapters are written in "old" Apple Logo. However, differences between Apple Logo and Apple Logo II arise only in disk-handling commands and in the editor. Tip 12 contains a table of commands used in these chapters.

8

Think about This (for Fun)
How can you put your left hand in your right-hand pants pocket and your right hand in your left-hand pants pocket, both at the same time?

Think about This (Seriously)
What other kinds of skills can students learn while learning to program?

"To the strongest and quickest mind it is far easier to learn than to invent."
Samuel Johnson

"Learn to live, and live to learn."
Bayard Taylor

"Unlearning is harder than learning."
anonymous

Welcome to Logo

8.1 Objectives

For the successful completion of this chapter, you should be able to

1. Explain how learning in a Logo environment differs from most classroom learning (Introduction to Part Three).
2. Define the features and benefits of a microworld and give an example (Introduction to Part Three).
3. Define the characteristics and utility of a "powerful idea" and give an example (Introduction to Part Three).
4. Boot Logo and load a Logo file from a disk (Section 8.3).
5. Move between text and graphics screens (Section 8.5.1).
6. Print words and numbers (Section 8.4).
7. Calculate basic arithmetic operations (Section 8.4.1).
8. Move the turtle around on the screen to create polygons (Section 8.6).

8.2 New Terms

MICROWORLD	SENTENCE (SE)	HEADING	POWERFUL IDEA
CONTROL S, L, T	SETHEADING (SETH)	LOAD	CLEARSCREEN (CS)
REPEAT	CONTROL F, Y, X	HOME	CIRCLER
CLEARTEXT (CT)	FORWARD (FD)	CIRCLEL	PRINT (PR)
BACK (BK)	ARCR	``	PENUP (PU)
ARCL	[]	PENDOWN (PD)	SETPC
+ – * /	RIGHT (RT)	SETBG	LEFT (LT)

8.3 Booting Up Logo

The Logo diskette that comes with this text is not a copy of the Logo language but a data disk containing sample programs and tools referred to in these chapters. (Side one of the diskette has been formatted with Apple DOS 3.3, for use with Apple Logo. Side two has been formatted with Apple ProDos1.1, for use with Apple Logo II.) You will need to use your own copy of Apple Logo (or Apple Logo II).

Slip your copy of Apple Logo into drive 1 and turn on your machine. The Logo program pauses in the midst of booting to allow you to insert a data disk with your own Logo work on it. If you do not have a disk, simply press the RETURN key and Logo will finish loading. When the Logo software pauses and asks you for your own disk of files, you should remove the Logo language disk and replace it with the data disk and press the RETURN key. Make sure that the disk label is facing up. Logo will check the directory (CATALOG) of the disk you have inserted.

After Logo has finished reading disks, it will print you a greeting in the upper left-hand corner of the screen: WELCOME TO LOGO. Beneath this is a question mark. That question mark is a Logo prompt, or cue. It means that Logo is ready and waiting to act on any instructions you type in.

8.3.1 A Note to ProDos Apple Logo II Users

If you are using Apple Logo II (ProDOS 1.1), insert the data disk with the ProDOS label facing up. ProDOS users need to inform ProDOS of the "volume prefix" on the disk, so that ProDOS can direct the Logo language to the right drive. (The volume name is created when you format the diskette). The volume name of the data disk is /LOGO-PROGS. Enter the following Logo commands (Logo passes the information to ProDOS):

```
SETPREFIX "/LOGOPROGS
```

Do not leave a space between the " and the / and the word LOGO. You should see the disk drive lights come on as ProDOS searches the drives for a diskette labeled LOGOPROGS. Once it finds it, it will tell Logo to default to that disk drive for all disk drive commands, or until you SETPREFIX to a different volume.

8.3.2 Whom Are You Calling Primitive?

The Logo programming language is made up of commands and operations that send instructions to the computer. These built-in commands are called *primitives*. By stacking primitives together you create programs to do more complicated programming tasks than can be done by any one primitive alone. In the next chapter, you will learn how to increase Logo's vocabulary by building new commands and operations for Logo to use; the ones you create are called *procedures.*

There are some very common instructions that are not Logo primitives. These commands are also very difficult for beginners to create by themselves. To help out, most versions of the Logo language come with a file containing these and other commonly used procedures. This file is usually called the TOOLS file. You can find out the names of files on your disk by entering this command: ? CATALOG (Apple Logo II users must remember to reset the volume prefix with the SETPREFIX command if they want to view the catalog of a different disk.)

Unfortunately, the TOOLS file contains many, many procedures (including many mathematics functions, such as cosine). Each one will take time to load and will use of space in RAM. Not all of them are useful to you. To help out, some of the more useful tools procedures have been stored on the data disk that comes with this text. If you CATALOG the textbook disk you will see a file listed as AIDS. Enter these instruction to move a copy of the AIDS file from the disk into computer RAM:

```
LOAD "AIDS
```

As Logo copies the procedures from AIDS into the RAM workspace, it prints the name of each procedure and the word DEFINED. This means that that procedure is now available for you to use; Logo will treat it like a primitive.

8.3.3 A Very Few Words about Syntax

The *syntax* of a programming language is analogous to the concept of grammar in the English language. It is a set of arbitrary standards for communicating. Just as German and French have their own grammars, so too each programming language has its own peculiar syntax. The Logo syntax has very few grammar rules, and they are very simple. There are two that you need to know for this chapter. First, Logo does not need line numbers; it carries out your instructions in the order that you typed them in, from left to right and from top to bottom. Second, Logo uses blank spaces to mark the beginning and ending of words or numbers.

8.3.4 A Few Words about Typos

Every programmer makes typographical errors or changes his or her mind while typing programming instructions. And every programming language has some sort of line editor capable of carrying out limited corrections on the line of code before it is been entered (sent to the computer via the RETURN key). The Logo line editor, like most, is very limited. After all, a programming language is not intended to be a word processor.

Logo also has the luxury of a separate full-screen editor with many more options for editing many lines of Logo at a time or a whole program. You will be introduced to it in Chapter 9. Meanwhile, learn to use the line-editing commands available to you; some of them will also work in the full-screen editor. (You may also try the lazy approach to typos. Press the RETURN key. Logo will complain that it does not understand your garbled line of instructions. Ignore the error message and type your instructions over again.)

LINE EDITOR COMMANDS:

RIGHT ARROW KEY	moves one space forward
LEFT ARROW KEY	deletes one character to the left
CONTROL + F	deletes the character at the cursor
CONTROL + Y	deletes (yanks) that part of the line to the right of the cursor
CONTROL + X	erases ("X's out) the whole line that the cursor is on
CLEARTEXT (or, CT)	erases or "clears" the whole text screen

8.4 Introduction to the Text Screen

When you first boot up Logo, it starts in the text screen, printing a greeting to you: WELCOME TO LOGO. You can write back with a printing command: PRINT (abbreviated PR). The PRINT command needs to be given an "input" (data that you give it). It needs to know what you want it to print. You can print a single word or a list of words, such as a sentence. To print a single word (or letter) attach one quotation mark to the front of the word (to the front only, with no space). To print a list of words, enclose them in square brackets. The exception to this rule is for a number. A single number does not need a quotation mark attached to the front of it unless you mean it as a word, not as a number, as the *007* in *Agent 007*. However, a list of numbers does need to be surrounded by brackets.

TRY IT NOW

Note what happens with each command.

```
? PRINT "AGENT
? PRINT [AGENT]
? PRINT 007
? PRINT "007
? PRINT [HELLO TO YOU LOGO.]
? PRINT [MY NAME IS BOND, JAMES BOND.]
? PRINT [1 2 3 4 5]
```

8.4.1 Arithmetic Operations

Logo carries out arithmetic operations by evaluating number statements in the same order you do, from the deepest level of parentheses outward. Use the common symbols for arithmetic operations— + − * /—and use parentheses to control the order in which operations are carried out.

```
(3 + 4) * 5          would equal 35
3 + (4 * 5)          would equal 23
```

These symbols are Logo operations. That is, they create output in the form of a number. Unless you tell Logo what to do with that output Logo will complain: I DON'T KNOW WHAT TO DO WITH the answer. That statement is a friendly "error message." It gives you a bit of a hint about what's wrong: Logo needs more commands to take care of the leftover output. You can use the one command you know so far, the PRINT command, to tell Logo you just want the answer printed on the text screen.

8.4.2 A Word to ProDos Users

Apple Logo II, the ProDos version of Logo, differs slightly from Apple Logo. Here's your second peculiarity. Logo II requires a space around the division sign, /, like this: 50 / 2. Old Apple Logo does not: 50/2. Strange, but true.

TRY IT NOW

Before you enter each line, predict what Logo will print.

```
? PRINT 12 * 12
? PRINT .5 - .02
? PRINT 100 * (50 - 25)
? PRINT 365/7
```

8.4.3 Extra for Experts: How Logo Evaluates Instructions

In the spirit of the Logo philosophy, here's a challenge for those who dare: combining words and arithmetic operations to print out more than one chunk of text. How can you get Logo to print *Agent 99*, where the *99* is the output of a calculation, 100 – 1 ?

If you guessed the following, try it. Can you see why it's wrong?

```
? PRINT [AGENT] 100-1
```

Yes, PRINT can only handle one input. It prints the contents of the list, *Agent;* then the PRINT command is through. Logo then executes the operation 100–1. It outputs *99,* but it does not know what to do with the *99.* You need to find a way either to get PRINT to take more than one input or to combine *AGENT* and *99* into one chunk.

SENTENCE (or SE) is an operation that takes two "chunks" of input and outputs them as one chunk. PRINT can then handle that one chunk. Try this:

```
? PRINT SENTENCE [AGENT] 100-1
```

Now, the real challenge is whether or not you understand the way Logo interpreted this line. (Figure 8.1 illustrates this explanation.) Logo processes your instructions from left to right. So, in the example above, Logo first encounters the command PRINT and looks to the next word for the one chunk of input that PRINT needs. Instead of a usable input, Logo encounters another Logo operation, SENTENCE. It temporarily suspends its attempt to PRINT and carries out the SENTENCE command. SENTENCE requires two inputs, so Logo looks to the next two chunks for usable input. [*AGENT*] is a usable chunk, a list with one

? PRINT SENTENCE [AGENT] 100-1

PRINT

SENTENCE

[AGENT]

100-1

99

SENTENCE [AGENT] 99

PRINT   [AGENT 99]

Figure 8.1   How Logo Evaluates Instruction

word on it. However, *100–1* is not usable yet because it too contains another Logo operation. SENTENCE must also halt temporarily while *100–1* gets evaluated. *100–1* results in the output *99;* SENTENCE now has its two inputs: [*AGENT*] and *99.* It combines them into one chunk, *AGENT 99,* and outputs that. Now PRINT has its one chunk, and it prints *AGENT 99* on the screen.

8.5 Bring on the Turtle

To bring up the turtle graphics screen instead of the text screen, type CONTROL S (by holding down the CONTROL key and simultaneously pressing the S key). The S stands for split screen; this screen is partly graphics screen and partly text screen. You should see a triangular cursor sitting in the middle of the screen, and four lines above the bottom of the screen you should see the familiar ? prompt indicating that Logo is ready and waiting for your instructions. These last four lines of the monitor are actually the bottom part of the text screen. You can therefore see the Logo instructions you type.

8.5.1 Moving between Text and Graphics

To get to a full graphics screen, with no text lines, type CONTROL L. (Think of L as an abbreviation for LONG screen.) Try it now. Notice that you have lost the ? prompt at the bottom of the screen; you can no longer see what you are typing. This makes typing very difficult, unless you are a perfect typist. Go back to the split screen mode (CONTROL S). To get back to the full text screen, type CONTROL T (the T is for text screen.) Notice that the text screen remains exactly the way you left it. Moving between screens does not cause them to be erased.

8.5.2 Walking the Turtle

When the graphics screen is called up by CONTROL S or CONTROL L it appears as you last left it. If you haven't drawn anything, the graphics screen is empty, and the turtle cursor is sitting in the middle of the screen. This spot is called the HOME position. If the graphics screen has been drawn on and needs to be cleared, typing CLEARSCREEN (or CS) will erase the screen and place the turtle in the home position. If you type CLEARSCREEN while in the text screen, you will call up the split screen, cleared of graphics and text, with the turtle centered.

The turtle has a head and a rear. The pointed end of the triangle indicates the direction the turtle is heading. Right now it should be heading up, toward the top of your monitor. If you command the turtle to move forward, it will move straight up. To move the turtle forward type FORWARD (or FD) and the number of "steps" you want the turtle to move. To move it backward, type BACK (or BK) and the number of steps you wish the turtle to move.

Notice that when the turtle moves it leaves a "pen" trail everywhere it goes unless you tell it to pick up its pen by typing PENUP or the abbreviation PU. To leave a mark again you need to put the pen back down: PENDOWN, or PD. You can send the turtle home from anywhere on the screen by typing the command HOME. But the turtle will leave a trail behind it unless the pen is up.

TRY IT NOW

Clear the screen so that the turtle is centered and the graphics screen is empty. Using the turtle commands you've learned so far, count the number of turtle steps needed to cross the screen from the bottom to the top.

8.5.3 Turn Here

It's not very exciting moving up and down without turning. The turning commands are simple: RIGHT (or RT) and LEFT (or LT). They turn the turtle toward its right or left side, not toward your right or left.

These commands require input from you telling the turtle how far right or left to turn. Although the input is a number, it represents degrees of a circle, not steps. (Remember that a circle has 360 degrees.)

To understand these two commands better, try acting them out as if you were the turtle. Stand up and follow directions. Turn right 360 degrees. Did you turn toward your right in a complete circle? You should find yourself facing the same direction you started in. Turn left 180 degrees. 180 degrees equals half of a complete circle. A 180-degree turn is an "about face." You should find yourself facing the exact opposite direction you started in. Now continue to turn toward the left, but go left 90 degrees. Did you make a quarter turn?

Notice that you did not move forward or backward at all; you merely changed your heading. The same is true with the turtle. Now try turning the on-screen turtle with the RIGHT and LEFT commands. (You might want to clear the screen, CS, to start.)

**TRY IT
NOW**

Throughout these chapters command abbreviations will be used wherever possible. Try to learn the abbreviations and use them to save yourself from making typos.

        ? RT 360 LT 180 LT 90

What do you think this will do?

        ? LT 90 * 2

It is sometimes difficult to tell how far the turtle has turned, and which way it is facing. This is especially true after you have completed several turning commands in a row. In typically simple Logo style, all you need to do is ask the turtle which direction it is heading. The operation HEADING does not require any inputs from you. HEADING is an operation, like the arithmetic operations; it produces an output. In this case, the output is a number of degrees, where 0 means straight up—that is, in the home position. But Logo needs to know what you want it to do with the output from HEADING. Usually you just want it printed on the screen so you can read it. Use your handy PRINT command to tell Logo that you just want the answer printed on the text screen. Remember that PRINT needs one input; in this case it will use the degrees it gets from HEADING.

You can also turn the turtle to face in a particular heading with the command SETHEADING (or SETH). This command takes a number, the "compass heading" in degrees, that you want the turtle to face in. Remember that in the HOME position the HEADING is 360 (or 0) degrees. In the following TRY IT NOW exercise are several ways to get the turtle facing the same direction. (Notice that you do not need to put each instruction on its own line. You could put them all on one line if you wished.)

TRY IT
NOW

? CLEARSCREEN
? RIGHT 360 - 90   PRINT HEADING
? SETHEADING 360
? LEFT 90   PRINT HEADING
? HOME
? SETHEADING 270   PRINT HEADING

8.6 Building Shapes

By writing turtle commands and operations in a particular sequence you create patterns and objects on the graphics screen. Try to get used to the abbreviations, they can save you a lot of typing aggravation. Can you predict what these two sets of instructions will create?

TRY IT
NOW

Mystery Shape 1

? CS
? FD 60 RT 90 FD 60 RT 90 FD 60 RT 90 FD 60 RT 90

Mystery Shape 2

? CS
? FD 50 RT120 FD 50 RT 120 FD 50 RT120

8.6.1 Repeat That Please

There is a lot of repetitive typing required in the Logo lines above. Blocks of commands are repeated again and again. Fortunately, Logo has a short-cut primitive that makes this sort of programming a lot easier. (It is also easier on Logo.) The REPEAT command needs two inputs from you in order to know how often to repeat and what you want repeated. The first input is a number that represents the number of times to repeat; the second input is a list of the instructions you want repeated. Remember, lists are enclosed in square brackets. Watch how this REPEAT command simplifies the box and triangle above.

TRY IT
NOW:

? CS REPEAT 4 [FD 50 RT 90]
? CS REPEAT 3 [FD 60 RT 120]

8.6.2 The Rule of 360

What direction is the turtle heading at the end each drawing? How can you check? (Hint: ask it to tell you what direction it is heading in.)

There is another way to figure out the turtle's heading. Add up the total degrees the turtle has traveled from its original position. To draw the box, the turtle has made a 90-degree turn at the edge of each of four sides. 4 sides × 90 degrees = 360 degrees. To draw the triangle, it turned right 120 degrees for each of three sides. 3 × 120 = 360. In both cases the turtle has traveled a total of 360 degrees, or one complete circle, ending up heading in the same direction it started in.

Any closed shape you draw will require the turtle to make one full turn around to its original heading. This fact is referred to by Logo programmers as the Rule of 360 or the Total Turtle Trip Theorem. You can make use of this information to create regular (equal-sided) polygons. After drawing each side, the turtle turns a little before moving forward to draw the next side. So, once you know the number of sides you wish your polygon to have, you can divide up the turtle's "total 360-degree trip" by the number of turns it needs to make. This will tell you how many degrees the turtle should turn each time.

**TRY IT
NOW**

Use your REPEAT command to save yourself some typing. Make Logo do the division for you. Remember that the math operations create output that can be used by other commands, such as LT and RT. (You will probably want to clear the screen between shapes.) Predict the shape:

```
? REPEAT 5 [FD 30 LT 360/5]
```

What is the angle of each turn? How can you find out?

```
? PRINT 360/5
```

```
? REPEAT 7 [FD 30 RT 360/7]
```

Now you create an octagon and a 15-sided polygon.

8.6.3 Draw Your Turtles into a Circle

Did you notice a pattern in the way the shapes looked as you built more and more sides into the figures? What is happening to the angle of turn in the polygon? Can you figure out how to produce a circle?

TRY IT
NOW

Can you predict this shape? (Hint: 360/360 = 1)

> ? REPEAT 360 [FD 1 RT 1]

Can you make the circle smaller? Think about the circumference.

> ? REPEAT 360 [FD .5 RT 1]

Even though there is no Logo circle primitive, there are Logo procedures that will allow you to control more easily the size of your circles. CIRCLER is a short procedure that takes one input, a number that represents the radius of the circle. CIRCLER draws a circle by turning the turtle toward its *right*. CIRCLEL is exactly the same, but it moves the turtle off toward its *left* side.

There are two more useful "ready made" graphics procedures. They allow you to manipulate partial circles, called *arcs*. ARCR and ARCL are the two procedures. Just as with the circle procedures, the last letter of the procedure name indicates the direction the turtle will be turning: R for arcs toward the right, L for arcs toward the left. Think about what the turtle would need to know to draw an arc. ARCR and ARCL both need two numbers from you as inputs. The first number specifies the radius of the whole circle; the second number is the length of circumference you want drawn for a circle of that size.

TRY IT
NOW

Clear the screen and try creating circles with these new commands. Get creative. Pick up the turtle pen and draw concentric circles. Try to create a figure eight.

> ? CS CIRCLER 50 CIRCLEL 30
> ? CS LT 90 ARCR 30 180 ARCL 30 180

Don't clear the screen between drawings. Use the repeat command and see what sort of designs you can create.

> ? REPEAT 5 [ARCL 10 30 ARCR 10 30]

BUG
SMASHER

Is Logo responding with "I don't know how to" CIRCLER, CIRCLEL, ARCR, or ARCL? Remember, these commands are not Logo primitives but rather short little programs (procedures). To make use of these procedures, you must have them loaded into your Logo workspace (RAM). Did you load the AIDS file, as described at the beginning of this chapter? If not, go back and do it now.

8.6.4 Getting Fancy with Screen Commands

If you are using a color monitor, you are in luck. Logo allows you to have a lot of fun with colors. You can set background color and pen color with two simple commands. SETBG takes one input, a whole number between 0 and 5 inclusive, and will change the color of the screen to match the color associated with that number. SETPC also takes a number between 0 and 5, and will alter the color of the trail the turtle leaves behind on the screen. Obviously, if you set the background and the pen to the same color, you will not be able to see the turtle or its trail.

TRY IT NOW

Create a color chart for your own reference by trying out these commands. Here's one to start off with.

```
0 = _ BLACK _____
1 = _____
2 = _____
3 = _____
4 = _____
5 = _____
```

8.7 Posers and Problems

These questions are intended to provide you with practice applying the concepts and programming instructions covered in this chapter. You should also consider the programming questions as a model of how to evaluate student programming knowledge. Notice the distinction in what's required of the responses from DEBUG, PREDICT, and PRODUCE.

1. Concept Check. Dr. Papert's gears are a microworld modeling of proportion. Describe another microworld (not necessarily electronic.)

   What makes it a microworld?
   What powerful ideas can it teach?
   Explain the Rule of 360. Use it to create a line of instructions that would draw a pentagon.

2. Debug. Each line of code below contains one or more major errors. Rewrite the instructions so they will run without errors.

```
? PRINT 'GREETINGS' EARTHMAN
? [FD15 RT90]
? REPEAT [I AM THE WALRUS.]
? 100 * 100
```

3. Predict. Predict the output from each line of instruction. You may draw your answer or write a description. Check your work on the computer.

```
? REPEAT 24 [I AM THE GREATEST PROGRAMMER IN THE UNIVERSE. ]
? PRINT SENTENCE [DOG] [HOUSE]
? CS REPEAT 2 [ARCR 20 180 ARCL 20 180 ]
? REPEAT 12 [FD 20 RT 30]
? PR (365/7) /12
```

4. Produce. Demonstrate your mastery of the Logo commands in this chapter by writing instructions that will create these effects. Although you should try to do this without the computer, of course it is "okay" to experiment on the computer. For best results, work with a partner. When you have solved each one, be sure to jot down the Logo programming instructions you used so you can repeat your success for others. (There's more than one way to do these.)

> Fill the screen with the alphabet.
> Fill the screen with a giant circle.
> Place a square inside the circle. (Clever people will resort to their mathematics knowledge for help, but it's not necessary.)
>
> Create a half moon.
> Write your initials.
> Calculate the sales tax on this book and print the answer on the screen.

5. Extra for Experts. Give these a try. (Hint: think about the components.)

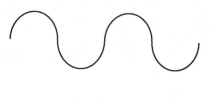

9

Think about This (for Fun)
I have two U.S. coins that total $0.55. One of them is *not* a nickel. What are the coins?

Think about This (Seriously)
Could the proliferation of microcomputers in the school and home alter the traditional classroom setting as we know it? If so, how?

"Don't put off for tomorrow what you can do today, because if you enjoy it today you can do it again tomorrow."
James A. Michener

The Old Shell Game . . . Just Watch the Turtle

9.1 Objectives

For the successful completion of this chapter, you should be able to

1. Create a procedure in the editor and transfer it to Logo (Section 9.4).
2. Take a procedure into the editor, revise it, and transfer it back to Logo (Section 9.4.6).
3. Explain "debugging" as a powerful idea (Section 9.5.1).
4. Explain "modular" programming as a powerful idea (Section 9.5.2).
5. Explain "variables" as a powerful idea (Section 9.6).
6. Create a procedure that uses two variables (Section 9.6).
7. List the titles of procedures in your computer workspace (Section 9.7).
8. List the procedures in your computer workspace (Section 9.7).
9. Erase procedures from your computer workspace (Section 9.7).
10. Save your Logo work on disk; catalog and erase disk files (Section 9.8).

9.2 New Terms

PROCEDURE	THING (:)	ERASE (ER)	DEBUG
PO	SAVE	EDIT (ED)	POTS
CATALOG	TO	POPS	ERASEFILE
END	CONTROL KEYS: C, G, A, E, N, P, D, X, Y, O		

9.3 Procedures, the Building Blocks of Logo

In the last chapter programming tasks were carried out in the inter-active mode, where each line of Logo code is executed the instant after you press the RETURN key. This kind of immediate feedback is useful when testing ideas or figuring out programming problems. However, once a set of instructions have been worked out, it can be tedious for the programmer to have to type them in one line at a time each time the design is created. If you find that you are beginning to feel these frustrations, you are ready to write, edit, and revise bigger "chunks" of Logo instructions.

Several lines of Logo instructions can be packaged together as a program called a procedure. When you create a Logo procedure you give it a name, such as BOX. To carry out the BOX instructions, simply type the procedure name, BOX. Logo will read and execute the set of instructions in the BOX procedure. To run a program in BASIC, you must use an execution command, RUN. Logo does not use an execution command. This difference is not a trivial one. When you write new Logo procedures you are defining new commands for Logo to use; you are expanding the Logo vocabulary. In a way, as you continue to create new Logo procedures, you customize the Logo language for your own purposes.

9.3.1 Just What Is a Procedure?

A procedure is a set of Logo instructions that produce some effect or carry out some task. A procedure always has a name and two markers that identify the beginning and end of the procedure. The first line of all Logo procedures begins with the word TO followed by a word the programmer has chosen to use as the name of the procedure—for example, TO BOX. The last line of all Logo procedures is the single word END.

9.3.2 Notes on Procedure Names

Remember that Logo reads spaces as markers for the beginning and ending of words. If you wish to have a procedure name that contains more than one word you must tie the words together with a period, like this: TO REALLY.BIG.BOX or TO EQUILATERAL.TRIANGLE. Often new Logo programmers (adult or child) like to name procedures after themselves or their favorite rock star—for example, TO BRUCE.SPRINGSTEEN. While this is amusing it can be very confusing and frustrating when the programmer cannot remember what the BRUCE.SPRINGSTEEN procedure does. Use descriptive names for procedures!

To get you started in procedure writing, the remainder of this chapter will contain tasks and examples for you to carry out on the computer. Stop now to boot up your copy of Logo; then remove the Logo language disk and insert the data disk that came with this text.

9.4 Where to Do It

There are two places where you can write Logo procedures. The safest and easiest place is in the Logo editor. The editor is a small word processor attached to Logo. The creators of Logo included the editor to make it easier to write and revise lines of code. In the editor you have a greater number of more powerful commands for erasing, moving, and inserting text than you do when you type lines of code in interactive Logo.

The second place where you can write a Logo procedure is in Logo itself. However, you do not have as many word-processing moves as you have in the editor. Also, novice programmers tend to get lost when using this method. (It is primarily intended as a short cut that allows experienced programmers to jot down programming solutions they have worked through in the interactive mode.) See Tip 12 for a description for using this method.

9.4.1 The Logo Editor

The main advantage of writing your procedures in the editor is the availability of more editing commands than exist in the Logo language. You have probably already experienced some of the limitations of editing in interactive Logo. For one thing, you can edit only the line that your cursor is on. In the editor you can move the cursor around to whatever line or part of the line you need to change. Almost all the Logo line editing commands are available inside the editor, and there are other, more powerful ones besides.

In the previous chapter you worked in the interactive mode creating graphic shapes and figures. You should transfer some of your interactive work into procedures. This will give you the luxury of executing complex designs by typing only a procedure name or two. By taking procedures back into the editor, you can more easily modify your designs.

9.4.2 Entering the Editor

Enter the Logo Editor by typing the Logo command EDIT or the abbreviation, ED. Notice that the screen changes; the top line reads LOGO EDITOR. The cursor is resting at the top line of the blank screen. You have already learned a few commands for editing in the last chapter. Those line-editor commands will also work in the Logo full-screen editor. These and additional commands are listed at the end of the chapter and in Tip 12. Notice that, for the most part, the editing commands use the CONTROL key in conjunction with a letter key; usually the letter key is the same as the first letter of an editing function. For example, to move the cursor to the *previous* line, use CONTROL-P; to move the cursor to the *next* line down, use CONTROL-N.

9.4.3 A Note to ProDos Users

If you are using Apple Logo II, a ProDos version of Logo, you have on-screen editing help available to you. Notice the three commands along the bottom of the screen. Hold down either of the APPLE keys, near the space bar, and press the ? key to get help with editor commands. To exit the on-screen help and get back to the editor simply hit the ESCAPE key on the upper left side of the keyboard.

TRY IT
NOW

Enter the editor and type in a copy of this procedure, errors and all.

```
TO  BOC
REPEAT  [FD30  RT  90]
END
```

Now use the full-screen editor commands to make corrections in the procedure so it reads like this.

```
TO  BOX
REPEAT  4  [FD  30  RT  90]
END
```

9.4.4 Exiting the Editor

After you type in your new Logo procedure you will want it passed back out to Logo so it can be used there. Procedures cannot be run in the editor; it is just a little word processor, not a programming language. To get your procedures back to Logo, leave the editor by holding down the CONTROL key and simultaneously pressing the C key. From inside the editor, CONTROL-C accomplishes two things: it gets you out of the editor and passes a copy of the procedure from the editor to Logo. Logo indicates that it has "accepted" the procedures from the editor by printing the procedure names followed by the word *defined*—for example, BOX DEFINED.

It is possible to exit the editor and not pass any procedures out to Logo. Sometimes this is useful if you have changed your mind about what you typed in the editor. CONTROL-G will "abort" your editing and place you back in Logo without passing any copies of the procedures in the editor.

TRY IT
NOW

Exit the editor and see if Logo accepts your procedure definition.

```
CONTROL-C  (to exit)
```

Does Logo respond with BOX DEFINED? If not, re-enter the editor. Check for typos. Did you remember to type END on the last line of your procedure? You may want to try moving back and forth between Logo and the Logo editor using these commands:

```
EDIT
ED
CONTROL-C  (accept: exit and pass procedures to Logo)
CONTROL-G  (abort: exit and don't pass anything to Logo)
```

9.4.5 A Few More Words about the Editor

The EDIT command is one of two ways to enter and exit the editor. EDIT always takes you to the editor the way you left it. When you enter the editor with EDIT you will see whatever you last left there. In this case, if you were to type EDIT, you would find the BOX procedure sitting there in the editor. This peculiarity is intended as an aid to the programmer. The Logo editor assumes that you are most likely to want to edit the last thing you wrote. However, sometimes that is not true. For instance, if it is your first trip into the editor since booting up, you will see a blank page.

The second way to enter the editor is by telling it the name of the specific procedure (or procedures) you wish to work on. If you wish to edit a procedure named SURFBOARD you can specify EDIT "SURFBOARD. (Remember that all Logo words used as names are tagged at the front with a quotation mark.) If you wish to work on more than one procedure in the editor, you can specify a list of names: EDIT [SURFBOARD SUN WAVE]. Remember that lists are enclosed by square brackets.

EDIT "(no name) will put you in the editor on an empty page. It is not necessary to start a new procedure on an empty page. You can simply use the return key to move your cursor down below the last procedure you wrote.

9.4.6 Editor Tricks

The editor is useful for more than correcting typos and revising Logo instructions. You can use it to save yourself time in creating new procedures. BOX, as it is defined so far, will generate a square with sides that are 30 steps long. Suppose that you wish to have a size-50 box. Revising the same BOX procedure will allow you easily to create different sizes of boxes without a lot of retyping. However, each time you revise BOX and exit the editor you will have written over the old version of BOX.

The trick is to create a box of a different size without wiping out the old box and yet save yourself all the extra typing. This is done by giving the procedure a different name. Then, when you exit the editor, Logo will have the new box name defined, and it will still have the old BOX sitting in workspace. Later in this chapter (Section 9.7) you will learn a few commands for checking the procedure titles in your workspace.

**TRY IT
NOW**

Enter the editor and revise the BOX procedure so that it will produce a square with sides of 50 steps each. Think: what part of the procedure needs to change? Where does Logo get the information about the length of the sides?

```
TO BOX
REPEAT 4 [FD 50 RT 90]
END
```

Exit and run the procedure to be certain it works. Reenter the editor. Move your cursor over to the end of the word BOX on the first line. Change the name of procedure, like this:

```
TO BOX. 50
REPEAT 4 [FD 50 RT 90]
END
```

Exit the editor with CONTROL-C. Now BOX.50 is defined. Enter the editor again. This time make the changes that will create a box of size 30.

```
TO BOX. 30
REPEAT 4 [FD 30 RT 90]
END
```

9.5 Powerful Ideas: Debugging and Modular Programming

In the last chapter you were introduced to the educational benefits ascribed to Logo programming. One of those benefits is growth in problem-solving skills and strategies as a result of two particular kinds of analytic programming experiences: debugging and modular programming.

9.5.1 When Is an Insect a Mistake? When It's a Bug

Rarely does the first version of a command or an entire procedure run exactly the way the programmer wanted and expected it to run. It does not matter whether you are a novice or sophisticated programmer; bugs arise and must be squashed. However, depending upon the tone set by the teacher, students will view a programming problem as either an error or a "snag." The distinction is not trivial.

For many students, "error" connotes not only wrongness but also the existence of a "right" answer. Students who feel that they are making mistakes tend to seek right answers from the instructor, redefine their programming goal to a safer one, or abandon what they had written in favor of starting over from scratch. They exhibit little analytical behavior, and they do not experience errors as useful data for revision.

On the other hand, the notion of snags implies something temporary and fixable. When students see problems as "bugs" instead of mistakes, they are more inclined to engage in revision behaviors: analyzing the results the "buggy" program produced, trying to identify the source of bugs, and devising and testing alternative solutions.

There are at least two teaching strategies that facilitate the development of debugging behaviors in student programmers. The first, and probably the most potent, is for the teacher to model those behaviors. Engage in genuine Logo projects of your own and share your struggles with your students. Cooperate in your programming efforts and share your programs and strategies. There is always more than one way to achieve the same programming result; show your students that you "see" classes of solutions rather than single "right answers." The second strategy is to focus attention on the messages Logo prints on the screen when it is confused by a program. Unfortunately, those messages are usually called "error messages," but in the Logo programming langauge they are particularly rich sources of information about the source and nature of the programming problem.

9.5.2 Mind-Sized Bites: A Modular Approach to Programming

When people are first introduced to writing graphics procedures they tend to begin attempting very complex designs—houses, people, cars, scenes. After working in the interactive mode, copying down lines of code that work, these novice programmers incorporate all lines of code into one very long procedure. Usually, the procedure contains at least one bug. However, finding the bug in a long procedure is much like finding a needle in a haystack. As an example, consider the SURPRISE procedure in the box below.

TRY IT NOW   Load the SURPRISE file from the disk. Take the procedure into the editor and examine it. Be sure you remember to exit the editor with CONTROL-C. Before you run the procedure, try to predict what it will do. (This procedure uses the CIRCLEL and CIRCLER commands. Are they loaded into your workspace?)

```
? LOAD "SURPRISE
SURPRISE DEFINED
? ED "SURPRISE
TO SURPRISE. SHAPE
CS PU
LT 90 FD 200 PD
REPEAT 4 [FD 50 RT 90]
REPEAT 4 [FD 30 LT 90]
LT 90 FD 15
CIRCLEL 5
BK 50
CIRCLEL 5
PU FD 150 PD
REPEAT 4 [FD 90 RT 90]
REPEAT 4 [FD 30 LT 90]
LT 90
FD 15
CIRCLEL 10
BK 70
CIRCLEL 10
END
```

Can you figure out the goal of the procedure? Can you describe the bug(s)? Where do you think the problem lies?

If you were to try to debug the SURPRISE procedure you would find it an unpleasant task. It would be difficult to figure out where to start looking for the programming bug; there are many lines of code and no apparent organization or sequence to the lines. It is difficult to tell how far Logo progressed through the procedure before it tripped on the bug. These difficulties are the result of trying to do too much in one program.

Reconsider the SURPRISE procedure. The truck scene it attempts to draw contains at least three distinct components: little truck, big truck, and the commands for setting up the turtle between trucks. By writing a separate procedure for each component, the programmer could much more easily test, debug, and revise his or her work until satisfied. When the components are ready to assemble, the programmer can focus on determining proper sequence and creating any additional linking procedures needed to smooth the transition from component to component.

TRY IT NOW   Take the SURPRISE procedure back into the editor and divide it up into the procedures representing the LITTLE.TRUCK, MOVE.PEN, and BIG.TRUCK. Insert new TO lines and END lines where needed.

```
TO LITTLE. TRUCK
CS PU
LT 90 FD 200 PD
REPEAT 4 [FD 50 RT 90]
REPEAT 4 [FD 30 LT 90]
LT 90 FD 15
CIRCLEL 5
BK 50
CIRCLEL 5
END
TO MOVE. PEN
PU FD 150 PD
END
TO BIG. TRUCK
REPEAT 4 [FD 90 RT 90]
REPEAT 4 [FD 30 LT 90]
LT 90 FD 15
CIRCLEL 10
BK 70
CIRCLEL 10
END
```

Run each procedure separately to locate the bug.

It sure is easier to debug these procedures one at a time than it is to find and eradicate the bugs in the SURPRISE procedure. Here's another benefit of the modular approach: you can reuse any of those procedures as you need it, without having to get the whole scene. For example, you could easily populate your scene with more trucks.

9.6 Powerful Idea: Variables

Besides the modular approach, another characteristic distinguishing good and less good programming is efficiency. An efficient program accomplishes its task in the least number of steps. One way to reduce steps is to identify a repeated pattern of steps and devise a pattern description that can be used over and over again as needed. An algorithm is just such a pattern description. And computer programs are really just algorithms. However, some programs are more useful than others because they are more widely applicable; their algorithms are flexible enough to fit a number of specific contexts. To be this flexible, algorithms often make use of variables. That is, they use symbols to stand for the specific values (numeric or alphabetic) that will be substituted for the symbols when the program is run.

Consider the BOX procedure used in this chapter. While it can be reused to generate boxes of various sizes, this requires either constant trips to the editor or the creation of many different sized boxes with unique names (such as BOX.50, BOX.30). Neither of these solutions to the problem of different-sized boxes is particularly efficient. However, if you examine each variety of box you will see a pattern of steps that is repeated in each and every box: REPEAT 4 [FD some number RT 90]. Would the angle of the box corners ever change? No, rectangles always contain four right (90 degree) angles. The size of the box changes as the length of the sides varies. In each different-sized box, the variable is the number of turtle steps given to the FD command.

With this information, you can now create a single BOX procedure that will operate as an algorithm to generate boxes of different sized sides, as needed. At the time the BOX procedure is run, you can specify the specific numeric value you wish FD to use for the length of the sides.

9.6.1 Using Variables in Procedures

Three things must be done to prepare a procedure for using variables. First, the programmer must invent and substitute a variable name where a specific value will be used. Second, the procedure must tell Logo the name of the variable. Third, it must tell Logo where to find the value to substitute for the variable name every place it sees that name in the procedure.

9.6.2 What's in a Name?

Earlier in this chapter, you saw how Logo allows the programmer to use long words when naming procedures. This is meant to encourage the use of natural English language words as labels for procedures and variables in order to make Logo programs more understandable to their programmers and to others with whom they might share their work. Take advantage of this opportunity; use meaningful names for your variables! Good names for the BOX variable are SIZE or LENGTH or STEPS; avoid names like X or LINDA.

Until you mark it as a variable, a name is just another word to Logo. The command THING, which is placed right in front of the variable name, indicates to Logo that this word is being used as a variable. Fortunately, there is a widely used abbreviation for the command THING, but it is a bit strange. It is a colon, placed right up against the front of the variable name, with no space between, like this—:SIZE, which is the same as THING SIZE.

9.6.3 Where to Find It

There is one other very important element to using variables in procedures. Logo must be told where to look for the value to substitute for the variable. In procedures, this is done by placing the variable on the very first line of the procedure, the TO line, like this—TO BOX :SIZE. This tells Logo two important pieces of information. First, it indicates that the procedure contains a variable with a particular name. Second, it tells Logo that the value for this variable will be given, along with the procedure name, at the time the procedure is run, like this:

```
? BOX 55
```

If you were to invoke the BOX without giving the additional information on the value for the variable, Logo would complain, "Not enough inputs to BOX," meaning that it knows from the TO line that it needs a value and that it did not get one. It cannot continue.

TRY IT NOW

Take the BOX procedure into the editor. Take out the number of turtle steps in the FD command and substitute your own variable name.

```
TO BOX :SIZE
REPEAT 4 [FD :SIZE RT 90]
END
```

Exit and run the program a couple of time with different values. Now there's a useful procedure!

```
? BOX 20
? BOX 50
? BOX 78
```

BUG SMASHER:

Did you use a colon, not a semi-colon?
Did you put the colon right up against the variable name without leaving a space?
Did you include the variable name on the TO line?
Did you exit the editor with CONTROL-C, not CONTROL-G?
Did you give a value (number) when you typed BOX?

9.6.4 Not Just for Graphics Anymore

In the last chapter you were introduced to the text screen and the PRINT command. As you might have guessed, procedures and variables are useful in text programming, too. And the same principles apply to describing the quality of text programs. The following GREET procedure is very limited in its usefulness. A generic GREET could serve more people by using a variable to stand for the specific name of the person being greeted.

There are some complications, however. If you use :SOMEONE in place of "James Bond," then you will break up the one input for the PRINT command into two parts. The first part will be the list of words, [Nice to meet you], and the second part will be the variable, :SOMEONE (or whatever variable name you use). Remember from the last chapter that PRINT expects one chunk of input. Look back to see how you can make one chunk out of two chunks of input.

TRY IT NOW

Load the disk file called "GREET from your data disk. The file contains a procedure to introduce a specific person, James Bond, to the computer. Take the procedure into the editor to examine it.

```
TO GREET
TEXTSCREEN CLEARTEXT
PR [HI THERE.  I'M A PROGRAM. ]
PR [NICE TO MEET YOU JAMES BOND. ]
END
```

Exit the editor and run the procedure.

```
? GREET
```

Modify GREET to accept variables. You will want to use the SENTENCE operation, something like this:

```
TO INTRODUCE  : SOMEONE
TEXTSCREEN CLEARTEXT
PR [HI THERE.  I'M A PROGRAM. ]
PR SE [NICE TO MEET YOU]  : SOMEONE
END
```

Exit. Test it. What do you think? Well, you might want to change the rest of the text a little too.

9.6.4 Beyond the Box

As you might imagine, it is possible to include more than one variable in a procedure. Suppose, for instance, that you wished to distinguish between squares and rectangles. Squares have equal sides, so BOX works just fine to produce squares. Rectangles have two sets of equal sides, but each set may be of a different length. Of course, both shapes have four right-angle corners, so that part won't be changing. The two variables for the rectangle are both lengths.

The same three steps you used to create your first one-variable procedure must also be taken to create a procedure with two variables. Think of variable names for the different side lengths. You could call them LENGTH1 and LENGTH2, or HEIGHT and WIDTH, or whatever descriptive variable name you wish. Be sure to list the new variable names on the TO line, after the new procedure name:

```
TO RECTANGLE :HEIGHT :WIDTH
```

Now substitute those variable names in place of the specific numeric values.

**TRY IT
NOW**

```
TO RECTANGLE :WIDTH :HEIGHT
REPEAT 2 [FD :WIDTH RT 90 FD :HEIGHT RT 90]
END
```

Don't forget to give two inputs for Logo to use in the procedure.

```
? RECTANGLE 30 60
```

9.7 Managing Workspace

If you have been following along with the text or experimenting some on your own, you have a number of little procedures floating around in your Logo workspace. Use these commands to keep track of what you have created.

These commands will display the contents of your workspace in one or another fashion.

POTS	stands for Print Out Titles. This command will display a list of all procedure titles currently available in the Logo workspace.
PO	stands for Print Out. This command is used with the name of a procedure (don't forget the ") and will display a listing of the procedure, line by line. Example: PO "BOX.50

These commands will erase parts of your Logo work from the workspace! Use them carefully; there is no "unerase" command.

ERASE (ER)	This command is used with the name of a procedure (don't forget the ") and will erase that procedure from the workspace. Example: ERASE "BOX.50
ERALL	This command is very dangerous. It combines the ERASE abbreviation with the word ALL, and the result is to erase everything you have created from the Logo workspace.

9.8 Disk Management

Now that you are writing procedures, you are ready to start "saving" your work on disk. Unless work is saved on disk, it disappears when the computer power goes off or, in this case, if you exit from the Logo language to work on something else such as AppleWorks.

At the beginning of this session, after booting up with the Logo language diskette, you were asked to remove that diskette and replace it with the one that accompanies this text. That disk contains the Logo programs and tools mentioned in these three chapters. There is also some space available for you to save your Logo work on disk. However, if you are going to continue working in Logo, you should prepare your own "data" disk for saving work. Use the Apple DOS to initialize a disk (see Tip 2). This disk can then be slipped into drive 1 after booting up with the Logo language disk. (Apple ProDos users must remember to use the SETPREFIX command described in the previous chapter.)

To check the current contents of your disk, type the command CATALOG. The drive light should come on as Logo talks to the DOS system, which in turn checks the disk. (Note: if your diskette is a newly initialized one, there will not be any titles listed. If you are using a ProDos formatted disk, you must first use SETPREFIX; see Tip 12.)

**TRY IT
NOW**

Check the contents of the Logo sample disk that came with this text.

? CATALOG

It should read

AIDS
BOX
GREET
SURPRISE
POLYGON

. . .ETC. . .

**BUG
SMASHER**

Do you have the disk in correctly (closed the door)?
Do you have the correct side up (ProDos version on back of disk)?

9.8.1 Save It!

Saving your work on a diskette allows you to recall that work back into the computer workspace anytime you need it—for example, to refine or modify an old procedure. Once you have saved your work, you can share it with others.

When you save your Logo work on disk you do so by creating a "file folder," which you will need to label or name. Of course you would have a chaotic mess if you used the same file name over and over for different files, or if you used odd or abbreviated names. Choose descriptive file names so that you can remember what is in the files. Think about the contents of the file. For example, the file named AIDS (on the textbook diskette) contains the CIRCLEL, CIRCLER, ARCR, and ARCL procedures. These are helpful toollike procedures, hence the file name AIDS.

If a file name already exists on diskette, you cannot save another file with the same name. You must either erase the file on disk or choose another file name. To erase a Logo file from the diskette, use the command ERASEFILE along with the name of the disk file that you want to destroy. Remember that ERASEFILE erases from the diskette and that ERASE erases from workspace. Just like ERASE, ERASEFILE is a dangerous command. Once you have erased from the diskette, there is no changing your mind.

The SAVE command places the new file folder in a "drawer" of files on the diskette. When you typed CATALOG, earlier, you saw a list of the files on the current diskette—that is, in the current drawer.

Saving your work can be a little tricky in Logo. When you type SAVE followed by the file name, Logo will gather up all the procedures in the workspace and put them in that file, and then copy the file onto the diskette. Many new Logo programmers wrongly assume that Logo can and will save one or two procedures of their choosing. Unless you have erased the procedures that you do not want saved, everything in workspace will be saved together in the same file. If you are not sure what is in your workspace, use the workspace management commands described earlier, especially POTS.

TRY IT NOW: Save the box procedures you have created in this chapter. It is a good idea always to start off the save process by checking the disk and the workspace.

        ? CATALOG

Remember that you cannot use duplicate names. Check the catalog of disk files.

        ? POTS

Check to see which procedures are still in workspace. Erase the ones you do not want to save.

        ? ER [BOX BOX.30 BOX.50 GREET SURPPRISE]

Check again to see what's left.

        ? POTS

Think about a descriptive file name for the group of procedures you will be saving.

        ? SAVE "TRUCKS

Everything left in workspace is now saved on the diskette under the file name Trucks (or whatever you called your file).

        ? CATALOG

You should see your file listed in the catalog. Always check that your SAVE command has worked before turning off the computer or erasing anything.

9.8.3 Bringing It Back

Saving does not erase anything out of your workspace. You should still have your procedures in workspace; check with POTS. And you have a copy of your procedures on the diskette listed under a particular file name. To retrieve files from the diskette, use the command LOAD, along with the name of the file you want to get. Remember to attach a quotation mark (") to front of the file name.

TRY IT NOW

Reload the file with your procedures using the LOAD command with the file name you used when you saved. (Be sure the disk is in the drive.) You should see the disk drive light come on as DOS reads the file out to Logo. Logo responds by reporting procedures names that it has accepted as defined.

```
? CATALOG
? LOAD "TRUCKS (or whatever name you used)
```

9.9 Posers and Problems

1. Concept Check. Describe something other than a computer program that you might have to debug. Are there any common strategies or methods in the two different contexts for debugging? What does this suggest to you about problem-solving skills?—about the teaching-learning of problem-solving skills?

   What makes debugging, modular programming, and using variables powerful ideas? What power is imparted to people who grasp these concepts?

   What use might these concepts have outside of programming or mathematics? How could you think in terms of variables in an English literature classroom? How could you debug a social studies concept?

2. Debug. Fix these procedures. Each one has two bugs, a syntax bug and a conceptual bug. Test your solutions and share them with your classmates. (Don't forget to CS between designs.)

```
TO BOX
REPEAT 4 [FD 50 RT :SIZE]
END

TO DONUT
CIRCLER 30
LT 90
FD 10
CIRCLER 50
END
```

3. Predict. For each procedure below predict the output Logo will display on the screen. Run each procedure to check your predictions. What will MYSTERY.SHAPE draw if you issue this command?

```
? MYSTERY.SHAPE 60
TO MYSTERY.SHAPE  :NUMBER
REPEAT  :NUMBER  [FD 30 RT 360 / :NUMBER]
END
```

What will Logo display if you use this COMPLEMENT procedure?

```
TO COMPLEMENT  :STAR
PR [HAS ANYONE EVER TOLD YOU THAT]
PR [YOU LOOK A LOT LIKE] :STAR
END
? COMPLEMENT EKIM BASSINGER]
```

Here's a tricky one. What will you get if you give Logo a list of two names to use with COMPLEMENT?

4. Produce. Demonstrate your mastery of variables by creating procedures to produce these effects:
   (a) A figure-8 whose size can vary.
   (b) The Happy Birthday song, so it can be sung to a particular person.

   (c)

10

Think about This (for Fun)
Using each number only once, arrange the figures 0, 1, 2, 3, 4, 5, 6, 7, 8, 9 so that their sum is 100.

Think about This (Seriously)
Should every student have an exposure to problem solving with computers through a required programming class before graduation from high school?

"The opportunities of man are limited only by his imagination. But so few have imagination that there are ten thousand fiddlers to one composer."
Charles F. Kettering

"The young do not know enough to be prudent and therefore they attempt the impossible—and achieve it, generation after generation." *Pearl S. Buck*

One Minute Logo—Make a List

10.1 Objectives

For the successful completion of this chapter, you should be able to

1. Explain "tools" as a powerful idea (Section 10.4).
2. Explain the difference between and uses of global and local variables (Section 10.7).
3. Create a superprocedure (Section 10.5).
4. Create and use a global variable (Section 10.7).
5. Accept input from the keyboard (Section 10.7.3).
6. Use a conditional operation to analyze input from the keyboard (Section 10.8).

10.2 New Terms

TOOL	FIRST	READNUM	SUPERPROCEDURE
LAST	TEST	GLOBAL VARIABLE	BUTFIRST (BF)
IFTRUE (IFT)	PONS	LOCAL VARIABLE	BUTLAST (BL)
IFFALSE (IFF)	READLIST (RL)		

10.3 You Are Here

In the last chapter you progressed from running individual lines of Logo code to creating and running small programs called procedures. This progression parallelled the growth in your programming goals. As your tasks became more ambitious, you experienced more bugs and the difficulties associated with finding and resolving them in long procedures.

Breaking up a long programming goal into several subgoals allowed you to focus on a one thing at a time. Building, testing, and debugging each procedure separately reduced the number of bugs you encountered and shortened the time it took you to find the problem underlying the bug. This powerful idea also gave you the freedom to reuse components more easily in other settings. For example, when the SURPRISE procedure was broken up into three component procedures, it became possible for you to use the big or little truck procedures on their own—for example, in other scenes. In the last chapter you also discovered a second powerful idea, variables. Variables let you get a lot more use out of each procedure by changing parts of it as needed.

Procedures with variables are more efficient programs because of their flexibility. Procedures that take mind-sized bites of a programming task are more efficient too, because they facilitate debugging and can be reused individually. What about procedures that are both modular and variable; shouldn't the combination of these two ideas result in even more efficient programming? Could the truck procedures, for example, use and benefit from the use of variables?

TRY IT
NOW

Examine the two truck procedures from the last chapter. (You may need to LOAD the disk file containing the truck procedures. If you cannot remember what you called the file, start with the CATALOG command.) If necessary, clean up the procedures to eliminate any pen moves that have nothing to do with making a truck. It is also a good practice to end by returning the turtle to its original position (RT 90 at the end of each procedure should do it).

```
TO LITTLE.TRUCK              TO BIG.TRUCK
REPEAT 4 [FD 50 RT 90]       REPEAT 4 [FD 90 RT 90]
REPEAT 4 [FD 30 LT 90]       REPEAT 4 [FD 30 LT 90]
LT 90                        LT 90
FD 15                        FD 15
CIRCLEL 5                    CIRCLEL 10
BK 50                        BK 70
CIRCLEL 5                    CIRCLEL 10
RT 90                        RT 90
END                          END
```

The two procedures are virtually identical. There are only three differences: the length of the sides in the square, the size of circles, and the back-up move between the two circles. You could substitute three variable names in place of each of those specific values, and then each time you ran the generic TRUCK procedure you would need to type in numbers you want to use. That could prove tricky. How will you remember what size wheel goes with what size truck bed?

In this case it is possible to tie the wheel size (circle) and back-up moves to the length of the truck bed. Look at the relationship among these parts in each of the two trucks. For example, the wheels (circle) are about one-tenth the size of the square. One variable could be used in all three places if that variable could be used in a mathematical term. Because of the way Logo evaluates lines of instructions, it is possible to incorporate math operations with variables to create terms, like this:

```
CIRCLEL :SIZE * .10
```

As Logo reads this line, it first comes to CIRCLEL. CIRCLEL is a procedure that expects one input, a number, which it uses to set the radius of the circle. But when Logo looks for the number right after CIRCLEL it next finds the operation THING (abbreviated as :) which tells Logo to substitute a value in place of the next word (SIZE). Logo inserts the value given when the procedure was first run, and evaluates it in the mathematical term :SIZE *.10, multiplying the value by .10. The result of the multiplication operation is passed back for CIRCLEL to use.

TRY IT NOW
Experiment with the possibilities below and record the results. Play with the values until you are happy with what you get. Does the procedure work well to create different-sized trucks? Share your procedure with your classmates. Discuss any differences in solutions. Which do you like best and why?

```
TO TRUCK :SIZE
REPEAT 4 [FD :SIZE RT 90]
REPEAT 4 [FD :SIZE * .3 LT 90]
LT 90
FD :SIZE * .5
CIRCLEL :SIZE * .10
BK :SIZE * 1.25
CIRCLEL :SIZE * .10
END
```

10.4 Powerful Ideas: Tools

You now have enough Logo knowledge to begin developing a whole set of objects that can be drawn and redrawn in different sizes. These objects can be used together with other procedures to create many scenes and designs. In a way, then, these "generic" procedures operate like tools. You use them to construct other things, and their variable quality makes them flexible.

10.4.1 Hand Me That Tool, Will You?

The idea of small programs operating as tools is a very powerful one. In fact, experienced programmers rely on tools to construct very sophisticated programs. They share tool programs with other programmers as they revise and update their "tool kits." So far the tools you have made are tools for drawing. They are useful for putting together pictures in turtle graphics.

Given your knowledge of math operations, procedures, and variables, you should be able to create a tool procedure that will carry out calculations for you. Here is an example:

```
TO  CUBE  : NUMBER
PR  : NUMBER  *  : NUMBER  *  : NUMBER
END
```

Actually, on the original Apple Logo language disk, in the file called TOOLS there are a number of useful mathematic and geometric procedures. You might want to investigate some of them. To do so, load the file, type POTS, and explore the procedure names that intrigue you. If you wish to add some of these tools to your own toolkit file, use the POTS and ERASE commands to pare your workspace down to only those tools you wish to save.

10.4.2 Tools and Teaching

In a way, a programming tool is simply a pattern of steps, or a strategy, to accomplish a task. The ability to recognize patterns and use them as strategies are both powerful problem-solving skills that are valuable outside the world of programming. Proponents of "programming as a problem-solving activity" argue that programming experiences help students acquire skills that can be generalized to other contexts for problem solving. Critics argue that educational research on programming has largely failed to demonstrate this; still others argue that programming skills bear little relationship to problem solving in other academic fields.

10.4.3 Cooperate with Collaborators

If you have attempted to construct a large and complicated Logo scene, you have, no doubt, sought the help of classmates or others. Programming provides ample opportunity for students to experience the value of collaboration. At the very least, a partner brings "fresh eyes" to debugging a program. Often, a partner has a useful tool to share. A strong team of programmers is made up of individuals with different strengths. For example, professional software development takes place in teams. Often the job is divided up, and subtasks handed out to teams with special skills or interests. The teams come together to share progress, problems, and suggestions. Collaboration and cooperation are not only useful programming methods; they are of benefit in all problem-solving situations.

10.5 It's a Bird. It's a Plane. It's Superprocedure.

With a series of procedures the programmer can create an entire Logo scene, like the TRUCKS scene. Yet, though you have reduced the programming and typing burden by using procedures, you still have had to enter each procedure name, in order, one at a time, to generate your scene.

Remember, though, that Logo treats procedures as if they were new words added to the Logo vocabulary. So far your procedures have been made up of Logo primitives (the words Logo comes with). Now you can make procedures that are made up of the new Logo words you have created, procedure names such as LITTLE.TRUCK. That is, you can create a procedure that makes use of other procedures. This is done by stacking the procedure modules on top of each other, like building blocks, in another procedure, called a *superprocedure*. Superprocedures call up other procedures, but they can also contain Logo primitives:

```
TO  TRUCK. SCENE
START SETPC 2
LITTLE. TRUCK
MOVE. PEN
SETPC 1
BIG. TRUCK
END
```

The TRUCK.SCENE superprocedure contains a primitive command, SETPC (setpencolor), as well as the names of four procedures (START, LITTLE.TRUCK, MOVE.PEN, and BIG.TRUCK). As long as these procedures are defined and available in the Logo workspace, the SUPERPROCEDURE will try to execute them one at a time in the order listed. To generate the entire truck stop scene you would need to type only the single command TRUCK.STOP and leave the driving to Logo.

Superprocedures are also very useful for building a single item with several parts to it, such as a truck. After all, the trucks you drew were made up of cabs, truck beds, and wheels. Each of these components could be contained in its own procedure. For instance, you may find it more aesthetically pleasing to use a variable square for the cab and a variable rectangle for the truck bed. You may want to make the wheels a fancy procedure that includes spokes or shows a three-dimensional view. Even though the "fancies" will present a new set of bugs, by working within one small procedure you will more easily squash those bugs. It is always better to break a procedure into several smaller procedures than to put too much together in one; try to keep each task in its own procedure.

10.5.1 Putting It All Together

This section pauses after all the new learning to let you try out ideas and information you have gotten so far and extend some of your skills by combining ideas.

Remember the "Rule of 360" you used to draw polygons in Chapters 8 and 9? It can also be applied here to devise superprocedures that generate neat designs. The rule described the total number of degrees in the turns the turtle makes to draw a closed shape (regular-sided polygon). As it turned out, the sum of the angles of each turn totalled 360, or a complete circle, bringing the turtle back to its original spot. To figure out the angle of turn you needed in a polygon of a particular number of sides, you divided 360 by the number of sides. This gave you the angle of turn the turtle needed to make between each side.

**TRY IT
NOW**

Load the POLYGON file from your disk. Take it into the editor to examine it. Notice that the TO line of this procedure lists two variable names. This means that Logo will be looking for two values when you use the procedure POLYGON. Also notice that a variable, :SIDES, is used in a mathematical term, just like the TRUCK procedure. Logo evaluates the term before passing the value on to RT.

```
TO POLYGON :SIDES :LENGTH
REPEAT :SIDES [FD :LENGTH RT 360/:SIDES]
END
```

Exit the editor and use POLYGON to create a pentagon, an octogon, a triangle. For instance,

```
? POLYGON 5 20
```

So far you have used REPEAT inside procedures to repeat instructions. Remember though, that new procedures you write and define are treated like new Logo words; you are expanding the Logo language. Any command you can use on a Logo primitive word you should be able to use on a defined Logo word (a procedure). Try REPEAT with a list containing the POLYGON procedure.

```
? REPEAT 10 [POLYGON 5 20]
```

This does not seem to result in a very interesting design; the turtle just retraces its steps over the first pentagon nine times. Imagine if you moved the turtle a bit before each copy of POLYGON.

```
? REPEAT 10 [POLYGON 5 20 RT 10]
```

**TRY IT
NOW**

Create a superprocedure that uses the REPEAT command and the POLYGON procedure so that you can easily return to edit and modify it later.

```
TO DESIGN
REPEAT 10 [POLYGON 5 20 RT 10]
END
```

Exit and test it.

```
? DESIGN
```

Now this is beginning to look interesting, but the turtle hasn't completed the design. The problem is, how can you determine the number of times to repeat the list of instructions?

At this point you should be having a "deja vu" experience. This same problem came up before when trying to figure out how much to turn the turtle to create the polygon procedure in Chapter 9. Can you discover the similarity between the two problem situations? In both cases the turtle is trying to make a closed shape. In the polygon procedure it is a many-sided shape; in this case it is a shape made up of many overlapping shapes. In making both closed shapes, the turtle should end up back at its starting point. Aha—the Rule of 360 might apply here. In the POLYGON procedure, the turn was part of a polygon shape; it occurred between sides. In this case, the turn is part of a multi-polygon shape; it occurs between shapes (polygons).

The Rule of 360 tells you that the number of turns to get back to the point of origin is a function of the number of degrees in each turn. There are ten degrees in each turn that the turtle makes between polygons, and 360/10 = 36. The turtle should need thirty-six repetitions of the 10-degree turn to finish off a closed shape. Modify the DESIGN superprocedure to try this solution.

TRY IT
NOW

```
TO DESIGN
REPEAT 36 [POLYGON 5 20 RT 10]
END
? DESIGN
```

Now that's pretty neat! But, it looks like that DESIGN procedure is pretty limited. It only makes one kind of design unless you enter the editor and change some of the numeric values. Are you having another deja vu experience yet?

TRY IT
NOW

```
TO DESIGN :TURNS
REPEAT :TURNS [POLYGON 5 20 RT 360/:TURNS]
END
```

Try the DESIGN procedure with a couple of different values. Don't clear the screen between tries.

```
? DESIGN 30
? DESIGN 60
```

Notice that it is not necessary to fiddle with the POLYGON subprocedure. It is still turning out pentagons. The interesting part of the DESIGN procedure is in the angle of turns between the pentagons.

10.5.2 Extra for Experts

Earlier you altered the shape and size of the POLYGON by using different values for the variables SIDES and LENGTH in the POLYGON procedure. But now that the POLYGON is buried inside the DESIGN how do you get to those POLYGON variables? Remember that the TO line of a procedure is where you declare variables that will be given inputs when the procedure runs. All you need to do to the DESIGN procedure is add those POLYGON variables to the TO line and substitute them in place of the specific numbers you used in the first version of DESIGN. How many inputs do you need to give Logo now when you run DESIGN?

TRY IT
NOW

```
TO DESIGN :TURNS :SIDES :LENGTH
REPEAT :TURNS [POLYGON :SIDES :LENGTH RT 360/:TURNS]
END
? DESIGN 30 10 30
? DESIGN 20 8 50
```

10.6 The Voice of the Turtle: List Processing

Turtle graphics are only one aspect of Logo. The nongraphic side of Logo can be as interesting to explore. Most people erroneously refer to the text side of Logo as *list processing.* However, as you now know, lists are also used in turtle graphics. The REPEAT command requires a list of instructions so that it knows what to repeat. The EDIT command can read a list of procedure names that you want to take into the Logo Editor. To specify the use of a list with either of these two commands you have been surrounding the words on the list with square brackets, like this:

```
REPEAT 4 [FD 100 RT 90]
EDIT [CAB TRUCK.BED WHEEL]
```

You have also used lists with the PRINT command and the operation SENTENCE. The words on these lists were real English words that you wanted to use as English words in a message.

```
PRINT [MY NAME IS BOND, JAMES BOND.]
```

So, you actually know a lot about lists. You know they are identified by the square brackets that surround them. You know they can contain English words, Logo commands, or procedure names.

10.6.1 But What Are They Good For

Lists are extremely useful items in Logo. You can use lists in many of the same ways you would use words. In the last chapter you were introduced to procedures with variables. You used variables to stand in for numbers—in TRUCK and RECTANGLE, and for words—in GREET. You can also use variables to stand for lists of input. This is especially useful for text procedures, where people's names or other verbal information may take more than one word. Sticking words together with periods, as in GREET "JAMES.BOND just does not look right. But the name "James Bond" is two words, and GREET expects to substitute one thing in place of the variable :SOMEONE.

Logo treats a list as one thing, and a list can contain one or more words. You can use a list as input to the GREET command by surrounding with square brackets the words you want treated as one whole thing. Take a second look at GREET with a list for input.

TRY IT   You may need to reconstruct that procedure (see Chapter 9, Section
NOW   9.6.4).

```
TO  GREET  : SOMEONE
TEXTSCREEN  CLEARTEXT
PR  [HI  THERE.  I'M  A  PROGRAM. ]
PR  SE  [NICE  TO  MEET  YOU]  : SOMEONE
END
```

Have a little fun by trying "James Bond" in Bond's own style.

```
?  GREET  [BOND,  JAMES  BOND]
```

10.6.2 A List of Lists

Logo lists can also contain other lists. It may help to think of an analogy
from everyday life. When you create a list called FAVORITE.FOODS you
might list items like this:

```
[OYSTERS  AVOCADOS  YOGURT]
```

However, you may want to include a food item that is made up of more
than one word, such as BAKED POTATOES. You can keep the two
words together as one item by putting them on their own list, just as
you did with James Bond's name in the previous section: [BAKED
POTATOES]. But to include this on the food list, you would need to
embed [BAKED POTATOES] in the midst of the other objects.

```
[OYSTERS  AVOCADOS  YOGURT  [BAKED  POTATOES] ]
```

Notice where the brackets are. Each list is surrounded by its own set
of brackets. As far as Logo is concerned, that list of favorite foods contains four things:

> the word OYSTERS
> the word AVOCADOS
> the word YOGURT
> and the list [BAKED POTATOES]

10.6.3 Take It Off!

So far you have used lists to repeat instructions or to print English sentences and words. You can also pull lists apart to use items one at a time for other purposes. Four operations are used to break up lists: FIRST, LAST, BUTFIRST, and BUTLAST. These four operations can also be used to break up Logo words.

FIRST and LAST do just what they say. They each expect one input, either a list or a (Logo) word. Given a word, like *OYSTERS*, FIRST will output the first letter of that word, *O;* LAST will output the last letter, *S.* Given a list, like *[OYSTERS AVOCADOS YOGURT [BAKED POTATOES]]*, FIRST will output the first item on the list, the word *OYSTERS;* LAST will output the last item on the list, in this case a list, *[BAKED POTATOES]*.

BUTFIRST (BF) and BUTLAST (BL) operate in a similar fashion. BF outputs all *BUT* the *FIRST* letter of a word or all *BUT* the *FIRST* item on a list. BL outputs all *BUT* the *LAST* letter of a word or all *BUT* the *LAST* item on a list. BF [OYSTERS AVOCADOS YOGURT [BAKED POTATOES]] takes off the first item, *OYSTERS,* and outputs the remaining list, *AVOCADOS YOGURT [BAKED POTATOES]*. BL [OYSTERS AVOCADOS YOGURT [BAKED POTATOES]] knocks off the last item and outputs the remaining list, *OYSTERS AVOCADOS YOGURT*.

10.6.4 A Few Words about Operations

You may have noticed that FIRST, LAST, BF, and BL were called *operations* in this last section, and they produced something called *output.* Up to now most Logo instructions have been referred to as *commands.* The difference between commands and operations is the kinds of work they do. Commands create effects; FORWARD, PRINT, SETPC are all commands. Operations, on the other hand, actually create something that can be used by another Logo instruction—output.

When you use an operation you must tell Logo what to do with the output it creates. If you do not, Logo whines, "I don't know what to do with . . ." For example, SENTENCE creates output by taking two separate items and passing them along as one item. In the last few chapters SENTENCE has been used in conjunction with PRINT to get two things printed:

```
PR SE [THE ANSWER IS] 42.
```

If you used SE without PR, Logo would have complained, "I don't know what to do with THE ANSWER IS 42."

TRY IT
NOW
Stay in the interactive mode and try these operations. Predict the result before you try each of these lines.

```
? PR FIRST "SANDY
? PR BF "SANDY
? PR LAST [[PEGGY SUE] DON JT ESTELLA]
? PR BL [[PEGGY SUE] DON JT ESTELLA]
```

Invent some lists and words of your own and try them out until you feel comfortable using them.

10.6.5   Stack 'Em Up

You can stack up these Logo operations to get some interesting results with lists. Think about it. Use FIRST FIRST and you ought to get the first item of the first item on the list. PR FIRST FIRST [OYSTERS AVO-CADOS YOGURT [BAKED POTATOES]] gives you *O*. Use LAST FIRST and you ought to get the last item of the first item on the list. PR LAST FIRST [OYSTERS AVOCADOS YOGURT [BAKED POTATOES]] gives you *S*. What about this:

```
PR FIRST LAST [OYSTERS AVOCADOS YOGURT [BAKED POTATOES]]
```

To understand truly the way these stacked operations work, you will need to review your understanding of how Logo processes lines of instruction. Figure 10.1 shows how Logo would have read that last example.

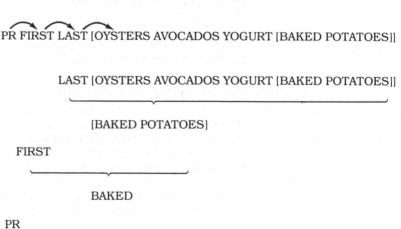

Figure 10.1

Logo reads PR. PR takes one input; Logo looks at the next thing on the line for a word or list to give PR. Instead, Logo finds another instruction, FIRST. It temporarily suspends work on PR and tries to carry out FIRST. FIRST takes one input, and Logo again looks for a word or list to use with FIRST. No, there is another instruction, LAST. Logo must suspend work on FIRST to try and carry out LAST. So far there are two instructions on hold. Fortunately, Logo finds a usable input for LAST, the list *[OYSTERS AVOCADOS YOGURT [BAKED POTATOES]]*. LAST operates on the list and passes Logo the output *[BAKED POTATOES]*. Now Logo has a usable piece of input for the FIRST it had put on hold. FIRST operates on the output from LAST, *[BAKED POTATOES]*, and yields the first item, *BAKED*. This is usable input for PR, and it now displays the word *BAKED* on the screen.

TRY IT NOW

Can you predict the results of the following lines of code? It may help you to parse the lines with a pencil, like this:

```
? PR LAST BF [[PEGGY SUE] DON JT ESTELLA]
? PR FIRST BF [[PEGGY SUE] DON JT ESTELLA]
? PR BL BL [[PEGGY SUE] DON JT ESTELLA]
```

Of course you can use these list and word manipulators inside procedures, like this:

```
TO DISCUSS.FOOD :FOOD.LIST
PR SE [THE FOOD I LIKE BEST] IS FIRST :FOOD.LIST
PR SE [MY SECOND FAVORITE FOOD IS] FIRST BF
:FOOD.LIST
END
? DISCUSS.FOOD [OYSTERS AVOCADOS
YOGURT [BAKED POTATOES]]
```

Or at the time the procedure is run, like this:

```
TO GREET :SOMEONE
PR [HI. I'M A COMPUTER PROGRAM.]
PR SE [NICE TO MEET YOU] :SOMEONE
PR [I'VE ALWAYS ADMIRED YOUR WORK.]
END
? GREET FIRST BF [[WILLIAM SHAKESPEARE]
[JOHN MILTON] [THOMAS PYNCHON]]
```

Now this is getting interesting. But, if you happen to have a long list of things to input, it can be rather boring to use this procedure.

10.7 Global Variables: A Life of Their Own

Up to now you have used variables to keep the procedures flexible. The actual values substituted for the variables have been given to Logo along with the procedure name. When the procedure finished, the value for the variable disappeared. To reuse the procedure has required you to create the value for the variable again. For example, if you ran DIS-CUSS.FOOD with the input list *[OYSTERS AVOCADOS YOGURT [BAKED POTATOES]]* as the value of :FOOD.LIST, the value of FOOD.LIST disappears when the procedure is done. Enter PR :FOOD.LIST and Logo will respond *FOOD.LIST has no value.*

Unlike most other programming languages (except Pascal) Logo allows you to create a variable and a value for that variable without using a procedure. The resulting variable has a life of its own in your Logo workspace. It remains there until it is erased or changed. Sitting in workspace, this variable can be used by any procedure that contains the variable name. This kind of variable is called a GLOBAL variable because of its omnipresence. In contrast, LOCAL variables have a limited reach; they are tied to their local procedure.

The operation MAKE creates a global variable. MAKE takes two inputs. The first input is the word you want to use as the name of the variable. The second input is the value you want that variable to have—a word, list, or number.

```
MAKE "FOOD.LIST [OYSTERS AVOCADOS YOGURT
[BAKED POTATOES]]
```

You won't see the result of this command. Like the procedures you create, a global variable sits in workspace, invisible, until you use it. You can check on it by asking Logo to print the current value of the variable, like this: PR :FOOD.LIST. If you want to check the current value of several global variables you can use the command PONS, which stands for Print Out NameS.

**TRY IT
NOW**

Here is a list that many students have enjoyed.

```
?MAKE "MONSTERS [GODZILLA [KING KONG] MOTHRA
[CREATURE FROM THE BLACK LAGOON] [KILLER TOMATOES]]
?PONS
```

Now that the MONSTERS variable has been established, you can play with it over and over again.

```
? PR BF  : MONSTERS
? PR FIRST BF  : MONSTERS
```

Can you figure out how to extract CREATURE FROM THE BLACK LAGOON from the list? Think: how many items need to be knocked off from the front of the list? How do you knock items off a list?

```
? PR FIRST BF BF BF
```

Ah, but, there is a shorter way to get to that creature!

If you want to change a global variable, simply remake it. Your output will write over the old one. Commands and operations used with the global variable will not alter the value; only another MAKE can do that. Add a monster to the list by remaking the list, like this:

```
?MAKE "MONSTERS [DRACULA GODZILLA [KING KONG] MOTHRA
[CREATURE FROM THE BLACK LAGOON] [KILLER TOMATOES]]
?PR  : MONSTERS
```

You can create global variables out of pieces of other global variables. Make a global variable to include just CREATURE FROM THE BLACK LAGOON.

```
? MAKE "SOMEONE LAST BL  : MONSTERS
? PR  : SOMEONE
```

Logo reads MAKE and looks for the first of two inputs to use with MAKE. It finds the first input, a name, marked with the quotation mark—"SOMEONE. It looks for a word, list, or number for the second input and finds an instruction. So Logo must temporarily suspend work on MAKE while it tries to execute the operation LAST. LAST must wait for BL. BL operates on the value of MONSTERS and outputs all but the last item, [DRACULA GODZILLA [KING KONG] MOTHRA [CREATURE FROM THE BLACK LAGOON]]. LAST operates on this list and outputs the last item, [CREATURE FROM THE BLACK LAGOON]. Now Logo has a usable second input for MAKE, and it creates the variable SOMEONE with the value [CREATURE FROM THE BLACK LAGOON]. Notice that nothing has happened to the value of MONSTERS.

10.7.1 Using Global Variables with Procedures

Wouldn't it be fun to use the monstrous value of SOMEONE in the GREET procedure. However, to use a global variable, you will need to modify your local variable procedure. Procedures with local variables are procedures that need to be given inputs to substitute for their values when they run. Procedures that use global variables do not need to be given inputs for their variables; Logo will look in the workspace for the values. You have used the TO line of your procedures to indicate that values will be given at the time the procedure is run. So, it is the TO line that must be modified. Remove the variable names from that line, and the procedure will run without inputs. When it gets down to a line where a variable name appears, Logo will look in the workspace for a global variable with the same name. The value of that global variable will be substituted in the procedure.

**TRY IT
NOW**

Take GREET into the editor and modify the TO line.

```
TO  GREET
PR  [HI.  I'M  A  COMPUTER  PROGRAM.]
PR  SE  [NICE  TO  MEET  YOU]  :SOMEONE
PR  [I'VE  ALWAYS  ADMIRED  YOUR  WORK.]
END
```

After you exit the editor, you might want to check on the variables in workspace before you run GREET.

```
?  PONS
?  GREET
```

10.7.2 The Global Advantage

While it is very useful to be able to change a variable value without rerunning a procedure, the real utility of global variables is in the availability to change more than one procedure at once. This is especially powerful for a superprocedure, where a variable might need to be used over and over again in some of the different procedures contained in the superprocedure.

**TRY IT
NOW**

Start by creating a second procedure to use with GREET in a CHAT superprocedure.

```
TO  CONVERSE
PR  SE  [DON'T  YOU  JUST  HATE  THIS  WEATHER,]  :SOMEONE
END

TO  CHAT
GREET
CONVERSE
END
```

Before you execute CHAT, you might want to check on your global variable with PONS.

10.7.3 Let Me Ask You Something

Your procedures are getting fairly sophisticated now that you have global variables available to you. But, you, the programmer, are still the one deciding the value of the global variable. To make your programs even more flexible, you need to have the program ask the program user for the values of the variables. That is, you need a procedure that can accept input from the keyboard in the middle of the program, a program that can carry on a genuine conversation with someone, like this:

> Logo: What's your name?
> User: Linda
> Logo: Nice to meet you, Linda

READLIST (RL) is a very sophisticated operation that has three important steps to it. First, it temporarily halts Logo; after all, the user has to be able to get a word or two in edgewise. Second, it gathers up all that the user types until the user hits the RETURN key; then it places that input on a list. Third, it outputs that list to Logo to use with another command or operation.

READLIST is often used in conjunction with MAKE to create a variable that can be used in the procedure, like this:

```
        TO  GREET
        PR  [HI.  I'M  A  COMPUTER  PROGRAM  NAMED  GREET.]
        PR  [WHAT'S  YOUR  NAME?]
=>      MAKE  "NAME  RL
        PR  SE  [OH.  NICE  TO  MEET  YOU,]  :NAME
        END
```

Realize that Logo doesn't stop and wait for input at the end of the question line. Logo reads the PRINT statement on that line and carries it out. Logo goes to the next line (see arrow). It reads MAKE and looks for two inputs, a name for the variable and a value. It finds a word it can use for the first input, "NAME. Then it runs into READLIST, not a usable second input for MAKE. Logo suspends work on MAKE to carry out the READLIST (RL) operation. When Logo reads READLIST it stops the procedure to wait for the ENTER key. If the user gets up and walks away, the procedure will continue to sit there, unfinished, waiting for a carriage return. When the carriage return comes, RL puts the input in a list and hands the list to Logo. In this particular case, Logo is looking for a second input for MAKE, so that is why it uses the list from RL. MAKE has created a global variable that now can be accessed by the procedure. When Logo gets down a line and runs into :NAME it looks to global workspace for the value associated with the variable called "NAME and substitutes that value.

Each time you reuse READLIST it waits for a new input. If you are using READLIST with MAKE, you will be remaking the global variable each time Logo runs that line. You can run GREET over and over with different people at the keyboard, and the MAKE and RL combination will always yield the new user information.

**TRY IT
NOW**

Why not write a procedure to ask users who their favorite MONSTERS are? Rerun this procedure over and over again giving a different answer to the question. It may help clarify what is happening if you type a PR :MONSTER command in between re-runs.

```
TO ASK.MONSTERS
PR [OK, SO WHO'S YOUR FAVORITE MONSTER?]
MAKE "MONSTER RL
PR [HAS ANYONE EVER TOLD YOU THAT YOU]
PR SE [LOOK A LOT LIKE] :MONSTER
PR [BUT THAT'S OKAY BECAUSE.]
PR SE :MONSTER [IS MY FAVORITE MONSTER TOO.]
END
```

10.7.4 Increase Your Reading Power

It is very important to realize that READLIST puts input into a list. Even if the user types only a one-word response, that word is placed in a list. If the user types nothing, just hits the RETURN key, READLIST produces what is called an empty list, [ ]. This is important to pay attention to if you plan to use the FIRST, LAST, BF, or BL operations with the READLIST output: FIRST [YES] is quite different from FIRST "YES.

There is another useful operation for accepting input from users. READNUM functions very much like READLIST, but with an important difference. It does not put the input on a list; it assumes it is a number. This is useful for writing procedures that will use input as numbers, not words—for example

```
TO PERCENT
PR [GIVE ME A PERCENT, LIKE THIS, 80]
PR [AND I WILL PRINT THE DECIMAL FRACTION,]
PR [LIKE THIS, .8]
MAKE "NUMBER READNUM
PR :NUMBER / 100
END
```

If you had used READLIST instead of READNUM you would have faced a bug when Logo tried to divide 100 into a list. It can only divide numbers. Of course, you could still use READLIST, but you would need to take the number off the list before you reached the division instruction. Here are two different ways of doing that:

```
      TO PERCENT
      PR [GIVE ME A PERCENT, LIKE THIS, 80]
      PR [AND I WILL PRINT THE DECIMAL FRACTION,]
      PR [LIKE THIS, .8]
=>    MAKE "NUMBER FIRST RL
      PR :NUMBER / 100
      END

      TO PERCENT
      PR [GIVE ME A PERCENT, LIKE THIS, 80]
      PR [AND I WILL PRINT THE DECIMAL FRACTION,]
      PR [LIKE THIS, .8]
      MAKE "NUMBER RL
=>    PR (FIRST :NUMBER) / 100
      END
```

In the second example, the parentheses help Logo and you understand the order of operations. Otherwise you both might try to print the FIRST character of :NUMBER/100, though you would still run into the problem of dividing into a list instead of a number. In other words, the first method is the more efficient one.

10.8 Okay, On One Condition . . .

Welcome to the last set of new Logo instructions in this text! The best has been saved for last. Now that you can write interactive programs that accept input from the keyboard, you are ready to evaluate that input and respond with conditional instructions. Here are two samples of dialogue between a program with conditional instruction and two different users. Notice that the program's response depends upon what the user types. Somewhere in the program Logo makes a decision between two choices, based upon some criterion.

```
WHAT'S YOUR AGE
? 6
OH, A SPRING CHICKEN.
        . . .

WHAT'S YOUR AGE?
? 101
REALLY, YOU DON'T LOOK IT!
```

10.8.1 If-Then Logic

No, Logo does not understand English; it only understands the conditions TRUE and FALSE. However, you can easily evaluate statements that will result in the output TRUE or FALSE. Then, based upon that output you can direct Logo to take specific actions. There are several ways to work with conditionals, and this chapter will only introduce you to one very straightforward method.

The whole conditional experience makes uses of three operations: TEST, IFTRUE (IFT), and IFFALSE (IFF). TEST is an operation that expects one input, the word TRUE or the word FALSE. It gets this input by evaluating statements like these:

> `100/5 = 20`   would output TRUE.

> `:NAME = "LINDA`   would output TRUE only if the value of the variable called NAME is currently equal to the word LINDA. This is one of those instances where it really matters whether you have used READLIST or FIRST READLIST to MAKE your variable.

> `:NAME = "LINDA`   would output FALSE if the value of NAME is [Linda] or 56 or "DONALD.

After receiving the TRUE or FALSE input, TEST waits to pass on its information to either operation IFT or operation IFF.

The IFT and IFF operations are very interesting ones. They are only activated by output from TEST. If TEST is holding the word TRUE, Logo will read the IFT line but will skip over the IFF line. If TEST is holding the word FALSE, Logo will skip the IFT line and read only lines that begin with IFF. Both IFT and IFF expect one input in the form of a list of instructions to carry out. Of course, brackets must surround the list.

TRY IT NOW

Create this procedure in the editor and give it a try. Notice that the lists on the IFT and IFF lines have a double set of brackets. This is because of the PRINT statement which is also using a list. You have a list within a list on both those lines, but you are fairly comfortable with that idea, right?

```
TO BE.RUDE
PR [WHAT'S YOUR AGE?]
MAKE "AGE READNUM
TEST :AGE < 29
IFT [PR [SPRING CHICKEN!]]
IFT [PR [OR A LIAR.]]
IFF [PR [REALLY, YOU DON'T LOOK IT!]]
END
```

Notice that you can add as many IFT's or IFF's in a row as you need.

Make use of your knowledge from other sections of these chapters. The example in the box above used only PRINT commands for the response. You know that lists could contain other lists and commands, or even other procedure names. In fact, if you find that you are writing a whole lot of instructions in the "then" part of your IFT or IFF lists, you should create a separate subprocedure with that information and then just list the procedure name in the IFT or IFF list.

10.8.2 On Your Own

These three chapters have given you a tiny bit of insight and experience into the Logo language and philosophy. You have plenty of Logo knowledge to experiment with for quite some time.

10.9 Posers and Problems

1. Concept Check. Reflect upon your Logo (and other) programming experiences. List some of the behaviors you engage in that might reasonably be called problem-solving behaviors. Describe a problem-solving situation, other than in programming, in which these behaviors would prove useful.

   As a class, construct a working superprocedure that makes use of the TEST IFT IFF operations. Treat it like the script of a play with subprocedures as acts. Appoint a director to call upon students to act out each subprocedure (by drawing Logo output on the board).

2. Predict. Write the response Logo will make when given this procedure and the execution line that follows it. (Don't erase between lines of instructions; the effects are cumulative.)

```
? MAKE "COMPUTER "APPLE
? PR :COMPUTER
? MAKE "COMPUTER "IBM
? PR :COMPUTER
? MAKE "COMPUTER [APPLE IBM COMMODORE]
? PR :COMPUTER
```

3. Debug. Rewrite this procedure eliminating bugs. Be sure to share solutions in class. (Hint: about seven bugs here!)

```
TO BRAG
PR [WHAT'S THE GREATEST PROGRAMMING LANGUAGE?]
MAKE :ANSW READNUM
TEST IF :ANSW = "LOGO
IFF PR [WHAT A TURKEY. LOGO'S THE BEST.]
IFT PR [NICE TO MEET ANOTHER BRILLIANT MIND.]
IFT PR [OR A LUCKY GUESSER.]
END
```

4. Produce. Using modular programming, construct a superprocedure and necessary subprocedures to generate the building design from Chapter 9.

   Use a superprocedure to reconstruct the Happy Birthday (Chapter 9 Posers and Problems) song. Be sure your program asks whose birthday it is before it starts singing.

Get together with a partner to construct a procedure that asks a simple question about Logo. Have the class assemble all the procedures produced into a superprocedure.

```
TO QUIZ
GREET
. . .
END
```

FOUR

A Golden Treasury of Practical Tips

TIP ONE

The Apple Computer and How to Use It

The Apple II Family of Computers

The Apple II microcomputer was first introduced in 1977 and has become one of the most popular computers used in education. Among the reasons for this popularity are its flexibility and expandability. An Apple owner can begin with a modest investment and gradually upgrade the system as his or her interest and budget allow.

Over the past eight years, the Apple II has seen many changes. The original Apple II included only 16K of RAM and a 40-column screen with uppercase characters only. This changed when the Apple II+ was introduced in 1979 with 48K of memory, expandable to 64K. In 1981, the Apple IIe came on the scene with 64K of memory, expandable to 128K, uppercase and lowercase characters, and an optional 80-column screen. All of these features—128K, 80 columns, and uppercase and lowercase characters—were combined into a portable computer, the Apple IIc, in 1984. This model also includes a built-in disk drive, a printer interface, and a communications interface for about one-third the 1977 cost of an Apple II system. In 1986, the Apple IIgs was introduced. This top-of-the-line system features advanced color graphics and sound. Its RAM is expandable to eight megabytes, and a variety of disk drives and other peripherals is available.

The variety of Apple II models and components makes it difficult to describe all the possible combinations. Therefore, this text will limit the discussion to the typical system found in schools:

1. Apple IIe with 64K of RAM
2. 80-column card and monitor
3. Floppy disk drive (5.25 inch)
4. Dot matrix printer

The "Core" of the Apple

From the exterior the Apple resembles a typewriter with a keyboard but no place to put the paper. Inside the case of the Apple are the integrated circuits, known as *IC's* or *chips,* that make it operate. Figure A.1 illustrates the core of the Apple IIe.

Figure A.1

The functional work unit is the microprocessor chip, which is located centrally in the computer. Surrounding the microprocessor are memory chips, peripheral slots, and other electronics necessary for the operation of the Apple.

Two types of memory are found in most microcomputers. ROM, read-only memory, has programs already stored in it by the manufacturer. These programs may be read but not changed in any way. They are permanent and are never lost, even when the power is turned off. In contrast, RAM, random-access memory, is read-and-write memory. It may be read or changed (written to). When the power is turned off, anything stored in RAM is erased.

In the Apple II +, the Apple IIe, the Apple IIc, and the Apple IIgs, ROM contains the programs that make the computer operate (the operating system) and the Applesoft language interpreter. The latter will convert Applesoft BASIC statements and commands to meaningful codes to which the microprocessor can react.

In the Apple II, the predecessor of the Apple II +, ROM contained the operating system and the Integer BASIC language. If you wish to use such a system with this text you will need either the Applesoft Firmware card, which contains the same ROM as the Apple II +, or the Language System, which contains 16K of RAM. The Language System works by loading the Applesoft BASIC interpreter into its RAM from the disk drive. Note: although the Applesoft language can be loaded into RAM on the Apple II, it will not allow the user access to high-resolution graphics, and some of the examples in this book will not function properly.

The Apple IIe is available with 64K (65,536 characters) of storage, and can be expanded up to one million characters of RAM. This memory is used to store a program, the program's variables, the images of the text screen, the low-resolution graphics screen, and the high-resolution graphics screen. When using a disk drive, the DOS (Disk Operating System) containing the instructions to transfer data and programs between the Apple and the drive, is loaded into RAM.

Eight slots are provided inside the Apple IIe, one toward the left front and the other seven toward the back. The latter are numbered 1 through 7 and are used to connect the Apple with peripheral devices. The slot toward the front, however, is the exception. It is used only for the 80-column card or the extended 80-column card, which contains an additional 64K of RAM. Slots 1 through 7 are used for communicating with external devices such as printers (usually slot 1), other computers (slot 2), and disk drives (slot 6). Other, less common peripherals include graphics tablet, clock, voice synthesis, voice recognition, plotter, and music synthesis. The remaining integrated circuits in the Apple's core are used to generate the screen display, decode the keyboard input, and create sounds on the Apple's speaker. As with all electronic appliances, severe damage or shock can result from liquids' being spilled inside the Apple. Care should be exercised to avoid any spills.

The Monitor (Television)

The Apple II will output to any monochrome or color monitor. (Of course, color graphics cannot be displayed in color on a monochrome monitor.) Alternatively, either a black-and-white or a color television can be used. A monitor will generally produce a sharper picture than a television; however, it is slightly more expensive. If a television is used, it is connected to the Apple with a radio frequency (RF) modulator that converts the Apple's video signal to a television signal. The modulator is connected from inside the Apple to the television antenna leads. If a monitor is used it is connected directly to the video output plug at the right rear corner of the Apple.

The Disk Drive

The floppy disk drive is the "file cabinet" system of the Apple. It is capable of storing 143,360 characters of information (programs and/or data) per diskette and can retrieve a single piece of information in 5/100,000 of a second. The disk drive is connected to the Apple through an interface called a disk controller, which is plugged into slot 6 inside the Apple. Two drives can be connected to one controller, in which case they are usually labeled drive 1 and drive 2.

The Dot Matrix Printer

A variety of printers can be connected to the Apple through an interface plugged into slot 1. The most common and least expensive printers use a pattern of dots to print the characters on the paper, hence the name "dot matrix printer." The cost of printers ranges from approximately $400 to several thousand dollars. The most popular printer used with the Apple IIe is the Imagewriter printer.

How to Use the Apple with This Book

A companion to this book is a diskette containing all of the sample files described in the various chapters. To utilize all of the sample files fully, you will also need an AppleWorks diskette, an Apple Logo diskette, and a DOS 3.3 System Master diskette. Although some of the programs will work on the Apple II and Apple II+, a 64K Apple IIe system with an 80-column card and at least one disk drive or an Apple IIc system is needed to be able to run all the examples.

It is recommended that the reader use this diskette in conjunction with the text in order to study the examples. It is further recommended that additional diskettes be used to store the files you develop from the "Posers and Problems." The following sections will explain how to boot up the Apple, use a printer, and what to do if you get into trouble.

Booting Up

Using the appropriate diskette (System Master, or AppleWorks, or Apple Logo) boot up the system as follows:

1. Open the door on disk drive 1.
2. Slip the diskette into the slot in the front of the drive with the diskette label facing upward. The edge of the diskette with the oval cutout should be toward the back of the drive.
3. Push the diskette gently into the drive until it is entirely inside the drive. Do not force or bend the diskette. Close the disk drive door.
4. Turn on the monitor.
5. Turn on the Apple by pushing upward on the switch located on the back of the computer on your left. The red light on the disk drive will go on, and the drive will make clicking sounds.
6. In a few seconds, the title of the diskette should appear on the screen.

The process of powering up the Apple is called *booting* DOS to experienced Apple users. The DOS, the disk operating system, is loaded from the diskette into RAM memory, and a predetermined program is executed.

How to Use a Printer

Since several printers may be used with the Apple II computer, the following instructions for using a printer are generalized. Should these instructions not work, refer to the printer's manual.

1. Locate the on/off switch on the printer and turn it on.
2. Check for a switch labeled *select* or *online/offline* and set for selected or online.

For BASIC:

3. Type PR#1 and depress the RETURN key. Subsequent text that appears on the monitor screen should also appear on the printer's paper.
4. When a "]" appears, printing may be halted by typing PR#0 and depressing the RETURN key. Locate a switch on the printer labeled *linefeed* or *formfeed.* Use this switch to eject the paper so that the printout can be removed from the printer. (Note: the printer may need to be deselected or offline to eject the paper.)

For AppleWorks:

3. Hold down the OPEN-APPLE key and simultaneously press the P key. Follow the directions on the screen, answering all the questions.
4. After printing is complete, locate a switch on the printer labeled *linefeed* or *formfeed*. Use this switch to eject the paper so that the printout can be removed from the printer. (Note: the printer may need to be deselected or offline to eject the paper.)

For AppleLogo:

3. Type .PRINTER 1 and press the RETURN key. From now on, any text that appears on the monitor screen should also appear on the paper in the printer.
4. To turn off the printer, type .PRINTER 0 and press the RETURN key. Locate a switch on the printer labeled *linefeed* or *formfeed*. Use this switch to eject the paper so that the printout can be removed from the printer. (Note: the printer may need to be deselected or offline to eject the paper.)

The above instructions require that the printer interface be plugged into peripheral slot 1 inside the Apple. This is its normal location. In BASIC, the default print line length is 40 characters, the same as the Apple's screen line length. Most printers can print 80 characters per line. To print 80 characters type the following sequence of keys (this procedure is needed only for BASIC):

1. Type PR#1 and press RETURN.
2. Type I while holding down the CTRL key.
3. Type 80N and press RETURN.

What to Do When All Else Fails

Booting DOS Manually

Because of the number of possible configurations of Apple systems, the above instructions will not always boot the system. If you follow the instructions for booting up, and the disk light does not go on, you can manually boot the DOS as follows:

1. On the Apple IIe and Apple IIc, simultaneously hold down the OPEN-APPLE key and the CONTROL key and press the RESET key.
2. If a "]" or ">" appears on the screen, type PR#6 and press the RETURN key.
3. If a "*" appears on the screen, type 6; then type P while holding down the CONTROL key. Finally, press RETURN.

Getting Back to BASIC (Applesoft)

Through a number of ways it is possible to get out of Applesoft BASIC (designated by a ")" prompt) and into either Integer BASIC (designated by a ">" prompt) or into the Apple monitor mode (designated by a "*" prompt). Follow these directions to return to Applesoft:

1. If a ">" appears on the screen type FP and press RETURN.
2. If a "*" appears on the screen type 3D0G and press RETURN. (That's a zero after the D.)

Halting a Runaway in BASIC or Logo

Sometimes when you run a BASIC program or take a listing of a program you desire to stop before it finishes. To do this type C while holding down the CONTROL key. In Apple Logo, type G while holding down the CONTROL key. DO NOT DO EITHER OF THESE IN APPLEWORKS.

The Last Resort

If you are using BASIC, and if all attempts to get yourself out of the jam you're in have failed, try pressing the RESET key and following the previous instructions for getting back into Applesoft. Please note that depressing the RESET key can have disastrous results with Apple-Works and Apple Logo. (Apple IIe and Apple IIc systems require the CONTROL key to be held down while pressing RESET.)

The ultimate correction for problems is to turn the power off and then boot up the Apple again. This will definitely erase the program in memory, but it will not affect the diskette so long as the red light on the disk drive is not lit when you turn off the power.

If you cannot get the companion diskette to this book to work correctly, reread "How to Use the Apple with This Book" on page 243 to make sure that the Apple you are using is configured correctly.

TIP TWO

Initializing (Formatting) Diskettes

Blank diskettes must be initialized (formatted) before they can be used on the Apple computer. Different software packages have different ways to initialize diskettes. This tip will present three sets of instructions for initializing diskettes using Applesoft BASIC and DOS 3.3, AppleWorks, and Apple Logo.

Initializing a Diskette Using Applesoft BASIC and DOS 3.3

1. Boot the Apple System Master diskette or any diskette previously initialized by the following procedure.
2. Remove the System Master and insert the new blank diskette into the disk drive.
3. Enter the following program, or any BASIC program of your choice:

```
NEW
10 HOME
20 PRINT "your name"
30 PRINT "the date"
40 END
```

4. Type INIT HELLO and press the RETURN key. The red light on the disk drive will go on, and the drive will whirr for about two minutes.
5. When the "]" character appears on the screen, remove the diskette and label it appropriately.

Initializing a Data Diskette Using AppleWorks

1. From the **MAIN MENU** on the AppleWorks Desktop, press the DOWN ARROW key four times to highlight option "5. Other Activities" and press the RETURN key.
2. The **OTHER ACTIVITIES** menu should now appear on the screen. Again, press the DOWN ARROW key four times to highlight option "5. Format a blank disk" and press the RETURN key.
3. The **DISK FORMATTER** instructions should now appear on the screen. The formatter will use the disk drive shown on the top line of the screen, usually Drive 2. Type in a name for your data disk. You may use as many as 15 letters, numbers, and periods, but the first character in the name must be a letter. For example, Fred Stone might want to name his disk "FREDS.FILES". After typing in your disk name, press the RETURN key.
4. Insert the **BLANK** diskette into the disk drive shown on the top line of the screen. Press the SPACE BAR to begin formatting. When the process is complete (about one minute), the screen will display "Successfully formatted."
5. To return to the MAIN MENU, press the ESCAPE key three times.

Initializing a Data Diskette for Apple Logo

Warning: an Apple Logo data diskette cannot be initialized after Apple Logo has been loaded; it must be initialized prior to loading Logo.

1. Boot the Apple System Master diskette or any diskette previously initialized by the following procedure.
2. Remove the System Master and insert the new blank diskette into the disk drive.
3. Enter the following program, or any BASIC program of your choice:

```
NEW
10 HOME
20 PRINT "LOGO DATA DISKETTE"
30 PRINT "the date"
40 END
```

4. Type INIT HELLO and press the RETURN key. The red light on the disk drive will go on, and the drive will whirr for about two minutes.
5. When the "]" character appears on the screen, remove the diskette and label it appropriately.

TIP THREE

How to Copy a File

Occasionally you will need to copy a single file from one diskette to another. A file on a diskette can contain a program or data. The procedures to copy a BASIC program file, a BASIC data file or a Logo file, and an AppleWorks data file are all different. Choose the appropriate procedure below for your needs:

BASIC Programs

1. Boot the Apple System Master diskette or other suitable DOS diskette. Insert the diskette that has the program file you wish to copy into drive 1. Type the following instruction replacing *filename* with the name of the file you wish to copy:

   ```
   LOAD filename    [press RETURN]
   ```

2. Remove the diskette containing your program and insert into drive 1 the diskette to which you wish to copy the program. This diskette must be initialized. Type the following instruction:

   ```
   SAVE filename    [press RETURN]
   ```

BASIC Files and Logo Files

Copying a BASIC data file or a Logo file requires the use of a file copy program. To perform this function, a file copy program, FILEM or FID, can be found on the Apple System Master diskette. This program will also copy BASIC program files.

1. Boot the Apple System Master diskette.
2. When the "]" character appears on the screen, type RUN FILEM and press the RETURN key. If you have an older Apple System Master diskette, you may have to type BRUN FID and press the RETURN key. The programs are identical.
3. When the menu appears, choose option "<1> COPY FILES" by typing 1 and pressing the RETURN key.
4. Answer the questions on the screen as follows (press the RETURN key after each answer):

SOURCE SLOT? **6**

DRIVE? **1**

DESTINATION SLOT? **6**

DRIVE? **1**   [enter a 2 if you have two drives]

5. When the prompt FILENAME?, appears, enter the name of the file that you want to copy and press the RETURN key.
6. Follow the directions on the screen for inserting the diskettes into the disk drives. If you are using only one disk drive, you may have to switch the source and destination diskettes several times, so be careful not to insert the wrong diskette at the wrong time. If you are using two disk drives, place the source diskette in drive 1 and the destination diskette in drive 2.
7. When the copy is complete, press the SPACE BAR to return to the menu. You can continue to copy additional files by following steps 2 through 6, or you can type a 9 and press the RETURN key to quit the FILEM program.

AppleWorks Data Files

1. From the MAIN MENU on the AppleWorks Desktop, highlight option "1. Add files to the Desktop" and press the RETURN key.
2. Insert the data diskette that has the file you wish to copy into drive 2 (the source diskette). Press the RETURN key to select option 1 from the ADD FILES menu.
3. Use the ARROW keys to select the file you wish to copy and press the RETURN key to add the file to the Desktop.

4. Remove the source diskette and insert the diskette on which you want the file copied (the destination diskette) into drive 2. Hold down the OPEN-APPLE key and simultaneously press the S key to save the file on the destination diskette.

Remember: You may be violating the copyright law if you make a duplicate copy of a program.

TIP FOUR

How to Make a Back-Up Diskette

It is always a good practice to make back-up copies of data diskettes just in case something unforeseen happens to the original diskette. The following procedure will allow you to copy the entire contents of an Applesoft BASIC program diskette, an AppleWorks data diskette, or an Apple Logo file diskette. This procedure uses the COPYA program found on the Apple System Master diskette.

1. Boot the Apple System Master Diskette.
2. When the "]" character appears on the screen, type RUN COPYA and press the RETURN key. This runs the Apple disk duplication program.
3. Press the RETURN key three times. The screen should say

```
ORIGINAL   SLOT:  6
           DRIVE:  1
DUPLICATE  SLOT:  6
           DRIVE:  DEFAULT = 2
```

4. If you have one disk drive, type 1 and press RETURN. If you have two disk drives type 2 and press RETURN.
5. When the message "PRESS 'RETURN' KEY TO BEGIN COPY" appears, press the RETURN key.
6. The program will instruct you when to insert your *original* diskette and when to insert your *duplicate* (back-up) diskette. If you have only one drive, you will have to switch diskettes several times. Be careful that you follow the directions and have the correct diskette in the drive; otherwise you may ruin your original diskette. If you have two drives, you won't have to swap diskettes.

TIP FIVE

Care and Treatment of Diskettes

The programs and data you store on diskette are valuable. You have an investment in them—either time or money or both. Eliminate troubles by following these simple precautions:

1. Handle a diskette by the jacket (plastic cover) only. Do not allow anything to touch the exposed area of the diskette.
2. Never subject a diskette to a magnetic field; it may erase the diskette. Setting your diskette on top of a TV or printer could cause problems.
3. Keep diskettes flat. Do not fold, bend, or crimp. If you store them in a three-ring binder, use plastic holders designed for this purpose.
4. Insert diskettes carefully into the disk drive. Don't use unnecessary force.
5. Store diskettes in their envelopes away from liquids, dirty or greasy surfaces, and dust. In the classroom, chalk dust can cause serious problems with diskettes.
6. Do not expose diskettes to extreme hot or cold temperatures. Car dashboards and trunks are diskette killers.

TIP SIX

Routine Microcomputer Maintenance

The worst enemy of a microcomputer is dust. Dust easily enters the ventilation holes of the monitor, disk drive, keyboard, system unit, and printer. The dust builds up and affects electrical contacts within. Disk drives are particularly subject to damage by dust. The disk head can be permanently damaged by dust particles, as can floppy diskettes inserted into a dusty drive. The best precaution is a dust cover for each computer, printer, and disk drive. This is not always practical or possible in an educational setting (like a lab of twenty computers.) However, if a computer is going to be sitting unused for a period of time (summer vacation, for example) it should be covered with a cloth or plastic sheet.

The second worst enemy of a computer in the classroom is dirty fingers. The keyboard and monitor seem to be the major collection sites for grease and grime. The monitor, keys, and computer case should be cleaned at frequent intervals. An all-purpose cleaner can be used, but it should not be sprayed directly on any of the computer components. The spray could get inside the unit and cause an electrical short. Turn off the computer and spray the cleaner on a paper towel. Clean the area by wiping it with the wetted towel.

Here are some tips for preventive maintenance of specific components.

System Unit

At least once a year, more frequently if the computer is moved a lot, remove the lid on the Apple's system unit (make sure the computer is turned off and unplugged), touch the power supply to discharge any static electricity, and push gently on each integrated circuit (chip). The chips gradually work out of their sockets and do not make good contact. At the same time, remove all circuit boards plugged into the mother board. Clean the edge connectors of each board with an eraser or denatured alcohol.

Keyboard

Clean the keys as needed by spraying an all-purpose cleaner on a towel and working it between the keys. Be careful not to spray or drip any liquid into the keyboard.

Monitor

Clean the screen as needed with glass cleaner. Again, do not spray cleaner directly on the screen. Spray it first on a towel and then wipe the screen. Monitors that have anti-glare screens should be cleaned in accordance with the manufacturer's directions. The use of glass cleaner on an anti-glare screen could damage it. If in doubt, try using denatured alcohol, but be careful not to get any on the plastic case, as the alcohol will bleach it.

Disk Drive

Once a year have an experienced service technician clean the disk heads and adjust the disk speed. This routine service can be a "do-it-yourself" project, if you are so inclined. Computer stores sell disk head cleaning kits and programs to test disk speed. Ask your dealer for advice. Some Apple disk drives do not require this maintenance as frequently as others.

Printer

Most printers require routine oiling and lubricating. Check your printer's manual. Printheads and daisywheels have a limited life. If your print quality is poor, you may need to replace the printhead. Replace the ribbon when needed with the correct replacement. Dot matrix printer ribbons use a special ink that lubricates the tiny pins in the print head. Substitution of a typewriter ribbon could reduce print head life.

TIP SEVEN

The Sixteen Most Common Hardware Problems and How to Troubleshoot Them

Problem	Probable Cause	Possible Cure
MONITOR		
No picture.	Not plugged in.	Plug into wall outlet.
	Not turned on.	Turn on monitor.
	Cable between computer and monitor disconnected.	Check cable to be sure it is properly connected.
Flickering picture.	Loose or defective cable between computer and monitor.	Wiggle cable to see if that affects the picture. Tighten connection or replace cable.
Image flickers and characters on screen change.	Static discharge or power surge.	Use an antistatic mat under your work area and/ or use a surge protector.
Image goes faint or gets smaller.	Voltage drop or "brown out."	Quit using the computer until the power returns to normal.
DISK DRIVE		
Red light doesn't go on, and drive makes no sounds.	No power.	Make sure Apple is plugged in and turned on.
	Loose or disconnected cable to computer.	Check cable between drive and computer if possible.

Problem	Probable Cause	Possible Cure
Red light goes on, drive makes clicking noises, but computer won't boot.	Diskette inserted incorrectly.	Check to see if diskette is right side up with oval cutout to back of drive.
	No DOS on diskette.	To boot the drive, the diskette must have been initialized or formatted. Try another diskette.
Programs load incorrectly or disk errors occur.	Disk heads dirty.	Clean with disk cleaning kit or have dealer service disk drive.
	Disk heads not aligned properly.	Have dealer service disk drive.
	Disk speed too slow or too fast.	If familiar with the procedure, adjust the disk speed. Otherwise have dealer service disk drive.

KEYBOARD AND SYSTEM UNIT

Problem	Probable Cause	Possible Cure
Simply won't work, power light does not go on.	Not plugged in.	Plug into wall outlet.
	Fuse is blown.	Check fuse and replace if necessary.
	Bad power switch.	Turn on and off several times and check to see if power sometimes goes on. Have dealer replace if switch bad.
Programs halt unexpectedly, characters change on the monitor, program statements get lost.	Bad or loose RAM or ROM chips.	If possible, open system unit and press RAM and ROM chips to reseat them (sometimes they get loose.) Run a RAM test and replace bad chips, or have dealer service unit.
Key sticks.	Something was spilled in the keyboard.	Pry off the key cap and spray a small amount of silicone lubricant. If this doesn't work have dealer replace key or keyboard.

PRINTER

Problem	Probable Cause	Possible Cure
Doesn't print, makes no noises, power light not on.	Not plugged in.	Plug into wall outlet
	Not turned on or bad power switch.	Check power switch.
	Printer's fuse blown.	Check fuse and replace if necessary.

Problem	Probable Cause	Possible Cure
	Printer's case not on correctly.	Many printers have switches to make sure the case is on. Check to see if case or cover is on tightly.
Doesn't print, but power light on.	Printer not "on line."	Check online or select switch to make sure it is on.
	Cable between printer and computer loose, disconnected, or bad.	Make sure you are using the right cable and that it is securely plugged in.
	No paper or bad paper-detection switch.	Make sure the paper is loaded correctly and that the "paper out" switch is working.
	Incorrect printer interface protocol.	Have knowledgeable person check the switches on the printer and the interface to see if they are correct.
Prints, but printing is faint.	Worn out ribbon.	Replace ribbon.
	Form thickness not adjusted properly.	Check printer manual and adjust for proper thickness.
Prints, but printing smudged.	Forms thickness not adjusted properly.	Adjust for thicker paper.
	Ribbon installed wrong.	Check to see if ribbon is threaded correctly.
Prints, but doesn't feed paper. Everything printed on one line.	Interfacing switches set incorrectly.	Check printer manual and set appropriate switch to add a linefeed at the end of each line.
	Form feed belt loose or broken.	Have dealer tighten or replace belt.
Prints, but always double spaces.	Interfacing switches set incorrectly.	Check printer manual and set appropriate switch to not add a linefeed at the end of each line.
Prints, but prints the wrong characters.	Interfacing switches set incorrectly.	Probably the printer is set for a different data speed (baud) than the computer. Check and set appropriately.
Prints, but printing not consistent, light or dark at top of letter or one side of page.	Ribbon jammed or not feeding properly.	Check to make sure ribbon is feeding correctly. Replace ribbon if necessary.
	Platten not aligned properly or worn out.	Have dealer service the printer.
	Print head defective.	Have dealer service or replace the print head.

TIP EIGHT

Considerations for Evaluating Software

It is estimated that there are at least 10,000 educational computer programs available in the United States. As you can imagine, some are good, some are poor, and some are in between. In order to begin to review software with a critical eye, one must have a reference point. The following *Ten Essentials of Educational Software* are criteria for evaluation.

    1. Software should utilize the unique capabilities of the computer. If the use of the computer as an adjunct to the instructional process cannot be justified, then why use it? Ask yourself: What does this software do on the computer that can't be done in some more traditional manner? Is the computer being used as a simple page turner or in place of flash cards?

    2. Software should be pedagogically sound. Is the program based on a learning or instructional theory appropriate to the subject matter and cognitive level of the student?

    3. Software should reflect current and valid curriculum. Is the curriculum content of the software consistent with the curriculum content of the classroom instruction? Does it meet the curriculum goals of the school program?

    4. Software should be free of any errors. Are there technical programming errors? Does the software have spelling, grammatical, or content errors?

5. Software should provide a positive learning experience. Is reinforcement immediate and positive? Students should receive as many positive rewards as possible. Many programs make the mistake of rewarding failure with cute graphics or sounds. Students intentionally fail in order to see the results. Other programs humiliate the slower students by responding with sour tones when they are repeatedly incorrect. Software should never contain insulting references to the student's progress, such as "You dummy" or sexual, racial, or religious slurs.

6. Software should be easy to use. Are the instructions clear, concise, and consistent? Can the instructions be easily remembered or recalled if the student forgets them? Is the operational skill level consistent with the age of the students? Does the student always know what she or he is expected to do next? These human design factors should all be answered with a Yes.

7. Software should allow for teacher options. Can the teacher select the number of questions or the length of the learning session? Can the teacher modify the instructional sequence such as by turning off the sound or changing the reward? Can the teacher exchange his or her own questions for the questions in the program? These options may be desirable in some circumstances.

8. Software should motivate the learner. The student should be motivated to be a learner in other educational settings as well as a learner on the computer.

9. Software should provide supplemental written materials. Are there written instructions for the software? Is there a teacher's guide describing the author's goals, objectives, instructional strategy, and classroom evaluation? Are there worksheets, handouts, exercises, tests, and so on?

10. Software should provide back-up capability. Educational software is costly and can be easily damaged. Can a back-up copy be made from the program or will the publisher provide a back-up copy? How much will the back-up copy cost and how long will it take to get it? Remember, back-up copies are to be used only if the original is damaged. We are all responsible for seeing that unauthorized copies of software are not used in the classroom. Besides being illegal, it sets a bad example for our students.

TIP NINE

Considerations for Setting Up a Computer Lab

Many school districts spend tens of thousands of dollars on microcomputers and software but neglect an important aspect of computing—the setting. Most administrators designing a computer lab or classroom computer workstation assume that the computers can be used with existing school desks and chairs. Ask any student who has had to use a computer in such a setting for more than a few minutes. Common complaints are backache, muscle cramps, and eyestrain.

These ailments can easily be avoided with a little ergonomic planning. Ergonomics is the science of making machines and people work in harmony. The following considerations should be kept in mind when designing an educational computer workstation.

Desks

The most important factor in choosing a desk for use as a computer station is its height. The desk should be adjustable. The height should be set so that the user's elbows are bent at a 90 degree angle when typing on the keyboard. For high school students or adults the proper height is about 26 to 27 inches off the floor. For primary students it is obviously much less.

The desk should also have some means of supporting the computer monitor, such as a shelf. Ideally this shelf should also be adjustable, but a fixed shelf is satisfactory. The shelf should raise the monitor so that the top of the screen is at eye level. If the monitor sits on top of the computer, it may be too low, resulting in strained neck muscles.

Special computer desks can be purchased from $60 to over $1000. The less expensive ones are designed for home use and usually won't stand up to the use and abuse in a school. A sturdy, well-designed computer desk will cost in the $250-to-$500 price range, a little steep for a school's budget (especially if you need 10 or 15 desks.) A less expensive alternative is a school table, 24 inches wide by 4 or 5 feet long with adjustable legs. These can be purchased from school furniture companies for about $50 and can be adjusted to the proper height for your students. The monitor's height can be adjusted by purchasing a separate monitor stand. This inexpensive accessory is available from computer dealers.

Chairs

The proper chair is as important as the proper desk. Most important, the chair should have good support for the lower back. Ideally, the height of the seat and the back support should be adjustable. A swivel chair on five casters with either no arms or short arms is recommended.

Special computer chairs can be purchased for from $400 to $500. Since most schools don't have $15,000 to spend on 30 chairs, some compromise must be made. A good alternative is a school chair selected to be the proper height to match the desk. School furniture companies make chairs in several heights. An upholstered foam seat and back rest are highly recommended because they will reduce fatigue. Such chairs are available for about $25. Most folding chairs should not be used, because they are usually too tall, improperly padded, and generally uncomfortable.

Printer Tables

Special printer tables are available for about $100. Most come with a slot cut into the table top to feed continuous form paper to the printer from a stack of paper beneath the table. Some have output shelves or baskets to stack the printed paper neatly.

The major consideration in selecting a printer table is whether it fits your printer. Is the slot cut in the right place? Is it wide enough for your paper? Do you even need a paper slot? Is the top the right size for your printer?

Reducing Glare and Eye Fatigue

To avoid glare, don't place the computer's monitor facing a window. Antiglare filters come installed on many monitors, or they can be added later. These filters are very helpful in reducing glare but require special cleaning when they get dirty.

Monitors that have tilt screens are most desirable. The screens can be adjusted to remove the glare. Reducing the glare is the first step to reducing eye fatigue.

Two other factors in eye fatigue are image contrast and sharpness. A color television is a poor choice for a computer screen. The sharpness (resolution) of the characters is poor, and the contrast is too great (usually white letters on a black background.) A monitor is the choice of computer professionals. If the computer work for the course requires a lot of reading of text on the screen, such as in a high school word processing class, either a green or amber tinted screen is recommended because its image is sharp and the contrast is easy on the eye muscles. Color monitors can used if color is an absolute necessity. However, only expensive RGB-type color monitors have as high a resolution as an inexpensive green or amber monitor.

Reducing Static Electricity

Carpeting in the computer classroom is desirable because it reduces the noise level in the room. However, it can be annoying if students build up static charges as they walk across the room. When they touch the computer they discharge the static electricity and may ruin their program or even damage the hardware.

Several solutions to the static problem are available. (1) Buy antistatic carpeting that has a grounded metallic fiber woven in the carpet. (2) Buy antistatic mats and place them under each workstation. (3) Spray the carpeting with a mild solution of liquid fabric softener and water (don't laugh—it really works); depending on the weather and climate you may have to spray daily, weekly or monthly. (4) Train students to ground themselves before using the computer. This can be done by touching a metal object like the chair or table leg after sitting down at the computer.

Eliminating Power Surges

Power surges can ruin your day and your equipment. A power surge is a sudden increase in voltage in the power running through the electrical wiring in the building. They are common in older school buildings. In its mildest form a power surge can alter the RAM, and you will have to reboot and start over. In worse cases, you can lose information on your disk or permanently damage the integrated circuits in the computer.

To prevent damage from surges, you can purchase surge protectors. These devices plug into a wall outlet, and then the computer is plugged into the surge protector.

Classroom Computer Security

One of the big problems facing most school computer labs is theft. Commercially available security pads are definite deterrents. A bottom plate is bolted or glued to the computer desk, and the security pad is bolted to the bottom of the computer. The computer is then locked to the table. This protects the computer but not the monitor or disk drive.

Special computer security devices are available that lock up the system unit, keyboard, monitor, and disk drive. These devices cost $250 and up but are very effective. They are designed so that the computers can be accessed for maintenance but not carried away. Each brand of computer requires a different security device, so check with your computer dealer before ordering.

The least expensive method of security is attaching padlock brackets to the cases of the computer, monitor, and disk drive. These brackets can be attached with screws or for better security with pop-rivets. Make sure that the screws or rivets don't interfere with any of the mechanical or electrical components. The units can then be chained and padlocked to the desk.

Considerations in Designing a Computer Lab

All the previous paragraphs are important in the environmental setting of a classroom computer. In addition to the above, some special considerations are necessary when developing a computer classroom or lab.

The most efficient arrangement is to have each of the computers set up against the side walls of the classroom. At the front of the room a blackboard, projection screen, and a demonstration computer with a 19″ to 25″ screen should be located. A slide or overhead projector can easily be positioned on a cart in the middle isle. This arrangement gives each student ample room at the computer and allows them to view the demonstration computer, projection screen, and blackboard with ease. The teacher can walk up and down the middle of the classroom and view each student's computer monitor to check progress.

If there are large windows in the classroom, shades or blinds must be available to darken the room for audiovisual presentations and to reduce the glare on the computer monitors. Tables of the proper height and comfortable chairs should be provided (see previous discussion). Carpeting is effective in reducing computer noises. Also be sure that sufficient electrical outlets and extension cords are available and that the circuitry will handle the power consumption of many computers. A typical microcomputer uses from 60 to 100 watts of electricity. Usually, ten to fifteen computers can be plugged into the same 15-amp circuit.

TIP TEN

Applesoft BASIC Language Summary

This reference defines the most commonly used statements and commands on the Apple computer. It is not a complete listing of all possible statements, nor does it present detailed descriptions of the action of each statement. The reader who requires such information is referred to the *Applesoft BASIC Programmer's Reference Manual*, available from Apple dealers.

The assumption of this guide is that the statements and commands as described are intended to be used on an Apple II, Apple II+, Apple IIe, or Apple IIc with a minimum of 48K of RAM and one or two disk drives, for which the controller card is located in slot #6. This configuration is very common. If the reader's system is not configured in this fashion, some of the following statements and commands will function differently than documented.

In the following summary the general format for each statement or command will be presented with an example (or examples) and a description of the action initiated. The conventions and abbreviations used are as follows:

<...>	Required element.
{...}	Optional element.
cond	Any logical condition.
dimension(s)	The maximum dimension(s) of an array.
expr	Any numeric constant, variable or expression.
file	Any legal filename (only the first 30 characters are used).
key	Any key on Apple keyboard.
line number	Any legal line number from 0 to 32767.
message	Any combination of characters.
statement	Any legal Applesoft statement.
string	Any string constant, variable or expression.
variable or var	Any legal variable described in "Summary of Variable Types," p. 275.
x	Any numeric constant, variable or expression defining a x-axis value.
y	Any numeric constant, variable or expression defining a y-axis value.

BASIC Statements

DATA   line number DATA <list of variables>

```
210 DATA 4.3,"A TO Z",10
```

Provides a program with data that can be stored into variables using the READ statement. In the example, 4.3 is a real number, "A TO Z" is a string, and 10 is an integer. (*See* READ.)

DIM   line number DIM <variable(dimension(s))>

```
10 DIM A(23),B(3,4),C$(4),D$(12,30)
```

Defines a variable that is capable of storing a list (single dimension) or a table (double dimension) of a specified length. In the example, A is a numeric variable with 23 possible entries. D$ is a string variable with a maximum of 12 rows and 30 columns.

END   line number END

```
32767 END
```

Terminates the execution of a program.

FOR   line number FOR <var> = <expr> TO <expr> {STEP <expr>}

```
45 FOR I=2 TO 10 STEP 2
```

Creates a "loop" that will execute all of the statements between a FOR and a NEXT statement a specified number of times. In the example, this loop would be executed for the values of I from 2 to 10 by 2's (2, 4, 6, 8, and 10). (*See* NEXT.)

GET   line number GET <variable>

```
70 GET X$
```

Inputs a single character from the keyboard without the character's being printed on the screen. Does not require the RETURN key to be pressed. In the example, the input character is stored in the variable X$.

GOSUB   line number GOSUB <line number>

```
220 GOSUB 10000
```

Unconditionally branches program execution to a subroutine at the indicated line number. When a RETURN statement is encountered in the subroutine, execution is returned to the statement immediately following the GOSUB. The example will cause the program to branch to the subroutine beginning at line 10000. (*See* RETURN.)

GOTO   line number GOTO <line number>

```
670 GOTO 10
```

Causes the execution of the program to branch to the indicated line number. In the example, program execution will branch from line 670 to line 10.

IF-THEN   line number IF <cond> THEN <statement>
line number IF <cond> THEN <line number>

```
55 IF A$ = "Y" THEN PRINT "CORRECT"
75 IF X < Z THEN 300
```

Causes the program to execute the indicated statement or branch to a line number if a specified condition is true. If the condition is false, the statement or branch is not executed, and the program continues with the execution of the next numbered statement following the IF-THEN. In the first example, the word CORRECT will be printed if A$ has the string value "Y." The second example will cause a branch to line 300 if the value stored in X is less than the value in Z.

INPUT   line number INPUT {string;} <list of variables>

```
240 INPUT "WHAT IS YOUR NAME "; NAME$
800 INPUT A, B, C
```

Inputs data from the keyboard to be stored into respective variables listed. Optionally, INPUT can print a string on the screen before waiting for input. The RETURN key must be pressed after the user has entered data. In the first example, the string *WHAT IS YOUR NAME* will be printed on the screen followed by a ? and the cursor. The string the user enters will be stored in NAME$. The second example will input from the keyboard three numeric values separated by commas and store them into A, B, and C respectively.

LET   line number LET <variable> = <expr>
          line number <variable> = <expr>

```
110 LET C = 100
120 P$ = "GREAT! "
130 A = 1/2 * B + H
```

Assigns the value of <expr> to <variable>. The word LET is optional. In the examples, the value 100 is stored in the variable C, the string *GREAT!* is stored in the variable P$, and variable A will have the value of one-half B plus H.

NEXT   line number NEXT <variable>

```
80 NEXT I
```

Terminates a loop begun by a FOR statement. The <variable> must be the same used in the corresponding FOR statement. In the example, line 80 will terminate the preceding statement 45 FOR I = 2 to 10 STEP 2. (*See* FOR.)

ON-GOSUB   line number ON <expr> GOSUB <list of line numbers>

```
30 ON X GOSUB 10000, 15000
```

Branches to the subroutine at the line numbers indicated based on the arithmetic value of an expression. In the example, the program will branch to the subroutine at line 10000 if X is 1 and to the subroutine at 15000 if X is 2. If X is less than 1 or greater than 2 the statement immediately following the ON-GOSUB will be executed.

ON-GOTO   line number ON <expr> GOTO <list of line numbers>

```
40 ON X-Y GOTO 500, 600, 700
```

Branches to the line numbers indicated based on the arithmetic value of an expression. In the example, the program will branch to line 500 if X−Y has a value 1, line 600 if X−Y has the value 2, and line 700 if X−Y has the value 3. If X−Y is less than 1 or greater than 3 then the statement immediately following the ON-GOTO will be executed.

PRINT   line number PRINT <list of variables>

```
890 PRINT "YOU GOT ";N;" QUESTIONS CORRECT."
```

Causes the computer to advance the cursor to the next line on the screen and print the values of the specified variables or strings. If, in the example, N had the value 9, *YOU GOT 9 QUESTIONS CORRECT.* would appear on the screen. See page 273, Text Formatting Statements, for more information.

READ   line number READ <list of variables>

```
465 READ X,Y,Z
```

Used in conjunction with the DATA statement to store data into variables within a program. When a READ statement is executed the program will set the variables listed to the next successive values in the program's DATA statements. The example will take the next three values from the DATA statements and store them in X, Y, and Z respectively. (*See* DATA.)

REM   line number REM <message>

```
10 REM   PROGRAM BY IMA TEACHER
```

Inserts a REMark into the program. The message only appears when the program is listed, not when it is run.

RESTORE   line number RESTORE

```
360 RESTORE
```

Returns the DATA list pointer to the first value of the first DATA statement allowing the DATA to be reread.

RETURN   line number RETURN

```
10450 RETURN
```

Terminates a subroutine and returns execution to the next numbered statement following the GOSUB that called the subroutine. (*See* GOSUB.)

Graphics Statements

COLOR   line number COLOR = <expr>

```
340 COLOR=7
```

Sets the color to be plotted in low-resolution graphics. <expr> is an integer between 0 and 15 that represents the following colors:

0 black	4 dark green	8 brown	12 green
1 magenta	5 grey	9 orange	13 yellow
2 dark blue	6 medium blue	10 grey	14 aqua
3 purple	7 light blue	11 pink	15 white

GR   line number GR

```
800 GR
```

Switches the display on the screen to low-resolution graphics (40 by 40 points) with four lines of text at the bottom. Clears the graphics screen to black and sets COLOR = 0 (black).

HCOLOR   line number HCOLOR = <expr>

```
460 HCOLOR=1
```

Sets the color to be plotted in high-resolution graphics. <expr> is an integer between 0 and 7 that represents the following colors:

0 black	2 violet	4 black	6 blue
1 green	3 white	5 orange	7 white

HGR   line number HGR

```
390 HGR
```

Switches the display on the screen to high-resolution graphics (280 by 160 points) with four lines of text at the bottom. Clears the graphics screen to black but does not change the value of HCOLOR.

HLIN   line number HLIN <x1>,<x2> AT <y>

```
1010 HLIN 5,25 AT 20
```

Draws a horizontal line on the low-resolution graphics screen at the y axis position <y> from the x axis position <x1> to the x axis position <x2>. The color will be that most recently set with the COLOR statement. In the example a horizontal line will be drawn from x = 5 to x = 25 at y = 20.

HPLOT   line number HPLOT <x>,<y>
line number HPLOT <x1>,<y1> TO <x2>,<y2>
line number HPLOT TO <x>,<y>

```
200 HPLOT 100,130
210 HPLOT 0,0 TO 279,159
220 HPLOT TO 150,10
```

Plots dots or lines on the high-resolution graphics screen using the color most recently set with the HCOLOR statement. The high resolution screen uses an x-y coordinate system with 0,0 in the upper left corner. In the first example, a dot will be plotted at $x = 100$, $y = 130$. In the second example, a line will be plotted from $x = 0$, $y = 0$ (upper left corner) to $x = 279$, $y = 159$ (lower right corner). In the third example a line will be plotted from the last point plotted to $x = 150$, $y = 10$.

PLOT   line number PLOT <x>,<y>

```
275 PLOT 20,30
```

Plots rectangular blocks on the low-resolution graphics screen using the color most recently set with the COLOR statement. The low-resolution screen uses an x-y coordinate system with 0,0 in the upper left corner and 39,39 in the lower right corner. The example will plot a block at $x = 20$, $y = 30$.

SCRN   line number <var> = SCRN(<x>,<y>)

```
620 Z=SCRN(27,5)
```

SCRN is a low-resolution graphics screen function that returns the color value of the graphic coordinates specified. In the example, Z will be set to the value of the color at $x = 27$, $y = 5$.

TEXT   line number TEXT

```
990 TEXT
```

Sets the screen to the text mode of 24 lines of text with 40 characters per line. TEXT does not clear the screen or HOME the cursor.

VLIN   line number VLIN <y1>,<y2> AT <x>

```
730 VLIN 0,39 AT 20
```

Draws a vertical line on the low-resolution graphics screen at the x axis position <x> from the y axis position <y1> to the y axis position <y2>. The color will be that most recently set with the COLOR statement. In the example, a vertical line will be drawn from $y = 0$ to $y = 39$ at $x = 20$.

Text Formatting Statements

COMMA (,)   line number PRINT <var>,<var>

```
370 PRINT QUANTITY, PRICE, TOTAL
```

Used in a PRINT statement to space data into 16-column fields. In the example, the value of the variable QUANTITY will be printed in column 1, the value of the variable PRICE will be printed in column 17, and the value of the variable TOTAL will be printed in column 33.

FLASH   line number FLASH

```
1500 FLASH
```

Sets the text printing mode to flashing characters. All text printed after this statement is executed will flash. NORMAL reverses this action.

HOME   line number HOME

```
10 HOME
```

Clears the text screen and returns the cursor to the HOME position in the upper left corner.

HTAB   line number HTAB <expr>

```
550 HTAB 27
```

Moves the cursor to the specified column number (1 to 40). The HTAB statement is usually followed by a PRINT statement. In the example, the cursor will be moved to column 27.

INVERSE   line number INVERSE

```
345 INVERSE
```

Sets the text printing mode to black on white characters instead of white on black. All text printed after this statement is executed will be printed in inverse. NORMAL reverses this action.

NORMAL   line number NORMAL

```
610 NORMAL
```

Sets the text printing mode to non-black characters. Reverses the action of the FLASH and INVERSE statements.

POS   line number <var> = POS(<expr>)

```
730 X = POS(0)
```

POS is the text function that returns the current horizontal cursor position from 0 (left margin) to 39 (right margin). Although <expr> is required, the expression has no effect on the results. In the example, X will be set to the current horizontal cursor position.

SEMICOLON (;)   line number PRINT <string>;<var>

```
840 PRINT "YOU GOT ";N;" CORRECT."
```

Used in a PRINT statement to position the cursor immediately after the string or variable preceding the semicolon. If N = 10 in the example, the printed line would read

```
YOU GOT 10 CORRECT.
```

SPC   line number PRINT <var>;SPC(<expr>);<var>

```
480 PRINT A;SPC(10);B
```

Used in a PRINT statement to insert a specified number of spaces between two variables when preceded and followed by semicolons. In the example, the value of A will be printed, followed by 10 spaces, and then the value of B will be printed.

SPEED   line number SPEED = <expr>

```
160 SPEED=200
```

Sets the speed at which characters are printed on the screen. The default speed is 255, which is the fastest system speed. Zero is the slowest speed.

TAB   line number PRINT TAB(<expr>);<var>

```
80 PRINT TAB(25);R
```

Used in a PRINT statement to move the cursor to the specified column where 1 is the left margin and 40 is the right margin. TAB can only move the cursor to the right. Use HTAB to move the cursor to the left. In the example, the value of R will be printed starting in column 25.

VTAB   line number VTAB <expr>

```
120 VTAB 18
```

Moves the cursor to the specified line number. The top of the screen is line 1, while the bottom is line 24. Usually the VTAB statement is followed by a PRINT statement. In the example, the cursor will be moved to line 18.

Summary of Variable Types

INTEGER   Variable name: single letter optionally followed by a single letter or digit followed by a % character.

> Range: −32767 to +32767.
> Examples: I%, B2%, GH%.

REAL   Variable name: single letter optionally followed by a single letter or digit.

> Range: −9.99999999 E+37 to +9.99999999 E+37.
> Examples: S, R5, DE.

STRING   Variable name: single letter optionally followed by a single letter or digit followed by a $ character.

> Range: 0 to 255 characters
> Examples: F$, K9$, XY$.

Note that variable names may be longer than two characters, but only the first two characters are significant. Consequently APPLE and APPLIANCE are the same real variable AP.

Summary of Operators

ARITHMETIC	+	Addition
	/	Division
	^	Exponentiation (raise to a power)
	*	Multiplication
	−	Subtraction or negation

LOGICAL	AND	Logical product
	NOT	Logical negation
	OR	Logical sum

RELATIONAL	=	Equals
	>	Greater than
	>=	Greater than or equal to
	<	Less than
	<=	Less than or equal to
	<>	Not equal to

| **STRING** | + | Concatenation |

███████████ ## Mathematical Functions

ABS   line number <var> = ABS(<expr>)

```
100 X = ABS(-6.75)
```

Returns the absolute value of <expr>. In the example, X=6.75.

ATN   line number <var>=ATN(<expr>)

```
100 X = ATN(1)
```

Returns the arctangent of <expr> in radians. In the example, X=.785398163.

COS   line number <var> = COS(<expr>)

```
100 X = COS(1)
```

Returns the cosine of <expr>. <expr> must be in radians. In the example, X=.540302306.

EXP   line number <var>=EXP(<expr>)

```
100 X=EXP(1)
```

Returns the value $e^{<expr>}$, where e=2.7182828183. In the example, X=2.7182828183.

INT   line number <var>=INT(<expr>)

```
100 X=INT(4.53)
```

Returns the greatest integer in <expr> which is less than or equal to <expr>. In the example, X=4.

LOG   line number <var>=LOG(<expr>)

```
100 X = LOG(2)
```

Returns the natural logarithm of <expr>. In the example, X=.693147181.

RND   line number <var> = RND(<expr>)

```
100 X = RND(1)
```

Returns a random number greater than or equal to 0 and less than 1. If <expr> is positive, a unique set of random numbers is generated. If <expr> is 0, then the last random number generated is returned. If <expr> is negative, the same set of random numbers will be generated every time the program is run.

SGN   line number <var> = SGN(<expr>)

```
100 X = SGN(-217.456)
```

Returns the sign of <expr>: +1 if positive, 0 if zero, and −1 if negative. In the example, X = −1.

SIN   line number <var> = SIN(<expr>)

```
100 X = SIN(1)
```

Returns the sine of <expr>. <expr> must be in radians. In the example, X = .841470985.

SQR   line number <var> = SQR(<expr>)

```
100 X = SQR(16)
```

Returns the square root of <expr>. In the example, X = 4.

TAN   line number <var> = TAN(<expr>)

```
100 X = TAN(1)
```

Returns the tangent of <expr>. <expr> must be in radians. In the example, X = 1.55740772.

String Functions

ASC   line number <var> = ASC(<string>)

```
100 X = ASC("APPLE")
```

Returns the ASCII code for the first character in the string specified. In the example, X = 65.

**CHR$**   line number <string> = CHR$(<expr>)

```
100 X$ = CHR$(65)
```

Returns the ASCII character specified by the numerical value of <expr>. In the example, X$ = "A".

**LEFT$**   line number <string> = LEFT$(<string>,<expr>)

```
100 X$ = LEFT$("APPLE",3)
```

Returns a substring of <string> from the first character to the <expr>th character. In the example, X$ = "APP".

LEN   line number <var> = LEN(<string>)

```
100 X=LEN("APPLE")
```

Returns the number of characters contained in <string>. In the example, X$=5.

MID   line number <string> = MID$(<string>,<expr1>,<expr2>)

```
100 X$ = MID$("NOW IS THE TIME",5,6)
```

Returns the substring of <string> that begins with the character specified by <expr1> and has a length of <expr2> characters. In the example, X$="IS THE".

**RIGHT$**   line number <string> = RIGHT$(<string>,<expr>)

```
100 X$=RIGHT$("APPLE",2)
```

Returns a substring of <string> consisting of the rightmost characters specified by <expr>. In the example, X$="LE".

**STR$**   line number <string>=STR$(<expr>)

```
100 X$ = STR$(24.07)
```

Converts the <expr> to a string. In the example, X$="24.07".

VAL   line number <var> = VAL(<string>)

```
100 X = VAL("365 DAYS")
```

Converts the <string> to a real or integer variable. The conversion will terminate when a non-numeric number is encountered. In the example, X=365.

BASIC and Disk Commands

CATALOG   CATALOG {,D<expr>}

```
CATALOG,D2
```

Prints a list of all the files on a diskette. Optionally the disk drive number, D<expr>, may be specified. In the example, a catalog of the diskette in drive 2 will be listed on the screen.

DEL   DEL <line number>,<line number>

```
DEL 350,400
```

Deletes line numbers from the program in memory starting with the first line number specified and ending with the second line number specified. In the example, line 350, line 400, and all of the line numbers between 350 and 400 will be deleted.

DELETE   DELETE <file>{,D<expr>};{,V<expr>}

```
DELETE BUTTERFLIES
```

Erases a file from a diskette. Optionally, the drive number or volume number may be specified. In the example, the file BUTTERFLIES will be erased from the diskette in the drive last used.

INIT   INIT <file> {,D<expr>} {,V<expr>}

```
INIT HELLO, V25
```

Initializes a blank diskette so that it can be used. The current program in memory will be saved as the <file> specified, and that program will be run when the diskette is booted. Optionally, the drive number or volume number may be specified. In the example, the diskette in the drive most recently used will be initalized as volume 25 with the program in memory stored as HELLO.

LIST   LIST {<line number>} {,<line number>}

```
LIST
LIST 300
LIST 1000, 2000
```

Lists lines of the program in memory to the screen. Optionally a line number or range may be specified. In the first example, the entire program will be listed. In the second example, line 300 only will be listed. In the third example, lines 1000 to 2000 inclusive will be listed.

LOAD   LOAD <file> {,D<expr>} {,V<expr>}

```
LOAD SNOW WHITE
```

Loads the specified diskette into memory. The current program in memory will be erased. Optionally the drive number or volume number may be specified. In the example, the program SNOW WHITE will be loaded into memory from the disk most recently used.

LOCK   LOCK <file> {,D<expr>} {,V<expr>}

```
LOCK MATH DRILL
```

Protects a file from being replaced or deleted accidentally. The UNLOCK command will reverse the action. Optionally, the drive number or volume number may be specified. In the example, the file MATH DRILL will be LOCKed on the diskette in the drive most recently used.

NEW

```
NEW
```

Erases the program and variables currently in memory. Used to clear memory before writing a new program.

PR   PR#<expr>

```
PR#6
PR#1
PR#0
```

Transfers output to the specified peripheral slot number. In the examples, PR#6 boots disk drive 1; PR#1 transfers all subsequent output to a printer assuming the printer interface is in slot 1; PR#0 returns output to the screen.

RUN   RUN {<file>} {,D<expr>} {,V<expr>}

```
RUN SPELL
```

Executes the program in memory if no file is specified. If a file is specified, memory is cleared, the file is loaded from a diskette, and the program executed. Optionally the drive number or volume number may be specified. In the example, the program SPELL will be loaded from the most recently used disk drive and executed.

RENAME   RENAME <file1>,<file2> {,D<expr>}{V<expr>}

```
RENAME PROGRAM 1,MUSCLES
```

Changes the name of <file1> to <file2> on a diskette. Optionally, the drive number may be specified. In the example, PROGRAM 1 will be renamed MUSCLES on the diskette in the drive most recently used.

SAVE   SAVE <file> {,D<expr>} {,V<expr>}

```
SAVE PICKLES
```

Saves the program currently in memory on diskette as the file specified. Optionally the drive number or volume number can be specified. If the file specified already exists on the diskette, it will be replaced by the program in memory unless it was LOCKed. In the example, the program in memory will be saved with the name PICKLES on the diskette in the drive most recently used.

UNLOCK   UNLOCK <file> {,D<expr>} {,V<expr>}

```
UNLOCK MATH DRILL
```

Removes the accidental-replace-or-delete lock on the file specified. Optionally, the drive number or volume number may be specified. In the example, MATH DRILL will be unlocked on the diskette in the drive most recently used.

Special Keys

APPLE Keys

> OPEN-APPLE
> CLOSED-APPLE

The APPLE keys are commonly used by application programs to signal special functions. They are actually substitutes for the game paddle buttons and are commonly used in arcade-game programs. (The APPLE keys are found only on the Apple IIe and Apple IIc.)

ARROW Keys

> LEFT ARROW (←)
> RIGHT ARROW (→)
> UP ARROW (↑)
> DOWN ARROW (↓)

The four keys on the Apple keyboard marked with a left arrow, a right arrow, an up arrow, and a down arrow are used to edit programs. The LEFT ARROW is used to delete characters previously typed in the current line. The RIGHT ARROW will reenter a character on the screen as though you were typing it. The UP ARROW will move up a line on the screen, and the DOWN ARROW will move down a line on the screen. The ESC key must be pressed before and after using either the UP ARROW or the DOWN ARROW keys. (The UP ARROW and DOWN ARROW keys are found only on the Apple IIe and Apple IIc.)

CAPS LOCK

> CAPS LOCK

The CAPS LOCK key locks the keyboard so that only uppercase letters will be printed on the screen. When the CAPS LOCK key is pressed a second time, the keyboard will be unlocked, and both uppercase and lowercase letters may be typed. (The CAPS LOCK key is found only on the Apple IIe and Apple IIc.)

CONTROL (CTRL)

> CONTROL <key>

The CONTROL key is used in conjunction with other keys to specify a variety of actions. To execute a CONTROL sequence, hold the CONTROL key down while simultaneously typing the other key. In the examples, CONTROL C will break the execution of a program and print the line number at which execution terminated, CONTROL G will sound a bell on the Apple speaker, and CONTROL X will delete the line currently being typed.

DELETE

DELETE

The DELETE key is commonly used in word processing programs to delete the screen character to the left of the cursor. The DELETE key has no function in Applesoft BASIC. (The DELETE key is found only on the Apple IIe and Apple IIc.)

ESCAPE (ESC)

ESCAPE

The ESCAPE key is most commonly used to edit programs. When the ESCAPE key is typed, the movable-cursor mode is entered. The ARROW keys are used to move the cursor up, left, right, and down. Once the cursor is positioned, pressing the ESCAPE key will return to normal mode. The LEFT and RIGHT ARROW keys can then be used to make edits.

REPEAT (REPT)

REPEAT <key>

The REPEAT key is held down in conjunction with another key. The other key will be repeatedly typed (only on the Apple II and Apple II +).

RESET

RESET
CONTROL RESET

The RESET key immediately halts the execution of a program and sets the screen to TEXT mode. If RESET is typed while a program is being saved on a diskette, the file may be damaged. The Apple IIe and Apple IIc require the CONTROL key to be held down while pressing RESET.

TAB

TAB

The TAB key is commonly used in word processing programs to move the cursor to a specified column on the screen. It has no function in Applesoft BASIC. (Found only on the Apple IIe and Apple IIc.)

ASCII Character Codes

The following codes are used in the CHR$ and ASC functions. Codes 97 through 127 and some punctuation characters are available only on the Apple IIe and Apple IIc.

Code	Character	Code	Character
0	CTRL @	64	@
1	CTRL A	65	A
2	CTRL B	66	B
3	CTRL C	67	C
4	CTRL D	68	D
5	CTRL E	69	E
6	CTRL F	70	F
7	CTRL G (bell)	71	G
8	CTRL H (left arrow)	72	H
9	CTRL I	73	I
10	CTRL J (down arrow)	74	J
11	CTRL K (up arrow)	75	K
12	CTRL L (form feed)	76	L
13	CTRL M (return)	77	M
14	CTRL N	78	N
15	CTRL O	79	O
16	CTRL P	80	P
17	CTRL Q	81	Q
18	CTRL R	82	R
19	CTRL S	83	S
20	CTRL T	84	T
21	CTRL U (right arrow)	85	U
22	CTRL V	86	V
23	CTRL W	87	W
24	CTRL X	88	X
25	CTRL Y	89	Y
26	CTRL Z	90	Z
27	CTRL [(escape)	91	[
28	CTRL \	92	\
29	CTRL]	93	]
30	CTRL ^	94	^
31	CTRL _	95	_
32	SPACE	96	`
33	!	97	a
34	"	98	b
35	#	99	c
36	$	100	d
37	%	101	e
38	&	102	f
39	'	103	g
40	(	104	h
41	)	105	i
42	*	106	j
43	+	107	k

Code	Character	Code	Character
44	,	108	l
45	-	109	m
46	.	110	n
47	/	111	o
48	0	112	p
49	1	113	q
50	2	114	r
51	3	115	s
52	4	116	t
53	5	117	u
54	6	118	v
55	7	119	w
56	8	120	x
57	9	121	y
58	:	122	z
59	;	123	{
60	<	124	|
61	=	125	}
62	>	126	~
63	?	127	DELETE

TIP ELEVEN

AppleWorks Command Summary

AppleWorks contains many specialized commands and functions. The following summary presents the most commonly used commands divided into three sections: word processing commands, spreadsheet commands, and data base commands. For a detailed description of these commands and others, see *AppleWorks Reference Manual* published by Apple Computer, Inc.

WORD PROCESSOR COMMANDS

Key(s)	Function
@ - C	Copy text (includes cut and paste)
@ - D	Delete text
@ - E	Change cursors
@ - F	Find occurrences of . . .
@ - H	Print screen
@ - K	Calculate page numbers
@ - M	Move text (includes cut and paste)
@ - N	Change name of file
@ - O	Options for print formatting
@ - P	Print document
@ - Q	See the Desktop Index
@ - R	Replaces occurrences of . . .
@ - S	Save current file to disk
@ - T	Set and clear tab stops
@ - Y	Delete from cursor to end of line

WORD PROCESSOR COMMANDS

Key(s)	Function
@ - Z	Zoom in or out to display or not display printer options
@ - ?	Get help
@ - SPACE BAR	Sticky space
ESCAPE	Cancels previous command
CONTROL - B	Begin or end bold face
CONTROL - L	Begin or end underline
RETURN	Mark end of paragraph
DELETE	Delete preceding character
▣ ▣ ▣ ▣	Move the cursor
@ - ▣	Back up a full screen
@ - ▣	Go forward a full screen
@ - ▣	Go to next word
@ - ▣	Go to previous word
TAB	Go to next tab stop
@ - TAB	Go to previous tab stop
@ - 1	Go to beginning of file
@ - 9	Go to end of file

SPREADSHEET COMMANDS

Key(s)	Function
@ - A	Arrange (sort) rows
@ - B	Blank an entry or entries
@ - C	Copy entries (includes cut and paste)
@ - D	Delete rows or columns
@ - E	Change cursors
@ - F	Find entries or text
@ - H	Print screen
@ - I	Insert rows or columns
@ - J	Jump to other window
@ - K	Calculate values
@ - L	Change layout of entries
@ - M	Move entries (includes cut and paste)
@ - N	Change name of file
@ - O	Options for print formatting
@ - P	Print spreadsheet
@ - Q	See the Desktop Index
@ - S	Save current file to disk
@ - T	Set or remove fixed titles
@ - U	Edit contents of an entry
@ - V	Set standard values and rules
@ - W	Create windows
@ - Y	Delete from cursor to end of cell
@ - Z	Zoom in or out to display or not display formulas
@ - ?	Get help
ESCAPE	Cancels previous command
RETURN	Accept entry
DELETE	Delete preceding character
▣ ▣ ▣ ▣	Move the cursor

SPREADSHEET COMMANDS

Key(s)	Function
@ - ◹	Back up a full screen
@ - ◸	Go forward a full screen
TAB	Go to next cell
@ - TAB	Go to previous cell
@ - 1	Go to beginning of file
@ - 9	Go to end of file
0–9, +, −, or .	Type a value
" or letters	Type a label

SPREADSHEET ARITHMETIC FUNCTIONS

Key(s)	Function
@ABS( )	Absolute value
@AVG( )	Arithmetic mean
@INT( )	Integer portion
@MAX( )	Maximum value
@MIN( )	Minimum value
@SQRT( )	Square root
@SUM( )	Sum of all the values

DATA BASE COMMANDS

Key(s)	Function
@ - A	Arrange (sort) a category
@ - C	Copy records
@ - D	Delete record or report category
@ - E	Change cursors
@ - F	Find records
@ - G	Add or remove group totals
@ - H	Print screen
@ - I	Insert record or report category
@ - J	Justify a report category
@ - K	Define a calculated report category
@ - L	Change record layout
@ - M	Move records
@ - N	Change name of file
@ - O	Options for print formatting
@ - P	Print report
@ - Q	See the Desktop Index
@ - R	Change record selection rules
@ - S	Save current file to disk
@ - T	Add or remove report totals
@ - V	Set standard values
@ - Y	Delete from cursor to end of entry
@ - Z	Zoom to single or multi-record layout
@ - ?	Get help
ESCAPE	Cancels previous command
RETURN	Accept entry
DELETE	Delete preceding character
◹ ◸ ◺ ◿	Move the cursor

TIP TWELVE

Logo Language Summary

Chapter Eight—Logo Terms

Turtle Commands

FORWARD (FD)   Command that expects one input, a number, and will move the turtle forward a given number of steps from its last heading.

        FD 10

BACK (BK)   Command that expects one input, a number, and will move the turtle backward a given number of steps from its last heading.

        BK 10

RIGHT (RT)   A command that expects one input, a number of degrees, and turns the turtle toward its right side a given number of degrees. Note that this command does not move the turtle forward or backward; it simply turns it in place.

        RT 90

LEFT (LT)   A command that expects one input, a number of degrees, and turns the turtle toward its left side a given number of degrees. Note that this command does not move the turtle forward or backward; it simply turns it in place.

        LT 90

CLEARSCREEN (CS)   A command that erases the graphics screen and returns the turtle to its HOME position in the center of the graphics screen.

HOME   A command that returns the turtle to its home position in the center of the graphics screen. If the turtle's pen is down when this command is given, the turtle will leave a trail as it is moves to the center of the screen.

SHOWTURTLE (ST)   A command that reveals the triangular turtle on the screen.

HIDETURTLE (HT)   A command that hides the turtle from view. This command does not prevent the turtle from leaving a trail.

HEADING   An operation that outputs the current compass direction the turtle is heading.

PR HEADING   Prints the current heading.

SETHEADING (SETH)   A command that expects one input, a whole number between 0 and 360, and faces the turtle in that direction. Note that this command does not move the turtle forward or backward; it simply turns it in place.

CIRCLER   A predefined procedure that can be loaded into your workspace from the Apple Logo file called TOOLS. This procedure expects one input, a number, which it uses in forming a circle toward the right with a radius equal to the given number.

> CIRCLER 20   yields a circle with radius 20.

CIRCLEL   a predefined procedure that can be loaded into your workspace from the Apple Logo file called TOOLS. This procedure expects one input, a number, which it uses in forming a circle toward the left with a radius equal to the given number.

> CIRCLEL 50   yields a circle with radius 50.

ARCR   A predefined procedure that can be loaded into your workspace from the Apple Logo file called TOOLS. This procedure expects two inputs, both numbers, and outputs an arc drawn toward its right side. The first number is used to define the radius of a circle, and the second number determines the size of the arc (piece of a circle circumference) equal to the given number.

> ARCR 30 180   yields a half-circle of radius 30.

ARCL   A predefined procedure that can be loaded into your workspace from the Apple Logo file called TOOLS. This procedure expects two inputs, both numbers, and outputs an arc drawn toward its right side. The first number is used to define the radius of a circle, and the second number determines the size of the arc (piece of a circle circumference) equal to the given number.

> ARCR 30 180   yields a half-circle of radius 30.

SETPENCOLOR (SETPC)   A command that expects one input, a number between 0 and 3, and resets the turtle's pen to the color corresponding to that number.

SETPC 2   sets the turtle's pen to red.

SETBACKGROUND (SETBG)   A command that expects one input, a number between 0 and 3, and resets the background color of the graphics screen to the color corresponding to that number.

SETBG 0   sets the background to black.

PENUP (PU)   A command to lift the turtle's pen so that it will not leave a trail when the turtle moves.

PENDOWN (PD)   Returns the pen point so that the turtle with leave a trail when it moves.

PENERASE (PE)   A command to replace the turtle's pen with an eraser so that it will erase all lines below it as it moves.

REPEAT   A command that expects two inputs, a number and a list, and repeats the instructions on the list a given number of times.

REPEAT 4 [FD 10 RT 90]

The turtle repeats four times, the instructions to go forward 10 and turn right 90 degrees.

[ ]   Square brackets are used to mark the beginning and end of lists (also see REPEAT for an example).

PR [HI THERE BOB.]

Text Commands

PRINT (PR)   A command that expects one input, a word, number, or list, and displays that input on the text screen.

PR "HELLO
PR [HI THERE BOB.]
PR 360/:NUM

SENTENCE (SE)   An operation that expects two inputs, words, numbers, or lists, and outputs them as one unit.

CONTROL-A   Moves cursor to beginning of line.

CONTROL-E   Moves cursor to end of line.

CONTROL-F An editing command that deletes a character to the right side of the cursor.

CONTROL-Y Deletes line to right of cursor.

CONTROL-K Erases line cursor is on.

CLEARTEXT (CT) Erases or clears the textscreen.

" Attached to the first character of a Logo word, used to designate Logo word.

```
PR "HELLO
```

Disk and Workspace Commands

CONTROL-S Changes screen to a combination of graphics and text screens (bottom four lines of screen are used for text).

CONTROL-L Changes screen to full graphics screen.

CONTROL-T Changes screen to full text screen.

LOAD A command that expects one input, a word or list, and loads the file or files from disk into workspace.

```
LOAD "TOOLS
LOAD [GREET TRUCKS AIDS]
```

Math Operations

+ An operation that expects two numbers and outputs their sum.

```
PR 50 + 50
```

— An operation that expects two numbers and outputs their difference.

```
PR 50 - 60
```

* An operation that expects two numbers and outputs their product.

```
PR 3.14 * 30
```

/ An operation that expects two numbers and outputs their quotient.

```
PR 360 / 12
```

( )   Used to force some commands and operations to take more than their expected number of inputs; also used to partition mathematics terms.

```
PR (20 / 24) * 100
PR (SE "HELLO "THERE "BOB)
```

Chapter 9—Logo Terms

THING (:)   An operation that expects one input, the name of a variable, and outputs the current value of that variable (the abbreviation : includes the " used to mark a word).

```
PR THING "LENGTH is the same as PR :LENGTH
```

ERASE (ER)   A command that expects one input, a word or list, and erases from workspace the variable(s) or procedure(s) named.

```
ER "TRUCKS
ER [LITTLE.TRUCK BIG.TRUCK]
```

PO   A command that expects one input, a procedure name, and prints out a copy of the lines in that procedure.

```
PO "TRUCKS
```

SAVE   A command that expects one input, a file name, and saves all global variables and procedures in workspace onto the disk in a file with the given name.

EDIT (ED)   A command that expects one input, a procedure name or a list of procedure names, and brings those procedures into the editor. Used without an input, ED returns to the most recent contents of the editor.

```
ED "LITTLE.TRUCK
ED [LITTLE.TRUCK BIG.TRUCK GREET]
```

POTS   A command whose effect is to print out titles or names of all procedures currently in workspace.

CATALOG   A DOS command that lists the contents of the disk.

TO   Used to define procedures. The first line of all Logo.

END   Procedures begin with TO, and the last line contains the single word END.

```
TO GREET
PR "HI
END
```

ERASEFILE   A command that expects a file name or list of file names and whose effect is to erase those files from the disk.

```
ERASEFILE "GREET
ERASEFILE [TRUCKS GREET]
```

CONTROL-C   A command that exits the editor and passes the contents of the editor to Logo.

CONTROL-G   An "escape" command that exits the editor without passing the editor contents to Logo (aborts the edit) or, when used while Logo is executing an instruction, will stop the processing.

Chapter 10—Logo Terms

FIRST   An operation that expects one input, a word, number, or list, and outputs the first letter of the word or number, or the first item of the list.

```
PR FIRST "FRED      yields F
PR FIRST [BOB TED CAROL ALICE]      yields BOB
```

LAST   An operation that expects one input, a word, number, or list, and outputs the last letter of the word or number, or the last item of the list.

```
PR LAST "FRED     yields D
PR LAST [BOB TED CAROL ALICE]      yields ALICE
```

BUTFIRST (BF)   An operation that expects one input, a word, number, or list, and outputs all but the first letter of the word or number, or all but the first item of the list.

```
PR BF "FRED     yields RED
PR BF [BOB TED CAROL ALICE]      yields TED CAROL ALICE
```

BUTLAST (BL)   An operation that expects one input, a word, number, or list, and outputs all but the last letter of the word or number, or all but the last item of the list.

```
PR BL "FRED     yields FRE
PR BL [BOB TED CAROL ALICE]      yields BOB TED CAROL
```

PONS   A command that lists the current names and values of all global variables currently in workspace.

READLIST (RL)   An operation that waits for a carriage return input from the keyboard, places all entered input on a list, and outputs that list.

PO   Stands for Print Out. This command is used with the name of a procedure (don't forget the ") and will display a listing of the procedure, line by line.

    PO "BOX. 50

ERALL   A command that erases all user-created variables and procedures from the Logo workspace.

Printing in Apple Logo

.PRINTER :N   Where :N stands for the slot number (between 1 and 7) of the printer; if in doubt, use .PRINTER 1 to access the printer. After you have entered this command, use the PO command to print out copies of procedures. .PRINTER 0 stops sending output to the printer.

Printing in Apple Logo II

PRINTPIC 1   Used to print a graphic picture on a dot matrix printer (number refers to printer slot).

DRIBBLE :N
NODRIBBLE   Where :N stands for the slot number (between 1 and 7) of the printer; if in doubt, use DRIBBLE 1 to access the printer. After you have enter this command, use the PO command to print out copies of procedures. NODRIBBLE stops sending output to the printer.

TIP THIRTEEN

Glossary of Computerese

Acoustic coupler   A form of modem attached to a computer to send and receive information using an ordinary telephone. (*See* Modem.)

ASCII   American Standard Code for Information Interchange. A standard that sets a code for every letter, numeral, and special character. Used by all microcomputers.

Back-up   A duplicate copy of the original data file or program.

BASIC   Beginner's All-purpose Symbolic Instruction Code. A language used by humans to tell computers what to do. BASIC was developed by Kemeny and Kurtz in 1963 at Dartmouth College and is now the most popular language available for microcomputers.

Bit   BInary digiT. The smallest unit of computer information. A bit represents a yes/no choice, a true/false distinction, or an on/off circuit. (*See* Byte.)

Branch   A departure from the main logic of a tutorial program to an instructional sequence geared to a higher or lower level. Also refers to a jump to another logical procedure in a computer program.

Bug   An error. A hardware bug is an equipment malfunction or a design flaw. A software bug is a programming error.

Bus   A connection that transfers data from one part of a computer to another.

Byte   The basic unit of information in a computer, usually consisting of eight bits. Each byte is capable of storing one character of information or a number from 0 to 255.

CAI   Computer Assisted Instruction. The use of computers to assist students with the educational process.

Chip   A small (one-half centimeter square), thin slice of silicon that contains a few dozen to tens of thousands of electronic circuit elements. (*See* IC.)

CMI   Computer Managed Instruction. The use of computers to aid in managing the instructional sequence. A CMI program typically includes testing of student performance, individualizing the instructional sequence, and prescriptive reporting to the instructor.

COBOL   COmmon Business-Oriented Language. The most common programming language used in business applications.

Command   A request to the computer that is executed as soon as it is received. (*See* Statement.)

Control character   Characters or commands obtained by holding down the CONTROL key (sometimes marked CTRL) while pressing another key.

Courseware   Software specifically written for educational applications.

CPU   Central Processing Unit. The main functional unit of the computer, controlling what the computer does.

CRT   Cathode Ray Tube. A computer video display. Refers to the monitor or television set on a microcomputer.

Cursor   A symbol placed on the screen to let you know where the next character typed will appear.

Data base   A systematic collection and organization of related information for access, retrieval, and update by computer.

Debugging   Detecting and correcting program errors.

Diskette   A small, flexible disk with a magnetic surface for recording data and programs. Sometimes referred to as a *floppy disk*.

Documentation   Instructions for a piece of software that may appear as written directions on the screen or as a printed user's manual.

DOS   Disk Operating System. A program that controls the interaction of the computer with one or more disk drives.

Dot matrix   A method by which some printers form characters as a pattern of dots, rather than solid lines.

Execute   To cause the computer to carry out a set of instructions. To run a program or a portion of a program.

Firmware   Software stored in ROM. (*See* ROM.)

Floppy disk   (See *diskette*.)

FORTRAN   FORmula TRANslator. A science-oriented programming language.

GIGO   Garbage In, Garbage Out. An acronym that implies that incorrect input results in invalid output.

Graphics   Information displayed in two- or three-dimensional form on the computer's screen or printed pictorially on paper.

Hard copy   Computer output printed on paper.

Hard disk   A rigid metal disk that stores data magnetically. A hard disk stores considerably more information and is faster than a floppy disk.

Hardware   The physical parts of a computer system.

Hollerith   Coding system used to represent letters, numerals, and special characters on a punched card.

IC   Integrated Circuit. An electronic device consisting of a plastic body surrounding a chip. The body protects the chip and provides leads to connect the chip to other components. (*See* chip.)

Input   Information arriving at a computer device. Also the act of entering information to a computer.

Interactive   The quality of a computer system that provides an immediate response and allows an immedate reaction by the user.

Interface   The connecting device between a computer and a peripheral device that allows the two to communicate.

Interpreter   A program that converts commands and statements written in a programming language to the native language of the computer.

I/O   An abbreviation for Input/Output.

K   Kilo. Refers to 1024 bytes of memory. A computer with 64K of memory has 65,536 (64 times 1024) bytes of memory.

Letter quality A type of printer that prints fully formed letters like a typewriter. The most common alternative is a dot matrix printer.

LSI Large Scale Integration. The technology of manufacturing integrated circuits with 500 to 20,000 logic gates, or 1K to 64K bits of memory.

Machine language (*See* Native Language.)

Mainframe A large, powerful computer typically with 256K to 2000K bytes of memory.

Memory The portion of a computer that stores information. (*See* RAM and ROM.)

Menu A list of options from which the computer user can choose.

Microcomputer A computer based on a microprocessor typically with 1K to 512K bytes of memory.

Microprocessor An integrated circuit that performs the task of executing instructions.

Minicomputer A medium-sized computer typically with 64K to 256K bytes of memory.

MODEM MOdulator-DEModulator. A device that allows a computer to communicate over telephone lines. It changes the digital data into tones. (*See* Acoustic coupler.)

Monitor A video display used with a computer. (*See* CRT.)

Native language The language that a computer was built to understand. Usually this language is inconvenient to use, and thus higher level languages such as BASIC, COBOL, FORTRAN, and Pascal are more commonly used.

Network A system of interconnected computers that share data and programs from a central source, usually a hard disk.

OS Operating System. A collection of programs allowing a user to control a computer. Typically the OS resides in ROM.

Output Information leaving from a device. Also the act of transferring information from the computer to a device such as a CRT, printer, or disk drive.

Pascal A programming language, named after the mathematician Blaise Pascal, used for structured programming solutions.

Peripheral A device that can send information to or receive information from a computer. Examples are printers, disk drives, modems, tape recorders, and monitors.

Printer   A peripheral device that makes hard copy output.

Program   A sequence of statements arranged in logical order to cause a computer to perform a certain task.

Programmer   A person who writes a program.

Prompt   A symbol that appears on the computer's screen to indicate that the computer is ready for keyboard input.

Punched card   An obsolescent means of storing information by punching holes in an index card. Its invention is attributed to Herman Hollerith in the 1890s.

RAM
Random Access Memory.   Internal memory of the computer that can be written to and read from. Typically data and programs are stored in RAM . This type of memory is erased when the computer's power is turned off.

RF modulator   An abbreviation for Radio Frequency modulator. A device converting the computer's video signal to a television signal that can be fed into a normal television set through the antenna leads.

ROM   Read Only Memory. A type of memory in which a program or information is stored once, usually by the manufacturer, and cannot be changed. Language interpreters and operating systems are commonly stored in ROM.

Run   To execute a computer program.

Save   To store a program or data somewhere other than in the computer's memory, such as on a floppy diskette.

Screen   A surface on which the computer displays information. (*See* CRT and monitor.)

Scroll   The feature of a screen that moves all the text upward to make room for another line of text at the bottom. Some computers or programs also allow text to scroll down for reviewing.

Software   Programs written for computer systems. Sometimes also refers to stored data.

Special character   A character that can be displayed by a computer but is not a letter or a numeral. For example, !@#$%& are special characters.

Statement   An instruction to the computer that is part of a program. A statement is not executed until the program is run. (*See* Command.)

String   A character string composed of letters, numerals, or special characters.

Subroutine   A portion of a computer program that defines a logical process and resides outside the main program. Control can be transferred from the main program to the subroutine repeatedly and is returned to the main program on completion of the subroutine.

Syntax   The rules outlining how statements should be written in a specific programming language.

Telecommunications   The transfer of information over telephone lines.

Teletype   A noisy, slow, obsolete computer terminal.

Terminal   A device consisting of a CRT and keyboard used to communicate with a computer.

Time-sharing   A computer system that allows more than one user to access the same computer simultaneously.

Turn-key   A computer system that is programmed to perform all necessary tasks as soon as it is turned on.

User   A human who interacts with a computer.

Utility program   A program that provides the user with a convenient way of performing a task. Intended to save time and eliminate the need to "reinvent the wheel."

Variable   A name for a storage location in which the values may vary during the execution of a program. Numbers or strings can be stored in variables.

Word processing   The process of recording, manipulating, editing, storing, and printing text.

TIP FOURTEEN

Answers to Selected Questions

Chapter 1

Think about This (for Fun)
ONE WORD.

Text Questions
Section 1.4.3

The output would be closepacked (printed with no separating spaces).

Section 1.5, Step 3

The blank space is needed to separate the comma from the name (value of N$). Otherwise, the comma and name would be printed closepacked.

Posers and Problems
1.
```
10 PRINT "Hello"
20 PRINT "What's your height in inches";
30 INPUT H
40 M = 2.54 * H
50 PRINT "You are" M "centimeters tall!"
60 END
```
2. 25, 4, 6, 0.666666667, 3
3. To prevent the text and variable values from being closepacked.
4. The semicolon closepacked the "?" printed by execution of the INPUT statement (60).

5. See PROGRAM 2.
6. NAME   SCORE   AVERAGE
   ←15 spaces→←15 spaces→
7. Enter and RUN the program.
8. 10 INPUT "What's your first name?";F$
   20 INPUT "What's your last name?;L$
   30 PRINT "Greetings, "F$" "L$ (Note the blank space after the comma and between the first and last name variables.)

Chapter 2

Think about This (for Fun)
A chair, a bed, and a toothbrush.

Text Questions
Section 2.3
Range of INT(91 * RND(1) + 5) = 95 to 5

Posers and Problems
1. REPLY is for numeric input (years).
   REPLY$ is for string input (state name).
3. Change PRINT statements 210 and 220 to ask for your age; change the *39* in statements 270, 310, and 350 to your age.
4. 360 RANUM = INT(5*RND(1) + 1)
   392 IF RANUM = 4 THEN FEEDBK$ = "You ol' meany!"
   394 IF RANUM = 5 THEN FEEDBK$ = "Boo to you!"
5. 120 PRINT "What state is the third"
   130 PRINT "largest by land area";
   150 IF REPLY$ = "CALIFORNIA"
       THEN PRINT "Orange you smart!"
   160 IF REPLY$ <> "CALIFORNIA"
       THEN PRINT "It's California!"
6. 5 INPUT "What is your first name?";F$
   450 PRINT "Bye-bye, " F$ "!"
7. X = INT(151 * RND(1) + 50)
8. 29 to 5, inclusive.
9. 10 INPUT "What is your height in inches? ";H
   20 IF H > 72 THEN PRINT "TALL"
   30 IF H < 60 THEN PRINT "SHORT"
   40 IF H > 59 AND H < 73 THEN PRINT "AVERAGE"
   50 END

10. 10 INPUT "Give me any number, 1 t0 10, inclusive => ";N
    20 A$ = " WAS ENTERED. "
    30 IF N = 3 THEN PRINT "THREE" A$
    40 IF N = 6 THEN PRINT "SIX" A$
    50 IF N = 9 THEN PRINT "NINE" A$
    60 IF N <> 3 AND N <> 6 AND N <> 9
       THEN PRINT "NEITHER 3, 6, OR 9" A$
    70 END

Chapter 3

Think about This (for Fun)
In.

Text Questions
Section 3.2.3

The semicolons in statement 60 closepack the display.

The values of the variables do not change.

Each READ assigned a new value to variable N. The value of variable C is increased by the value of N each time statement 30 or 70 is executed.

Posers and Problems

1. 10 FOR Y = 1 TO 10

    20 READ Q$, A, C$
    30 PRINT Q$ C$;
    50 IF A = R THEN 70

2.   5 DIM NAME$ (4) , SCRE (4)
    30 READ NAME$ (L) , SCRE (L)
    40 PRINT NAME$ (L) , SCRE (L)
    50 NEXT L

3.   6 SUM = 0
    32 SUM = SUM + SCRE (L) : N = N + 1
    60 PRINT : PRINT "The average score is" SUM/N

4. FOR R = 10 TO 1 STEP -1 starts the loop at 10 and counts in steps of − 1.

The comma in statement 40 tabs 15 spaces before PRINTing.

The semicolon in statement 60 closepacks the tails (note, however, that a space is enclosed with the *).

The PRINT at statement 80 cancels the closepacking effect of the semicolon in statement 60.

5. The minimum changes could be

```
LOAD PROGRAM4
  70 PRINT "MULTIPLICATION DRILL"
 420 ANSWER = N1 * N2
 430 PRINT N1 " X " N2 " = ";
SAVE MULDRILL <or a name of your choice>
```

6. The minimum changes could be

```
LOAD PROGRAM 4
  70 PRINT "DIVISION DRILL"
 410 IF N1/N2 <> INT(N1/N2) THEN 360
 420 ANSWER = N1/N2
 430 PRINT N1 " / " N2 " = ";
SAVE DIVDRILL <or a name of your choice>
```

Chapter 4

Think about This (for Fun)
6.

Chapter 5

Think about This (for Fun)
Period, question mark, comma, semicolon, colon, quotation mark, apostrophe, dash, exclamation point, asterisk, braces, hyphen, brackets, parentheses. . ? , ; : " ' — ! * {} - [] ()

Chapter 6

Think about This (for Fun)
If the tank is full in 60 minutes, it was half full a minute earlier, or at 59 minutes.

Chapter 7

Think about This (for Fun)
6.

8579   5789

Chapter 8

Think about This (for Fun)
Put your pants on backwards.

Chapter 9

Think about This (for Fun)
A 50-cent piece and a nickel (one of the coins is not a nickel—but the other one is!)

Chapter 10

Think about This (for Fun)
50–1/2 + 49–38/76 = 100

INDEX